Epworth Com

General E...
Ivor H. Jones

Isaiah 1–39

Epworth Commentaries

Already published

The Book of Job
C.S. Rodd

The Books of Amos and Hosea
Harry Mowvley

The Gospel of John
Kenneth Grayston

The First Epistle to the Corinthians
Nigel Watson

The Second Epistle to the Corinthians
Nigel Watson

The Epistle to the Galatians
John Ziesler

The Epistle to the Philippians
Howard Marshall

The Epistle to the Colossians
Roy Yates

The Epistle to the Hebrews
Paul Ellingworth

The Johannine Epistles
William Loader

In preparation

The Gospel of Matthew
Ivor Jones

The Book of Revelation
Christopher Rowland

ISAIAH

Chapters 1–39

DAVID STACEY

EPWORTH PRESS

ISBN 0 7162 0491 6

First Published 1993
by Epworth Press
1 Central Buildings Westminster
London SW1H 9NR

Typeset by Regent Typesetting, London
and printed in Great Britain by
Mackays of Chatham

CONTENTS

GENERAL INTRODUCTION

The *Epworth Preacher's Commentaries* that Greville P. Lewis edited so successfully in the 1950s and 1960s having now served their turn, the Epworth Press has commissioned a team of distinguished academics who are also preachers and teachers to create a new series of commentaries that will serve the 1990s and beyond. We have seized the opportunity offered by the publication in 1989 of the Revised English Bible to use this very readable and scholarly version as the basis of our commentaries, and we are grateful to the Oxford and Cambridge University Presses for the requisite licence and for granting our authors pre-publication access. They will nevertheless be free to cite and discuss other translations wherever they think that these will illuminate the original text.

Just as the books that make up the Bible differ in their provenance and purpose, so our authors will necessarily differ in the structure and bearing of their commentaries. But they will all strive to get as close as possible to the intention of the original writers, expounding their texts in the light of the place, time, circumstances, and culture that gave them birth, and showing why each work was received by Jews and Christians into their respective Canons of Holy Scripture. They will seek to make full use of the dramatic advance in biblical scholarship world-wide but at the same time to explain technical terms in the language of the common reader, and to suggest ways in which Scripture can help towards the living of a Christian life today. They will endeavour to produce commentaries that can be used with confidence in ecumenical, multiracial, and multifaith situations, and not by scholars only but by preachers, teachers, students, church members, and anyone who wants to improve his or her understanding of the Bible.

Ivor H. Jones

ABBREVIATIONS

ANE	Ancient Near East
ANET	*Ancient Near Eastern Texts*, 3rd edition,1969, James B. Pritchard (ed.)
AV	Authorized Version
BCE	Before the Common Era
CE	Common Era
ch., chs.	chapter, chapters
DSS	Dead Sea Scroll
ET	English translation
GNB	Good News Bible, 1976
Heb.	Hebrew, usually a reference to the Hebrew text
JB	Jerusalem Bible, 1966
JLG	*Joint Liturgical Group*
JSOT	*Journal for the Study of the Old Testament*
lit.	literally
LXX	Septuagint, i.e. a Greek translation of the OT
MS, MSS	manuscript, manuscripts
marg.	the margin of the text at the bottom of the page
MT	Masoretic Text, see footnote on p. 7
NEB	New English Bible, 1970
NIV	New International Version, 1979
NRSV	New Revised Standard Version, 1990
p., pp.	page, pages
REB	Revised English Bible, 1989
RSV	Revised Standard Version, 1946
RV	Revised Version, 1884
v., vv.	verse, verses

BIBLIOGRAPHY

Clements R. E., *Isaiah 1–39*, The New Century Bible Commentary, London, 1980

— *Isaiah and the Deliverance of Jerusalem: A Study of the Interpretation of Prophecy in the Old Testament*, JSOT Supplement Series, 13, Sheffield 1980

Hayes, John H. and Irvine, Stuart A., *Isaiah, the Eighth-century Prophet: His Times and His Preaching*, Nashville 1987

Herbert, A. S., *The Book of the Prophet Isaiah, 1–39*, Cambridge Commentary on the New English Bible, Cambridge 1973

Kaiser, O., *Isaiah 1–12*, SCM Old Testament Library, ET London, 2nd edition, 1983

— *Isaiah 13–39*, SCM Old Testament Library, ET London 1974

Mauchline, J., *Isaiah 1–39*, Torch Bible Commentaries, London 1962

Oswalt, J. N., *The Book of Isaiah: Chapters 1–39*, The New International Commentary, Grand Rapids, Michigan 1986

Partain, Jack and Deutsch, Richard, *A Guide to Isaiah 1–39*, London 1986

Sawyer, John F. A., *Isaiah*, vols. 1 (chs. 1–32) and 2 (chs. 33–66), The Daily Study Bible, Edinburgh 1984 and 1986

Scott, R. B. Y., *The Book of Isaiah*, The Interpreter's Bible, vol. 5, New York and Nashville 1956

Watts, J. D. W., *Isaiah 1–33*, Word Biblical Commentary, Waco, Texas 1985

— *Isaiah 34–66*, Word Biblical Commentary, Waco, Texas 1987

See also: *The Calendar and the Lectionary*, edited for JLG by Ronald C. D. Jasper (*JLG 1*, O.U.P. 1967) and *A Four Year Lectionary* (*JLG 2*, Canterbury Press 1990).

References to Josephus' *TheAntiquities of the Jews* and *The Wars of the Jews* are taken from the Whiston edition and involve three figures, book, chapter, and paragraph.

Note

This commentary is based upon the REB (Oxford and Cambridge, 1989), but readers would be wise to make frequent reference to other translations. Frequently the differences are remarkable; this indicates how difficult the art of translation is.

INTRODUCTION

1. Reading Isaiah today

This is a commentary for preachers and teachers and in many ways
it proceeds along traditional lines. That is to say, it works on the
assumption that the meaning of the oracles when they were first
spoken is of the greatest importance for assessing their meaning for
today. So this commentary asks questions about how the text came
to be in its present form. What were the original units? What were
the circumstances in which each unit was first spoken? Who said it?
Who heard it? What did the two parties understand by it? And then,
who remembered it, and wrote it down, and preserved it, and united
it with other units, and passed it all on, and who else inherited the
collection, and edited it, and re-applied it? And who, at last,
gathered the various collections together and produced the book of
Isaiah as we know it?

The fact that such questions can, and must, be asked shows that
the meaning of the text (and even the meaning of the various units
within the text) will never be easy to nail down. The person who
composed and published each original unit – in some but not all
cases, Isaiah himself – doubtless had a clear idea of what he meant;
but a devout disciple, living a century or two later, may well have
taken over the words and used them in a different sense to teach a
lesson for his own day; and then, of course, when all the editorial
work was done and the various collections had been joined together
to make our book of Isaiah, and that book had been united with other
books to form the Hebrew Scriptures, the meaning would have
moved on again, for each book in those Scriptures would inevitably
come to interpret the others for faithful Jewish readers. In due time
the authors of the New Testament made extensive use of the book of
Isaiah, finding yet further significance in it (see below on 7.10–17),
and so the process has continued down to the present day, the
present translation, and the present commentary.

Nevertheless, it is reasonable to contend that the original meaning, the author's meaning, if it can be ascertained, should exercise some kind of control over the meanings discovered by readers in later years, particularly if, as is surely the case with preachers, the book is regarded as a medium of revelation. The present commentary takes the meaning of the text in its ancient Israelite setting, or settings, very seriously, and this is why it is fair to call it traditional in its method.

Not everyone is entirely happy about this method. The process of searching out the original context can be extremely technical and its results uncertain. Can the context be all that important if the ordinary reader cannot know it and the scholar cannot be sure? Moreover, many people want to read the Bible, either as literature or as a holy book, without using complex and expensive commentaries. Cannot the text be allowed to speak for itself? Many OT texts, such as the psalms, are read profitably without the reader having any idea of who was the original author and what was the original context; cannot the same be true of Isaiah? These are searching questions and it would be folly to say that simple and direct reading is invalid. Nevertheless preachers particularly must be concerned about the question of authority, and, where the prophetic texts are concerned, the authority is inevitably connected with the situation that is being addressed.

Some texts have a completely internal integrity, that is to say, they can be read with profit without any reference to factors outside it. Ps. 130 speaks to the bereaved because of its profound understanding of the human condition; there is not the slightest need to ask who is being mourned and what he or she died of. But a reader of the speeches made by Winston Churchill in 1940, lacking knowledge of the circumstances in which he spoke, would miss most of the point. A tape recording of John Arlott's commentary on Bradman's last test innings is treasured by many cricketers, but it would be almost meaningless if one did not know who Bradman was and what his achievements were. The integrity of these texts depends on external factors, and most prophetic oracles come in the same category.

It is of the essence of Scripture that large parts of it deal, not with general truths, but with particular situations. There *is* great difficulty in recovering those situations, but those who take Scripture seriously cannot abandon the quest. Oracles do not float in the air, ready to be attached to any situation that arises. They are a word for a particular moment and their authority depends upon our being able to understand that moment. So the task must be pursued. The end is not to make all things crystal clear, which is impossible, but to make as much as possible as clear as possible and so to hear the authentic voice as clearly as we can.

We have to recognize, of course, that what Isaiah said to his compatriots about their problems at the close of the eighth century BCE will not relate immediately to our situation in the English-speaking world at the latter end of the twentieth century. And if an editor, beavering away at the text of Isaiah in, say, 550 BCE, found it necessary to edit and re-apply the material to suit the needs of his own contemporaries, how much more shall we need to do the same thing for our own day? Our preaching and our teaching must be addressed precisely and directly to our audience. So we have to operate a kind of formula: if the prophet said those words to those people in those circumstances, what should we say to our audience to convey the same message with the same power?[1]

This is not an easy task. There are no rules to ensure that all interpreters of goodwill arrive at broadly the same conclusions, because interpretation is necessarily subjective. At one time it was assumed that basic exegetical work was objective, though application to contemporary circumstances tended to be influenced by the author's own slant. That position cannot be maintained today. All literary enquiry is carried out from one particular standpoint and it is subjective. Even judgements about date and place of writing, audience, background, etc., are, in the end, settled by personal assessment. And if that is true of basic exegetical work, how much more is it true of the application of the material to complex modern situations?

To say that interpretation is subjective, however, is not to say that it is useless. Interpretation that is well-argued and endowed with insight can be immensely creative, though it does not have the kind of authority that belongs to a demonstrable scientific equation. Commentators interpreting Scripture are more akin to conductors interpreting a score or actors interpreting a role than to scientists tabulating conclusions. This factor becomes more clear when we recognize that, all across the world, interpreters are coming to the Bible today from avowedly committed standpoints and with no intention of being objective. Liberation theologians and feminist theologians are but two groups who regard objectivity, not as a

---

[1] Some readers may recognize in this formula a reworking of Leonard Hodgson's argument in *For Faith and Freedom*, vol. 2, Oxford 1957, p. 5.

virtue, but as exhibiting indifference to the true meaning of the text. What matters to them is how the Bible bears upon their situation, and by this standard, many of the fruits of objective enquiry are irrelevant.

Commentators of a previous generation would have thought ill of this development, but it can be defended on two grounds. In the first place, as we have seen, the so-called objectivity of the older commentators was no objectivity at all; it was simply the unacknowledged subjectivity of the Western academic tradition, which was presumed, quite wrongly, to be of universal validity. Secondly, the acquisition of knowledge, pure but impractical, serves no great purpose. The interpretation of the Bible should be a life-changing exercise, and if that is to happen, the Bible has to be read as if it were written for the reader's own particular moment.

It follows that the attempt to put forward the present commentary as a sound and adequate interpretation of Isaiah 1–39 for all readers in all situations would be disingenuous. More honestly, this is a commentary written by a male Methodist minister, living in comfortable circumstances in Cambridge, England, retired but still active, interested in academic work, and in worship and preaching from both the personal and social points of view. The commentary strives to be fair, accurate and logical, and it is hoped that the comment it offers will provide insights for many who come to the book of Isaiah from different starting-points, including those far removed from the author's own. But it is only one attempt among many. Every reader will have his or her own subjective concerns too, so that, if it is necessary for the author to say who he is, it is equally necessary for the reader to make an acknowledgment of his or her own point of view. Only in that way can the text of Isaiah be given a chance to work creatively.

This recognition of the inevitability of subjective attitudes is a relatively modern phenomeon in biblical study. It is much preferable to the practice which preceded it, whereby an author wrote, in effect, for his own constituency and readers chose commentaries from within the range of their own sympathies. In those circumstances presuppositions of all kinds, and one has to say prejudices, remained undisturbed and were maybe fortified. But we have come to recognize that both writing and reading are risky undertakings. If we pursue them properly, we never know quite what the end will be. When we recall how Isaiah has been read over the centuries, that surely is as it should be.

The growth of the book of Isaiah

Even a swift reading of the book of Isaiah reveals that the text is not homogeneous. Many different literary forms appear in no apparent order. There are oracles, both denunciations and promises, addressed to Judah, to other nations, to individuals; there are narratives in the third person about Isaiah and there are narratives in which Isaiah speaks of himself in the first person; there are monologues and dialogues, parables, songs, psalms, liturgies; there is a long historical passage in chs. 36–9 that looks as if it has been lifted straight out of II Kings; there is frequent vacillation between poetry and prose, as the REB wisely indicates, and there are many editorial formulae which begin sections, end sections, and comment on the text.

Almost immediately, then, we have to abandon the notion that the book is simply a faithful and consistent account of the life's work of one man. Instead we have to conceive of a long process, lasting about four hundred years, in which the book grew and grew. The first element was indeed the preaching of the prophet Isaiah; the last was the final text, as we have it now, divided into sixty-six chapters. What happened in between is a historical puzzle that we should dearly like to solve. Unfortunately, however, we do not have sufficient evidence to produce a firmly based and universally acceptable account of the growth of the book in those four centuries. This is a pity because it is always helpful if we can say with confidence that a particular passage comes from a particular period. But we are not completely helpless, and it is possible, with care, to put forward hypotheses that, while not solving all our problems, will help to illuminate the text and clarify its message. The details of this process will emerge as we work through the commentary, but it may be helpful if a brief summary is offered now.

There can be no doubt that there was a man called Isaiah who prophesied in Judah in the second half of the eighth century BCE, nor that many of his oracles are to be found in the book that bears his name. The starting-point, therefore, is the prophetic work of Isaiah, that is to say, his actual words, spoken on a particular day. Even during his lifetime, some of these words were written down. There are one or two references to writing in chs. 1–39 (8.1; 8.16; 30.8) which indicate that a written record would have been quite possible, and if it was possible, then it is almost certain that it was done.

Moreover Isaiah gained a huge reputation among the more per-cipient, if not during his lifetime, then soon afterwards, so that there would have been a strong reason for recording and collecting all that the great prophet had said and adding to it such records of events in his life as were available (e.g. 7.1–17; 20.1–6).

Something like this must have happened with all the prophets, but in Isaiah's case, the evidence points to a further factor of immense importance. The thrust of Isaiah's message did not end with him; nor was it simply recorded for posterity by his disciples. It created a tradition that inspired generation after generation of Hebrew thinkers so that his ideas, sometimes his actual words, were taken over and re-used and re-applied in all kinds of different circum-stances. Again, this happened to a lesser degree with all the prophets, but the Isaiah tradition was broader, it embraced more followers, and it inspired at least two other great figures who, while enunciating messages for their own day, stood so clearly within the Isaiah tradition that eventually their utterances were incorporated into the book of Isaiah without their names ever being recorded. The Isaiah tradition thus spans four centuries and makes it possible for us to speak of the book of Isaiah as having a character and identity of its own, despite the enormous range of contexts, authors, styles, etc. represented within it.

But this is to race ahead. The first task was collecting and preserv-ing the Isaianic material and discreetly adding to it. This is a point that sometimes disturbs students when they first come to read the Old Testament. It is one thing to recognize that editors arranged the material according to their own rules and purposes, as they plainly did, but quite another to accept that they incorporated into the Isaianic corpus material from their own day, composed long after Isaiah was dead. We simply have to shed modern ideas when we read the Old Testament. Modern authors modestly thank their teachers in their prefaces and then go on to say that responsibility for the work is all their own. Old Testament authors were even more modest. If the inspiration belonged to a great figure of the past, they were happy that he should have the credit and that they themselves should be forgotten. Whether they were right or wrong about this is hardly the point; that is what happened. So in the years after Isaiah died, the corpus expanded as the editors did their work.

The next step is to determine at what points in history Isaiah's witness would be especially relevant and therefore liable to re-use and extension. The first is the period about sixty years after his death when the Assyrian empire, under whose gloomy shadow Judah had existed throughout Isaiah's lifetime and about which he had frequently prophesied, was at last sinking to its knees. Isaiah had vigorously maintained that Yahweh would deal with Assyria. The events of 701, when Sennacherib was forced to withdraw from Jerusalem, seemed to vindicate him and now his words were coming true in the fullest sense. Nineveh fell in 612 and for a while Hebrew confidence ran high. That would be an appropriate time to import into the growing tradition the material from II Kings relating to the deliverance of Jerusalem. It may well be that other editorial work was done at the same time, because at no other period did Isaiah's policy of leaving it all to Yahweh seem more wise.

Less than two decades after these heady events, however, Jerusalem itself was in trouble and this time Yahweh did not save her. The city was sacked and many of the inhabitants were deported to Babylon. The Isaiah tradition began to look out of touch and those who went into exile faced the task of adapting it to the new situation. Signs of this are to be seen in the vigorous accusations that justified the awful punishment, in modifications of some of the previous rhetoric, such as we see in ch. 39, and perhaps in those passages where future hopes are detached from the immediate future and presented in an idealized form.

Remarkably, at this low, one might think desperate, point, the Isaiah tradition suddenly exploded into a new burst of vitality. A new prophet arose, steeped in the old traditions and ready to apply them to a new world which he saw coming over the horizon. 'Comfort my people', was his message, 'Speak kindly to Jerusalem'. We call this prophet Second Isaiah, for that is what he was. He was a new Isaiah, well versed in the wisdom of the old, but addressing an altogether new situation. In view of the profound shock that the exile brought, it shows great insight on the part of the editors that the work of this Second Isaiah was added to the Isaiah tradition as if there were no question that that is where it belonged.

The final act took place after the exile. The Isaiah tradition persisted, though no towering figure emerged to give it voice. There was a prophet, or perhaps several prophets, who laboured to understand the rather disappointing present in terms of the great promises of the past, and he, or they, undoubtedly made some bold moves. Third Isaiah, as we term the author, or authors, of chs. 56–66, is worth far more attention than he commonly receives, even if he lacks the charisma of his predecessors. In the century after the return from exile the last phases of editing took place. Probably chs. 24–27 were added and the shape of the whole book was finally determined. By the year 400 BCE this extraordinary amalgam of brilliant vision, faithful interpretation, and patient editing was complete.

3. *Isaiah, his life and times*

Isaiah, the son of Amoz (not to be confused with Amos, whose name is quite different in Hebrew), lived in Jerusalem in the second half of the eighth century BCE. He was a person of some importance in the community, who could converse with kings and other influential people without difficulty, though the notion that he was himself of aristocratic breeding has no foundation. According to his own account in ch. 6, he was called to prophesy, or maybe given a specific charge, in 742.[2] He was married and his wife is called a prophetess in 8.3 (though REB takes this to mean simply the wife of a prophet). They had at least two children, given clumsy symbolic names, Shear-jashub (7.3) and Maher-shalal-hash-baz (8.3). His last oracles relate to the affairs of the year 701. The colourful tradition, to which Heb. 11.37 probably alludes, that he was sawn apart with a wood-saw, on Manasseh's orders, and did not cry or weep, first appears in a Jewish text of the late first century CE.[3] It says much about how Isaiah and Manasseh were later regarded, but hardly counts as biographical information.

The eighth century began with Syria crippled and Assyria busy in the east. Consequently the kingdoms of Israel and Judah were able to expand and prosper. In the south, King Uzziah (783–42), also called Azariah,[4] subdued the Ammonites and the Philistines, built Elath, and re-fortified Jerusalem.[5] At some stage he contracted leprosy and

[2] The chronology of this period is problematic and scholars operate with different schemes, so students must be prepared for some variation between different books. The disparity is rarely more than ten years. See Hayes and Irvine, *Isaiah, the Eighth-century Prophet*, pp. 34–6 and my *Groundwork of Biblical Studies*, London 1979, p. 129.

[3] See H.F.D. Sparks (ed.),*The Apocryphal Old Testament*, Oxford 1984, pp. 793f.

[4] See marg. on II Kings 15.1

[5] These details are given in II Chron. 26, where it is also recounted that the king was struck with leprosy as a punishment for usurping the rights of the priesthood and burning incense. II Kings is none too kind to Uzziah. His achievements are dealt with only briefly in 14.21f. and 15.1–7.

had to live in seclusion; Jotham, his son, became regent. Judah was experiencing an economic revival similar to that observed by Amos in the north, though, because Judah had fewer resources, it was rather less splendid. Many and luxuriant were the offerings made in those years, but whether they represented piety and obedience was another matter.

The period of Assyrian weakness ended with the accession of Tiglath-Pileser III in 745. At first he busied himself with problems at home and on his northern borders, but the writing was already on the wall for the kingdoms of the west. Tiglath-Pileser acted in 738; he reduced Syria and took much of its territory to be an Assyrian province. The kingdom of Israel seems to have suffered from a death wish for, in these dangerous times, its leaders fell into intrigue and internecine strife. Pekah, the last king but one, foolishly joined forces with Rezin, king of all that was left of Syria, to form a pitifully weak coalition against Assyria. The two kings had the idea of compelling Judah to join them, and when Ahaz, now king of Judah, hesitated, they sent an army south to persuade him. This was the Syro-Ephraimite confederacy that provides the background for much of Isaiah's prophecy. The coalition failed. The details of the story are not entirely clear, but in 732 Damascus was sacked and the Syrian nation brought to an end. Pekah was murdered and replaced by the pro-Assyrian Hoshea, who reigned as an Assyrian puppet. He was no statesman and, on Tiglath-Pileser's death, he withheld tribute and turned to Egypt for help. The new Assyrian king, Shalmaneser V, came west to punish him, but died before the task was complete. There was no respite for Israel, however; Sargon II followed Shalmaneser and took Samaria in 721. The inhabitants were deported and disappeared from history (II Kings 17.6; 18.11). Only Judah was left.

The years of turbulence in the north corresponded with the first half of Isaiah's ministry. Uzziah had been followed by Jotham, who died just as the Syro-Ephraimite confederacy was launched, and it was left to Ahaz, his successor, to deal with it. Isaiah was untroubled by the threat from the two kings, but Ahaz seems to have lost his nerve. According to II Kings 16.7–9, he appealed to Assyria for help and sent off gifts from the temple treasury as well as from his own. It was an unnecessary action; Tiglath-Pileser would have acted anyway. It was also foolish. Political subservience meant ideological subservience, and within a year or two Ahaz had to modify the temple cult to placate the Assyrian king (II Kings 16.10–18).

Ahaz' son and successor was Hezekiah (715–687). He was fortunate at first in that again Assyria had problems at home, but around the year 711 Egypt was beginning to stir and Philistia was interested in revolt. Hezekiah was tempted to join them, but Isaiah opposed any such venture, particularly if it meant putting any faith in Egypt. The revolt took place, Egypt withdrew, and the Assyrians vented their wrath on Philistia. Jerusalem was left untouched. Hezekiah was fortunate again but only for a time. In 701 Assyria was on the march again. Tyre, Philistia, and even Egypt were defeated and then Sennacherib, Sargon's successor, turned on Judah. According to his own inscriptions, not necessarily true, he laid waste forty-six cities of Judah and shut up Hezekiah 'like a bird in a cage'.[6] Hezekiah had no choice but to sue for peace and pay a huge tribute (II Kings 18.13–16). Precisely what happened next is not clear. Isaiah prophesied that Sennacherib would hear a rumour and return home (II Kings 19.7; Isa. 37.7), but the story goes on to speak of a calamity in the Assyrian camp, 185,000 struck dead in one night by the angel of the LORD (II Kings 19.35f.; Isa. 37.36f.). Whatever the truth, Jerusalem was saved again. A fuller consideration of this event will be found in the introduction to chs. 36–9 below.

As far as religion was concerned, the times were no more stable and no less dangerous. There are a few cases in Isa. 1–39 where individuals were denounced for particular acts of apostasy. Hezekiah's flirting with Egypt, for example, was seen by Isaiah as disobedience to Yahweh and therefore as unbelief and folly. But most of the material from the prophecy relates to a more general infidelity. Isaiah's faith affirmed that Yahweh was unique and holy; he alone guided the universe; history was in his hands; the duty of kings and commoners was loyally to abide by his will. Worship must symbolize obedience and social forms must demonstrate the unity of Yahweh's people before him. This, however, could hardly be said to be the common faith of Israel. Other ideas were close at hand, notably in the shrines devoted to Baal. Baal was not a unique deity; he was not holy and separate; Baal was involved in the working of the universe together with his worshippers; together they made the fields and flocks fertile and the seasons revolve. Baal died and rose with the seasons, and in the shrines, the local monarch played this part for him. So kings partook of the divine nature, which in practice gave

---

[6] Sennacherib's annals record a victory over Egypt at Eltekeh and the sack of Ekron before the Assyrian king turned on Hezekiah (*ANET*, pp. 287f.)

them the rights of tyrants. Good for their courtiers, bad for the peasants. This is just how Jezebel wanted Ahab to behave.

On paper then the two cults were in formal and permanent opposition. The problem on the ground, however, was that the two cults had become muddled, Baalish practices and Baalish attitudes being put forward in the name of Yahwism. Isaiah's barbs, therefore, have larger targets than at first appears. The denunciation of the women in 3.16ff. does not mean simply that, in Isaiah's view, ostentatious dress was unbecoming. The passage attacks ostentation because it was one aspect of a social system that was linked with a view of kingship that in turn derived from a notion of the deity that was totally at odds with Yahwism. What lies behind many of the denunciations in Isaiah is a composite crime, showing itself in various particular ways, but rooted in a general readiness to flirt with Baalism and an unwillingness to trust Yahweh and accept his ordering of affairs. It is not right, therefore, to see Isaiah as a social reformer or a liturgical purist or a shrewd politician. He rages on these themes simply because they are the visible part of the iceberg. Fundamental infidelity is Israel's real tragedy.

4. *Theology: a necessary preamble*

That Isaiah of Jerusalem was a profound and creative influence in Hebrew thought, perhaps the greatest of the prophets, is hardly open to dispute. Without doubt Isaiah inherited many religious traditions from the past (e.g. belief in Yahweh's involvement in Israelite history, his choice of Zion, his approval of David), and without doubt he stood, together with his contemporary, Micah, in a prophetic tradition, epitomized by Amos, which was strong on social justice. Equally it is clear that the oracles of Isaiah stimulated both editorial and prophetic activity, the literary result of which is now to be found in the text of Isa. 1–39, side by side with the work of the master. It follows that it is not easy to give a systematic account of the theology of Isaiah himself. Only an incautious commentator would claim to be able to separate 'the genuine Isaiah' from the traditions that both preceded and followed him.

That raises the question of whether one should try. Years ago it was thought that divine inspiration rested only on a few favoured prophetic figures and that any line in a prophetic book which gave the appearance of emanating from another source should be discarded as inauthentic. Sorting the wheat from the chaff was an inexact science, but some scholars went to work with such confident enthusiasm that prophetic books were reduced to a few dozen verses. Today almost no one would approve of such a procedure. Whatever view we take of divine inspiration, it must be related to the whole literary, religious and social process whereby the book came into being. All kinds of people were involved in creating the book of Isaiah. To distinguish between the inspired and the uninspired, the authentic word and the inauthentic word, is neither possible nor desirable.

It is better, therefore, to consider the theological teaching of the book as a whole, and while acknowledging the enormous contribution of Isaiah himself, to accept non-Isaianic material as an essential part of the data. This process does not lead to a unified and consistent theological system, but who could expect such a thing from an ancient book that makes no claim to be systematic?

The deepest problem that the book presents to Christian readers is the prevalence of oracles of judgement, often stated vehemently and at length, and usually attributed to the direct action of Yahweh. Many of the oracles in the section 'Against foreign nations' come in this category, but there are plenty outside it (e.g. ch. 34). Can such oracles be associated with a God of compassion and forgiving grace? If not, then what can the book of Isaiah do for us?

The problem is serious and requires us, in the first instance, to look deeply at our own theology. For all the amazing technological advances made in the last two millennia, the disorder in human experience has not decreased very much. Plague, earthquake, famine and drought still bring death to millions; wars, massacres, and all kinds of oppression still abound. Today's theologian faces the same question as the authors of Isaiah: what is the meaning of it all? And what is the place of God in it? Our inclination, in handling this most searching question, is not to relate the appalling facts to God too closely. Wherever possible we attribute the tragedies to human sin, rightly so, but when drought and disease, which cannot reasonably be blamed directly on the human race, cause dreadful suffering in Africa, we draw back from the conclusion that they are positive divine acts. The result is that God, in our reckoning, is preserved from accusations of displaying unreasonable wrath, but, at the same time, he inevitably appears as slightly disconnected from his world; and theologians have to confess themselves mystified and uncertain about what is going on. To say, as we do, that God shares in the hunger of the hungry does not quite explain the provenance of the natural calamity that made them hungry.

One resolution of the problem, not entirely satisfactory, is that hope for deliverance is pushed forward into the next world. Those who are wrongly exalted now, will be brought low; those who suffer now will be relieved. A huge question mark has to be placed over this approach. It is a gross misunderstanding of biblical faith to think of eternal life chiefly in terms of compensation. Nevertheless it does provide the modern theologian with the opportunity to argue that horrors that cannot be explained in terms of this life, might be resolved in another.

Isaiah and his editors had no such hope. It is true that once or twice in the book, notably 25.8 and 26.19, there are references to a life beyond death, but they are brief comments and in no way do they affect the theology of the whole. God's dealings with the human race had to be worked out in the life of this world. Moreover Yahweh was not a disconnected deity. He ruled nature and he ruled history; he ruled them directly; and he ruled them in righteousness and justice. In Isaiah Yahweh is intensely involved and politically involved in human affairs. Judah's foreign policy was his concern. If Judah was willing to make alliances with Egypt without consulting Yahweh (30.1–3; 31.1–3), then she must expect discipline. This in turn means that war is his concern too. War was a holy matter (13.3; 34.2) and, if Yahweh commanded it, it must be carried out with the zeal appropriate to a holy task. There is a straightforward logic about all this. Yahweh, the righteous, confronts human wickedness. Therefore there has to be judgement. Any other result would be unjust. This view is held with full rigour, and this is what leads many of us to draw back from it.[7] Surely, we think, God is more inclined to forgive than to punish. But there is an obvious danger that our experience of grace will lead us to facile judgements about sin. The NT itself is not nearly as indulgent as we, in our liberality, are inclined to believe. Consequently Isaiah stands as a necessary corrective to a gospel that

[7] Most of us are ill at ease with too much rigour. J.H. Newman's famous dictum is valuable, not so much for its truth, which is dubious, but for the way it reveals to us our slightly sentimental view of sin. "She [the Catholic Church] holds that it were better for sun and moon to drop from heaven, for the earth to fail, and for all the many millions who are upon it to die of starvation in extremest agony, as far as temporal affliction goes, than one soul, I will not say should be lost, but should commit one single venial sin" (*Lectures on Anglican Difficulties, VIII*)

makes grace too cheap. The book may not always be right, and its proportions may need attention, but it begins in the right place and it does not shirk the hard decisions, nor sink into sentimentality.

Another factor to be remembered is that, in Isaiah's thought, there were no 'natural forces' that could be held responsible for some of the terrible things that took place. We try to distinguish between happenings that can readily be seen as the direct result of providential activity and tragedies, like floods, earthquakes and crop failures, that are simply the consequence of the way the world works. Isaiah could make no such distinction. There could be no earthquake in which Yahweh's will was not patent. Uncertainty on such points as this was no part of the prophet's view of the world.

If survival of death played little part in the prophetic schema, there was another cardinal doctrine which played a very large part, that is, the belief in rewards and punishments in this life. It is probably wrong to talk about doctrine where the prophets are concerned. They were practical thinkers, not theorists, but they were convinced that no person and no nation could escape from Yahweh's will. Blessing followed obedience; judgement followed rebellion. We tend to link this teaching with the book of Deuteronomy, but the ideas in that book were in the making long before it was found in the temple by Hilkiah in 622. Often in Isaiah the word 'therefore' follows an accusation and precedes a prophecy of doom. It follows that, when dreadful things happen, a cause must be sought in the behaviour of those being afflicted. Equally, when a people suffers as much as Israel at the hands of other nations, her prophets look to a righteous Yahweh to vindicate her. That means a confident expectation that the oppressor will soon bite the dust. The course of history is not formless; it follows a divine plan. In the end there will be a complete reversal of all present injustices (19.12). This will involve a great shake-up and probably much violence, but so it must be to establish the universal glory and justice of the Holy One, the end to which the whole book is pointing. Much of the harsh language can be explained in these terms.

There are a number of other considerations that bear on this subject which cannot be treated at length here but that must, at least, be mentioned. In the first place, Yahweh's judgement is always understood to be moral, righteous, and, therefore, necessary, and never capricious, vindictive and, therefore, unnecessary. The moral nature of the universe, and nothing else, demands the consequence. The judgement may be avoided if the nation repents, but then the moral logic is not broken. It would be broken if, for some idle reason, the awful consequence did not happen. Paul's notion of the wrath of God in Romans has an affinity with this view. Secondly, the moral nature of the judgements is emphasized by the fact that often the oracles are directed against Israel, Yahweh's own people, and the prophet's own people. Isaiah shows no sign of masochism; rather he agonizes over the fact that, by moral necessity, his compatriots are bound to suffer. Thirdly, some of the harshest language consists of warnings, not threats or prophecies. They are an attempt to prevent the dreadful consequences, not an announcement that they are inevitable. Fourthly, there is surprising magnanimity in some of these passages. The prophet does little gloating. He is able to show deep sympathy for nations who have in the past oppressed Israel and who have now to face their judgement. Fifthly, few of us entertain a doctrine of direct inspiration. However inspired Isaiah and his authors were, the words as we have them are not the words of God precisely. We must recognize that Isaiah and his editors were human and that, in choosing the words to speak or write, human passions played a part. Isaiah himself was one who suffered from Assyrian depredations. It is asking too much to suppose that his preaching should show no sign of it. Lastly, and perhaps most importantly, the book must be read as a whole. If some passages are full of judgement, others are full of grace. 19.16 may be unattractive, but look at 19.24f. Reading selected passages in separation from the whole is not the way to study Scripture. The whole book in its changing context provides our subject matter, and it is more likely to leave us with a sense of hope in the divine providence than of fear at the divine wrath.

5. *Theological themes in Isaiah 1–39*

The book is dominated by Isaiah's concept of Yahweh, revealed, to a large extent, in the designations, the Lord of Hosts and the Holy One of Israel, which are used throughout the book. The former is more common (very common in 1–39, but rare thereafter); it signifies great, mysterious and irresistible power. The title is ancient and there is some doubt about who the 'hosts' are. Possibly they are earthly armies that Yahweh controls, or armies of spiritual beings and heavenly messengers, or even the heavenly bodies themselves, regarded as divine in some ANE cults, but subjugated to Yahweh in Hebrew theology (cf. Judg. 5.20). Whatever the original meaning, the title affirms that Yahweh is a unique power and no one will stand in his way. The second title stresses two significant points. First, Yahweh is holy. The word 'holy' is of the utmost importance for Hebrew religion. It means separate, distinct, unique, beyond any comparison with any other thing or being, and, therefore, to be viewed with great awe and wonder. Holiness is a quality that does not apply to Baal, not because there are ethical differences between the two ideologies, though there are, but because Baal was involved with his worshippers in the operation of the created order, whereas Yahweh was above, over and beyond it. Secondly, this incomparable God was the Holy One *of Israel*. The qualification does not limit Yahweh, but it gives Israel a sense of privilege, of vocation and destiny and, one has to say, at times a sense of self-importance, that is without parallel in ancient religion. All nations believed they were important and all nations believed their gods were best, but no other nation came anywhere near Israel in grasping the idea of a God, who was unique, holy and all-powerful, and yet who could concern himself, in both grace and judgement, with the affairs of the small, fractious, inept and often disloyal people, that he was willing to call his own.

The fact that Yahweh called Israel 'my people' had a number of consequences. In the first place, the entity that stood before Yahweh was the whole people. It was not uncommon in the ANE for gods to have dealings with kings, with priests, with those who owned the land or staffed the shrines, but in cults of that kind, the peasants were simply serfs who supplied the labour without enjoying any corresponding rights. By contrast, Yahweh, the God of Israel, showed his concern for his *people*. Moreover he had provided the clearest possible guidance regarding social order for the people to whom he had committed himself. It was to be an order based on *mišpāṭ*, justice, and *ṣᵉdāqâ* (or *ṣeḏeq*), righteousness. These Hebrew words provide the standard whereby any ruler or any situation must be judged. Apart from them, there is no Yahwism.[8] Hence the onslaught on injustice (1.16f.; 1.23; 3.14–26; 5.8; 9.16; 10.1–4; 11.4; etc.) and the bitter denunciation of kings, rulers, officers, and the insensitive rich, that litter the pages of the prophecy.

Zion, the capital city, provides a focus for Israel's tragedy. The city

[8]'For Isaiah, the administration of justice displays most clearly man's attitude to God' (Gerhard Von Rad, *Old Testament Theology*, vol. 2, ET London 1965, p. 149).

was chosen by Yahweh to be the symbol of Israel's privilege. Yet, as the seat of government and the place of sacrifice, it is the scene of the worst abuses. The book of Isaiah struggles with this awful paradox throughout. Zion is the centre of Israel's hopes (4.2–6; 30.19) and ultimately of the hopes of all peoples (2.2–4); Zion will receive Yahweh's protection (7.1–9; 14.32; 29.5–8; 31.4–9); Zion will be the true exemplar of justice and righteousness (4.4f.), but, in the meantime, Zion will be scourged if she proves unworthy (3.16–26; 10.5–11; 29.1–4). Together with the holy city goes the throne established there. The house of David merited the same protection as Zion itself (7.2–9; 9.7; 37.35), but the occupant of the throne often failed to promote justice and righteousness; all too often he embodied the vices of ANE tyrants, instead of the virtues of Yahweh's chosen. For this reason hopes for the royal house were pushed into the future; the coming ruler would be the true son of David and establish a faithful and just society. So messianic prophecy is born (9.2–7; 11.1–5). It is interesting to note that the future anointed one is not given the title of king. Yahweh is the true king of Israel; the son of David, prince and governor though he may be, has only a derived authority. His function is not to lord it over the people but to lead them in obedience.

The medium by which Yahweh enacts his judgements and will achieve his promises is history. A constant theme of the book is that wilful rebellion against the will of Yahweh, however attractive its fruits, can only be destructive and painful. So appalling suffering, as, for example, in 1.4–9, is explained entirely in terms of Israel's sin. It is important to realize that this is not a pragmatic judgement – that the suffering of any period is in exact proportion to its sin – but a general theological principle – that wickedness leads to disaster. To emphasize this principle other possible causes of the disaster are ignored.

At no point is the prophet's framework of thought more at odds with modern ideas than here. When A.J.P. Taylor used to give his TV lectures on how wars began, the one word that you could be sure he would never use was God. Armies, rulers, treaties, land hunger cause wars; not God. Modern theists might disagree, but no serious theologian has been able to come forward with an account of the affairs of the twentieth century interpreted entirely, or even largely, in terms of divine action. Now it would not be true that OT writers paid no attention at all to armies, rulers, treaties and land hunger, but they are merely the minor characters, the stage, the scenery of the drama; the chief actor was Yahweh. Israel was not alone in the belief that military affairs were heavily dependent on celestial support, because all commanders sought the help and guidance of their deities. So battles became a demonstration of the superiority of one deity rather than of one military machine.

One might suppose that, in these terms, the obvious winner in Isaiah's day would be Ashur, the god of the Assyrians, and the obvious losers the deities of all the smaller nations that the Assyrians crushed. But Isaiah could easily brush aside such an observation. He was able to read the history of his day in terms of the unassailable majesty of Yahweh. If Assyria prospered, it was because she was 'the rod I wield in my anger' (10.5); when she had fulfilled her purpose, Assyria would face her nemesis for daring to presume that she had succeeded in her own strength (10.12; 30.31; 31.8). Modern theists might follow thus far, but few would be able to take the next step, for Isaiah contended that Yahweh did not need human co-operation; indeed, human schemes were likely to make things worse (28.14–22; 30.1–7; 31.1–3). What was needed from his people was total confidence and trust (7.4–9; 22.11; 30.15), which often they blindly refused (5.12). Isaiah's confidence in Yahweh at this point is simply awesome. If the will of Yahweh is to defend his people, then, with the enemy almost at the gates, all there is to do is to sit still and believe. In quietness and in confidence shall be your strength!

In the book of Isaiah we begin to see a picture of Yahweh, not simply as the lord of the occasional event (the escape from Egypt, the particular battle), but as the supreme lord of history, working out a plan that might involve any nation at any time (14.27). Syria and the northen kingdom are but 'two smouldering stumps' (7.4), Assyria is but a tool in Yahweh's hand (10.5), Egypt's affairs will be reordered by Yahweh (19.1–4), and so on. This does not amount to a world plan in which all events have their place (the notion of such plans lay far in the future), but rather to a scheme for securing the salvation of Israel, regardless of what other nations might attempt to do to frustrate it. Nations who suffer Yahweh's attentions do so, not because they themselves are important, but because their activity impinges upon Israel. It is inaccurate to call this monotheism, because it is a practical vision and not a philosophical theory; nor is it really a universal idea, but it does carry with it the presumption that other nations' gods have no power to affect Yahweh's progress. The gods are there, they exist, because they can be seen, but they have no practical significance.

As we have already noted, a large part of the book is concerned with judgement. Yahweh's will is flouted by his own people, and it goes without saying that other nations, who threaten Israel and parade their false gods, call forth denunciation, almost as often as their names are mentioned. Yahweh's wrath is thus frequently referred to (1.2–9; 5.1–25; 9.8–10.4; 10.12–19; 13.9–13; etc.) and the theme of the day of the LORD, when all scores will be settled, is vigorously expounded (2.12–22; 7.18–25; 13.6, 9; etc.). But it is not all gloom. Isaiah himself had little to enthuse over, but his disappointment with Israel did not destroy his belief in the ultimate good of Yahweh's purposes. So he leaves enough hints of better things to come for his successors to work out some very positive ideas. The day of doom for some will be a day of promise for others (22.20–25; 26.1–6). The messianic passages are somewhat idyllic (9.2–7; 11.1–5). There are some glowing prophecies of future salvation, even a salvation in which other nations might have a part (2.1–5; 11; 12; 19.16–25; 23.17f.; 25.6–8).

In this area, more than any other, the composite nature of the book shows through. Hopes of all kinds jostle each other, including even hopes of resurrection (25.8; 26.19), which indicates that to attempt to impose a unified system of belief on the book is the greatest possible error. Yahweh's power and Yahweh's concern for Israel provide the unity. The way this conviction is worked out varies from passage to passage, from context to context, and from editor to editor. Something similar is true of the well-known concept of the remnant. There is no single account of the remnant in chs. 1–39. Partly the idea appears in a practical form. Whatever the disaster, there will be survivors. Partly it appears as a theological principle: that Israel must suffer judgement for her sin and yet must survive, through a remnant, to inherit the promises. Then the overtone is sometimes positive, 'a remnant *will* survive', and sometimes negative, '*only* a remnant will survive'. And behind it all lies the baffling problem that, in crude historical terms, those who survived could not be equated with the righteous, nor those who suffered with the guilty. An understanding of the Hebrew idea of representation comes to our aid at this point. Some represent Israel in suffering, some in surviving, but both are Israel in the true sense. In that way Israel both suffers and survives.

There is profound truth in all the theological ideas in this book, not least when they are in conflict. The proper way to pay the book respect, therefore, is to study it line by line and passage by passage.

That is a far more rewarding method than to seek for a summary, which might have the merit of clarity, but, by that same token, would be quite false to the book itself.

6. Translators' trials

The perfect translation of the Bible for all occasions will never appear. This is partly because one translation is suitable for reading to large gatherings, another for use in small groups, and yet another for reading on the train. But there are other, deeper reasons why perfection will always be beyond us. In the first place, we cannot be absolutely certain what the text of the Bible *is*. We have hundreds of ancient MSS, including the DSS, and we have many ancient versions or translations; and though in all important matters they are the same, in detail they differ. So variant readings appear on every page of the student's Heb. Bible. The first task of a panel of translators, therefore, is to decide exactly what words they are going to read in any given passage. Inevitably other translators will disagree, and if unanimity disappears, it is impossible to think any more about perfection. REB, like some other translations, provides notes at the bottom of the page to reveal their greatest difficulties, but the truth is that there are many more difficulties than appear in the notes. It would be wrong to exaggerate the importance of this uncertainty; nevertheless the idea of a clear, immaculate and final Heb. text cannot be entertained for a moment.

A second difficulty is that no translator really knows the Heb. tongue well enough. To know a language well one must be able to read enough of it to build up a vocabulary of all the words in regular use and also the technical words associated with farming, building, soldiering, worshipping, travelling, etc. Unfortuately ancient languages rarely provide enough text to enable a scholar to do that. The Heb. of the OT went out of common use almost as soon as the OT achieved its final form, and though Heb. was preserved for worship and derivative forms of Heb. were used in later Jewish writing, to a large extent, for classical Heb., we have to rely on the Bible. That means inevitably that many words used by Hebrews in gossiping on street corners and haggling in the market are not now known to anybody. But, worse than that, we cannot always be sure of the meaning of words that *are* used. Meaning is determined primarily by usage and only secondarily by derivation. If a word occurs frequently in the OT, its meaning becomes clear, but there may still be a problem over the lack of an English equivalent. The term *nepeš* is an example. It corresponds to no English term and is difficult to translate; 'soul' is a poor approximation. But the word occurs hundreds of times in the OT, so it is possible to build up a picture of the idea. We can be sure that *nepeš* means something like 'livingness' or 'natural vitality', even though we do not have a word in English to translate it exactly. But what of those words that occur only once or twice in the Heb. Bible? If they are obviously related to some other form, we may guess confidently, but if there is no such relationship, guessing becomes very hypothetical. Much scholarship is devoted to this, but even the most competent linguists can be puzzled. At this point it is reasonable to turn to derivations to see if they help. If there is a similar word in a cognate language, that may mean that Heb. possessed a word derived from it. Forming hypotheses of this kind is a highly skilled matter, and it is still not very certain. Moreover the later meaning of words tends to move away from the earlier, so derivations have to be used with great care.

Then, of course, all translation is an art. Languages are social constructions formed over centuries and matching a sentence in one with a sentence in another borders on the impossible. It could be argued that no two people understand a sentence in the *same* language in exactly the same way. How often we say, "I didn't mean that". So we could go on, but we have said enough to show what a delicate area this is and how grateful we must be that there are translators who have the patience, skill and dedication to provide us with English Bibles.

It is important to recognize all these problems; this commentary does not go looking for them, but it cannot escape them altogether, and it would be wrong to try. Scripture comes to us in 'an earthen vessel'. The word of God is there, but we have to search and study diligently to find it.

Prophecies against Judah
1.1–5.30

The first five chapters are largely concerned with Judah and they envisage a dark future following from what appear to be social sins. The corruption shows itself in many forms, ingratitude, treachery, false worship, disobedience, oppression of the weak, and a general failure to promote justice. Much of this material can be safely attributed to Isaiah, though there are clear signs of editorial additions. The whole section is a collection of collections, reaching its present form in various stages.

Title
1.1

On the face of it, this verse provides the title for all sixty-six chapters, but by no means all of the book concerns Judah and Jerusalem and much of it relates to times long after the four kings named were dead.
  This title probably belonged to one of the smaller collections of oracles that make up the book (perhaps chs. 1–5, as REB suggests).

1.1 The very first word in the Heb. text makes an important point. The prophecy is a *vision*. Prophets in Israel were not regarded as deep thinkers who delivered oracles out of their own reflections, not even their own inspired reflections; they were people to whom Yahweh revealed particular truths. The prophet was, therefore, one who 'saw' what other people could not see. The name *Isaiah* means, appropriately, 'Yahweh saves'. The spelling of *Amoz* in Heb. differs from 'Amos' in both the first and the last letters, so there is no possibility of a link between them.

1

The ingratitude of Israel
1.2f.

The subject matter of 2f. is the same as that of vv. 4–9, but the form of address is different. In 2f. a prophetic herald speaks about the people; in 4–9 a prophetic onlooker berates them to their face. For this reason it is best to treat them as separate oracles.

1.2   The prophet acts as a herald proclaiming an assize. Yahweh is about to arraign his people before a court consisting of *the heavens and the earth*, which are somehow personified (cf. Deut. 30.19; Micah 6.1f.). The rebellion is no trivial matter and the judgement will be exhaustive and public. The prophet then goes on to speak Yahweh's words for him. The charge is disloyalty and ingratitude; the people have rebelled against the one who brought them up as children. The rebellion of a child against an earthly father was a serious matter (Ex. 20.12; Deut. 21.18–21); rebellion against Yahweh was infinitely worse. The verse indicates that the people of Israel were Yahweh's children in a sense that other nations were not. The premise of the argument is that Israel knows well that Yahweh is their God and that he has protected them like a father. The precise nature and date of this rebellion is not made clear, but this hardly matters.

1.3   The *ox* and the *donkey* are unreasoning creatures; they are guided only by instinct. Nor do they have a deep relationship with the farmer; he is simply their *owner* (lit. 'the one who has bought him') and their *master*. Nevertheless the animals recognize who feeds and protects them, and they always come faithfully home. Israel, on the other hand, with greater status and greater privileges, fails to display the same common sense. Wisdom and folly in the OT both have a moral sense. Lacking knowledge and having no discernment are moral failings.

Indictment of the nation
1.4–9

The prophet speaks as an unhappy observer of the contemporary scene. The wickedness of the nation provides no clue as to date, but vv. 7f. are fairly precise about the sad condition of Judah. Some calamity has struck the land, possibly an invasion. The occasion of the Syro-Ephraimite confederacy is improbable, because the northerners would hardly be described as *strangers* (v. 7) and they would not have sacked the land of a hoped-for ally. The invasion of Sennacherib in 701 BCE is more likely. He claims to have destroyed Hebrew cities, plundered the land, and besieged Hezekiah in Jerusalem (*ANET*, p. 288). Alternatively, the verses may indicate a natural disaster. There was an earthquake during the reign of Uzziah (Amos 1.1; Zech.14.5).

In these verses four great theological verities are drawn together. First, the wickedness of Jerusalem is affirmed at length with no suggestion of mitigating circumstances. Secondly, the absolute holiness of Yahweh is affirmed with no suggestion of weakness or indulgence on his part. Thirdly, pain and calamity are described as the inevitable consequence of the collision between wickedness and holiness. Fourthly, Yahweh has the last word, and it is a word of grace. Some will survive to be Israel and to inherit the promises.

1.4 A fourfold accusation; the terms used to describe Israel become increasingly more intimate: *nation, people, race* (the Heb. means 'seed', 'offspring', and so 'family'), *children*, whereas the predicates seem to get worse, beginning with sin and ending with depravity. The actual crime, though alluded to three times, remains unclear. The most probable explanation of the evil deeds implied by the terms *deserted, spurned,* and *turned your backs* is what we have called 'the composite crime' of deserting Yahweh for the Baalim (see Introduction, p. xxiii). *the Holy One of Israel* (see Introduction, p. xxviii) is a title used frequently in chs. 1–39 and taken up in chs. 40–55, one of the many indications that Second Isaiah was part of the Isaiah tradition. *Holy* means not so much moral and good as absolutely supreme and utterly authoritative. To spurn such a one is arrogant madness.

1.5 The nation is here described under the image of a badly beaten up body. The implication is that a lot of punishment has fallen on Israel already, which is another reason for opting for the date of 701 BCE. According to 5a the wounds are perversely brought upon Israel by herself; but she still continues to rebel and invite more punishment. Note again the irrationality of sinful behaviour. In 5c and d

3

there is a hint that the affliction was brought on by inner corruption rather than external beating. The image of *sores* might imply that; and *bruised* is not a good translation; the Heb. word means 'faint' or 'unwell', as with illness or menstruation. The verse raises the theological question of the wrath of God. It is much easier to suppose that, in God's moral world, sin leads inevitably to pain and loss, than it is to think of God reacting to affronts and deliberately punishing the sinner. But many passages elsewhere in the OT suggest the latter. The prophets, particularly, take the view that Yahweh was personally and sometimes punitively active in history. See 10.5f.

1.6   Three kinds of injury are indicated, caused by cutting, beating and whipping, which confirms that active punishment rather than inner corruption has taken place. So 6 points the same way as 5a. None of the wounds has been eased by nursing. The usual process would have been to squeeze out the matter, to use oil to lessen the pain and bandages to keep them clean (cf. Luke 10.34). This shocking language leads us to ask what kind of villainy could possibly justify such savage treatment. Was 'the composite crime' so awful? It is possible to argue that some syncretism was inevitable and that the view expressed in Deut. 7.1-6 was impracticable and excessive. Maybe, but Isaiah was a prophet. He was not making measured judgements on the contemporary situation; he was proclaiming a faith, a faith concerned with a holy God and a sinful nation. The message is that wilful rebellion against the holy God, however attractive its fruits may seem, can only be destructive and painful. He makes his point starkly.

1.7   We move from the image of the body to the actual condition of Judah at the time. Is the desolation the result of an earthquake or an invasion? *strangers* might refer to roaming bandits who plundered the ravaged villages; or it might, more probably, suggest the Assyrian army. The Assyrians stand out, even in the annals of those brutal days, for their cruelty and destructiveness. Frequently they made no attempt to colonize conquered territories but simply plundered them. In 7b we have a poignant picture of villagers fleeing to the woods and hills and watching while the marauders loot and burn their homes and barns. The marg. reveals that 7c involves a translator's guess. The Heb. does not give good sense (lit. 'as the overthrow of strangers'), but a slight change gives *Sodom* instead of 'strangers'. There are good reasons for making the change, but the reader needs to be aware that the translator is following conjecture.

1.8 Three similes are used to show how helpless *Zion*, that is Jerusalem, is. The first two refer to insecure structures. The *watchman's shelter* was made of branches pushed into the ground; it lasted no longer than the days of harvesting. *hut* is less precise; it means any old shack where one might pass the night. *cucumbers*, actually a kind of melon, were a valuable crop; when ripe a watchman was necessary. 8d changes abruptly from image to harsh reality.

1.9 Suddenly there is a leap in time and the speaker changes from the prophet contemplating the reality from within to an editor who knows what subsequently happened and looks back on it from a later time. The editor is concerned, not with Israel's wickedness, but with how Yahweh dealt with it; and the message is that, though Israel was deserving of utter destruction, Yahweh actually preserved a group of survivors to carry on the people's identity. *Lord of Hosts* – see Introduction, pp. xxviif.; *a few survivors* implies that a large part of the population had been slaughtered. *Sodom* and *Gomorrah* appear throughout the OT as symbols of utter corruption and divine retribution (see Gen. 18–19). Jerusalem had been as guilty as these two cities; nevertheless, by divine grace, the city and its population was not completely destroyed.

The futility of their sacrifices
1.10–17

This is a much quoted passage; it occurs in lectionaries as one of the lessons for Ash Wednesday, for Epiphany 6, and also allied to headings like 'The Right Use of the Sabbath'. It has been said to affirm the futility of outward forms of religion. The words 'vain oblations' of v. 13 (AV and RV) have been a gift to iconoclasts, but their exegesis is not sound. In the first place, a large part of the OT deals with festivals and sacrifices. If such outward performances are futile, all this material must be rejected, and Isaiah must be set over against Deuteronomy and Leviticus as representing a fundamentally different concept of religion. Careful study of the OT does not sustain such a contention. Secondly, the passage also appears to proscribe observance of the sabbath, gatherings for worship, and even prayer, which surely cannot be the true sense. Thirdly, the greatest figures of the OT, Abraham, Moses, and Elijah, to name but three, built altars to offer sacrifice. The answer is clear. What is decried here is not the external forms themselves but the performance of these forms by people whose lives were at odds with the offerings they were making. Fifty years ago it was argued that prophets and priests were in permanent contention on this matter, but this thesis has long since been rejected. It is more common today to argue that some prophets, at least, had an important place in the performance of the cult. Worship, in common with much formal behaviour, has no meaning by itself. It has meaning only as a dramatic symbol of a way of living. Sending flowers is an outward form; if the action represents true love, it is a delightful means of expressing it. But if the flowers are sent by an unfaithful partner as a means of deception, the act is hypocritical and deplorable. No one would conclude, however, that sending flowers is itself a dubious action. This passage, therefore, affirms an important theological principle: worship can never be justified purely in its own terms. The fact that it is liturgically correct, or aesthetically appealing, or lavishly presented avails nothing, important as some of these considerations may be. Worship is an expression of true devotion, otherwise expressed practically in fidelity, obedience, and just behaviour, or it is nothing. Worship is a means of giving voice, in an hour or so, to a devotion that is a permanent disposition and activity.

1.10   This oracle is put next to the previous one because of the link words *Sodom* and *Gomorrah*. Editors often use this device to link passages that are not related by date or subject matter. Evidently showy sacrifices are going on apace; the rich, at least, were prospering. As it would take the nation a long time to recover from the situation described in vv. 7f., we must assume that this oracle comes from an earlier period, before the Assyrian pressure was felt. Isaiah is addressing his contemporaries in Jerusalem. *the word of the LORD* is a common way of describing a prophetic oracle; it conveys the same idea as *vision* in v. 1. *Sodom* and *Gomorrah* are used as symbolic names for a very sinful people. *rulers* are magistrates and people of relatively low rank spread throughout the nation. They are singled out because they set the fashion in worship as in everything else. The poor were less guilty, presumably because they could not afford extravagant sacrifices and because the trendsetters had set a bad example. The Heb. for *teaching* is *ṭôrâ*. We know this word from Torah, the name for the first five books of the OT, which, since the fourth century BCE, have constituted the sacred Law of Judaism. In Isaiah's day, the Torah in that sense was still in the future, and the word simply meant 'instruction' and not necessarily the divine instruction referred to here.

1.11 *countless sacrifices* indicate self-indulgence as well as the shallow notion that Yahweh would be impressed by mere quantity. The word for *sacrifices* is a general term, but, as the next line refers to *whole-offerings*, we can infer that peace-offerings are meant here. Peace-offerings could be riotous occasions, for, though Yahweh and the priests were given a share, most of the carcase was eaten by the worshipper and his friends (Lev. 3; 7.11–21, 28–34). *whole-offerings* were not self-indulgent, as the whole carcase was burnt and the worshippers got nothing (Lev. 1), but they could still be ostentatious and hypocritical. *fat* and *blood* were the parts that were always offered to Yahweh (Lev. 3.16f.).

1.12 The division between verses is awkward and REB is right to include 12a in the previous sentence. *into my presence* raises an interesting question. In its original unpointed form the Heb. could mean 'to see my face', and one ancient version translates it this way; but Ex. 33.20 says that you cannot see God's face and live, and it is clear that there were early misgivings about this reading. The LXX assumed a different set of vowels and translated the verb as a passive, 'to be seen by me', though there is no word in the Heb. for 'by'. The MT took the same line.[1] REB gives the right sense without solving the problem. The LXX also has the idea of letting 12b stand as

---

[1] Hebrew was originally written without vowels; the actual sound of the words was preserved by oral tradition. In this case the consonants could be read as either active or passive, and evidently in early days there were alternative traditions. To remedy this Jewish scholars invented a system of vowels that were written below and above the consonants. The resultant text has been the standard text of the Hebrew Bible since the tenth century CE. It is known as the Masoretic Text (MT) from the word meaning 'tradition'.

a sentence on its own and REB follows this. REB then borrows *No more* from v. 13 and adds it to 12c making good sense of a difficult line. Compare RV and RSV which remain faithful to the Heb. and are much less clear. This illustrates one of the difficulties of translation. How far can other ancient versions be trusted when the Heb. is difficult? In this instance the LXX is helpful, but we need to be wary, because the LXX frequently reveals a mind of its own. *tread my courts* – the verb has a negative overtone suggesting that worshippers tramp about like cattle, desecrating the temple *courts*.

1.13   The language is very strong. The word translated *is abhorrent* is normally reserved for Baalish rites and other abominations. *the reek of sacrifice* is probably correct, though it might be 'incense'. Minor celebrations took place at *New moons* (I Sam. 20.5, 18, 24; II Kings 4.23; Ps. 81.3; Hos. 2.11; Amos 8.5), that is, the first day of the lunar month. *sabbaths* are deplored here despite the fact that the sabbath figures in the Decalogue; it is the sabbath observance of the people addressed that is the problem. It is they who render the *ceremonies idolatrous*.

1.14   *your festivals* refers to Passover, Weeks and Tabernacles, the three great festivals of the pre-exilic calendar.

1.15   Body language is always interesting. One supposes that in prayer the hands were open and turned upwards, partly to receive, partly to demonstrate that they do not constitute a threat as a clenched fist would (Ex. 9.29, 33; Ps. 44.20; 143.6). *countless prayers* – Matt. 6.7 is relevant here. There is nothing wrong with prayer, but if the person praying is morally unacceptable, adding prayer to prayer will not help. The *blood on your hands* is the first indication of the precise sin that makes their offerings unacceptable. Vv. 16f. explain it further. Those addressed are not accused of murder but injustice. To speak of *blood* may seem like hyperbole, but injustice to the poor in a relatively insecure society could well mean death.

1.16   Accusation ceases and exhortation takes over. There follows a list of eight imperatives providing the hearers with a programme for reform. It is interesting to note that the commands, *Wash and be clean,* depend upon a ceremonial image and may even require ceremonial action.

1.17 *justice* (Heb. *mišpāṭ*; see Introduction, p. xxviii) is one of the most important words in OT religion. It refers to the general standard of uprightness in society, not simply to the resolutions of the courts. No legal system can operate in a context of mafia-like intrigue; bribery and intimidation soon corrupt any system. The law must be supported by a universally accepted ethos of good faith. *justice*, therefore, refers to everyday behaviour, not simply to litigation. *uphold the rights* – this is the verbal form of the root from which the noun *justice* is derived and it covers the same range of meaning. *fatherless, widow* – in Hebrew society, these, together with immigrants and dispossessed Levites, are the people who are most likely to suffer, not simply personal oppression, but structural oppression from a society built on the patriarchal family. For this reason, Deuteronomy requires that these groups be especially protected. This is where *justice* comes in. There is no *justice* if the wealthy and the strong are prosperous (and very active in religious assemblies) and the weak and the poor suffer.

A divine appeal
1.18–20

The literary form of this short oracle is a speech by Yahweh himself, but we must not be misled. Theologically, all these oracles are the same – a divine message given through a human prophet. The fact that the oracles use different formulae, *it is the LORD who speaks* (v. 2), *listen to the word of the LORD* (v. 10), *says the LORD* (v. 18) and display different moods does not alter this. There is a change in tone. Yahweh speaks quietly, reasonably, graciously. Many commentators are concerned that v. 18, which seems to represent total grace (RV etc.), contradicts vv. 19f., which requires obedience. So they read 18 as a question, 'can they be white as snow?', or as an exhortation, 'let them be white as snow', or even as heavy sarcasm. REB takes 18 as showing the possibilities and 19f. as revealing the logic of righteousness, grace and judgement. This disposes of the contradiction and is a fair translation of the Hebrew.

1.18 *argue* – there are many ways of translating this verb. The idea of an argument between two sides in court (as in vv. 2f.) does not really fit the context here. 'Let us work this out between us' is the best sense. *scarlet, crimson* – these terms are not normally used to imply guilt in the OT, but they tie up nicely with 15e. *white* does appear for innocence, but not as often as one might expect. This actually makes the oracle stronger, because, when it was written, it was not using clichés.

1.19 No verse in the Bible sets out the prophetic and Deuteronomic teaching more clearly. The promise has two sides and the positive is put first. *to obey* – the Heb. verb usually means 'to hear'; it is a splendid example of the way in which Heb. gathers up a whole series of meanings in one word. The verb means 'to hear', 'to listen', 'to understand', and 'to obey'. All these elements are necessary if the word of Yahweh is to be taken with proper seriousness. *the best that earth yields* – the promised reward is thoroughly materialistic; it is neither 'spiritual', nor confined to the next world. The impressive account of spirituality, worship, and ethics found in the OT concerns itself with this earth. (Isa. 26.19 provides an exception which will be discussed when we come to it.)

1.20 This is the other side of the coin and it is equally materialistic. *The LORD himself has spoken* – once again the prophet claims no authorship for himself. The oracle leaves us asking the question: did it always work out like that? See the discussion in the Introduction, pp. xxvi, xxix.

Indictment of Jerusalem
1.21–23

The form of this oracle is that of a lament, a form often used in the psalms; it is a kind of dirge sung over the city. The subject matter suggests that these verses should be taken with verses 24–26. There is no external enemy; the trouble comes from within Israel. That suggests an early date before the Assyrian threat had appeared.

1.21 *faithful city* – was Jerusalem ever faithful? There were some gruesome actions even in David's day. The prophets sometimes idealized the past. Jerusalem is not named in the Heb., though there is no doubt that Jerusalem is indicated. The LXX inserts the word 'Zion'. *played the whore* – the same image is used again and again in the OT for those who desert Yahweh for Baal, committing 'the composite crime' (Introduction, p. xxiii). The fact that Baalish rites included ritual prostitution makes it peculiarly appropriate. Fidelity played a large part in the Hebrew understanding of morality. *the home of justice* – the place where there was fair dealing all round and not simply in the courts. *where righteousness dwelt* – there is an allusion here which is lost in English. In Gen. 14, the priest-king of Jerusalem was the mysterious Melchizedek; and when David conquered Jerusalem, he mysteriously acquired a new priest called Zadok. The Heb word ṣedeq, meaning 'righteousness', lies behind both names.[2] It is reasonable to infer that ṣedeq was part of a sacral or regal title belonging to Jerusalem. So *where righteousness dwelt* is a very pointed description.

1.22 These oracles are packed with images. They make the language vigorous, exciting and memorable, but they do not aid precision. *silver* and *fine liquor* probably stand for the qualities of justice and righteousness. Both can be adulterated, cheapened and spoiled.

1.23 The attack is focussed on the leaders of the community. *Your rulers are rebels* neatly preserves the alliteration of the Heb. The *rulers* were the product of the monarchical system which, though two and a half centuries old, was not regarded by everyone as entirely suitable for a godly people (see I Sam. 8.10–22). The older, tribal structure had no place for court aristocrats. Prophets seemed to have no difficulty in longing for a true son of David as king while still deploring court aristocrats. *associates of thieves* – the crime is not common theft but oppressive extortion, which takes place openly in unjust societies. *chases after* – they not merely expect bribes, but insist

---

[2] The consonants s, d and q are sometimes transliterated z, d and k.

on them. The *fatherless* and the *widow* can pay no bribes, so they are denied justice. This echoes v. 17; it describes a society far gone in corruption.

The standard of judgement expressed here is ever-topical. For preachers it means at least three things. First, social issues are important. Moral breakdown is not simply an individual matter; the city is corrupt as a single entity. Secondly, those promoted to positions of power bear a great load of responsibility for the moral health of the city. If they err, the city as a whole is lost. Thirdly, *justice* and *righteousness* are the cornerstones of a godly society.

The purging of Zion
1.24–28

If vv. 21–23 are the charge, vv. 24–26 are the sentence. Isaiah's indictment of his contemporaries is as forceful as that of Amos, but Isaiah is more ready to see the redemptive power of Yahweh at work.

1.24 *therefore* – a strong indication of a logical link between 21–23 and 24–26. *word of the* LORD – for the fifth time in the chapter the words that follow are attributed to Yahweh (cf. vv. 1, 2, 10, 18). The weight and certainty of the sentence are emphasized by the sonorous titles given to the judge. *the* LORD – not here the name Yahweh, which occurs in the next title, but a word meaning 'supreme governor', sometimes used of men and sometimes of God. *the* LORD *of Hosts* – see Introduction, p. xxviiif. *the Mighty One of Israel* – an ancient title (see Gen. 49.24) emphasizing power, even violent power, which occurs in 49.26 and 60.16, but nowhere else in the prophetic books. *secure a respite* – Yahweh is represented as being made uncomfortable by his enemies; colloquially, Yahweh has 'had enough'. *foes, enemies* – the people so described do not, of course, realize that this is what they are. To understand the word *vengeance* properly in its OT context, we need to divest it of the overtones of hate and passion. The true sense lies in the right of an offended person to seek a just requital.

1.25   Punishment turns into a promise of renewal. The verse recaptures the images of v. 22 and extends them. *act against* – lit. 'turn my hand' from supporting to chastizing. *potash* – a reference to some primitive smelting process for purifying metals.

1.26   As in v. 21, the past is idealized. The eschatological promise here is social and political – sound judges and counsellors. The inference, which can be confirmed again and again in the prophets, is that the nature of society is all-important to the vocation of the people of God. Once justice is established, the people become righteous and faithful. 26d recalls 21ab, perhaps conclusive proof that the two passages should be taken together. Here the pun is even more obvious; *Home of Righteousness* is in Heb. 'city of ṣeḏeq', but everybody knew that this was Jerusalem's proper character; it was the city of Melchizedek and of Zadok.

1.27   REB connects 27f. to 24–6, but the two verses may be a later addition made by an editor who knew how Zion's history had turned out. This would help to explain the difficult phrase, *her returning people*. Some commentators would make a break here and connect 27f. to 29–31, which are also regarded as a later addition. *Zion* – the city is named for the first time in the sequence that began in 21. *justice* and *righteousness* echo 21. *her returning people* could refer to those who repent; more probably it refers to those who would come home from deportation after some future catastrophe, and what more likely than the Babylonian exile? In either case, the new population will be free from the faults of the old.

1.28   A general warning that the restored city would not be free from absolute moral demands. *Rebels and sinners* and *those who forsake the Lord* are very inclusive categories; they include the overtly unfaithful as well as the hypocritical, the ruled as well as the rulers.

The positive side of the problematic word *vengeance* is evident here. Yahweh's wrath has a reforming purpose. The prophet does not expect the people to return to fidelity and obedience before they are taught a harsh lesson. Refining and purging are drastic metaphors. Again we are impressed by the moral seriousness of Isaiah. Where rebellion of such magnitude is concerned, the road to restoration will be painful and the moral demands will remain in place. Isaiah has no time for the soft doctrine, 'He will forgive; it's his business'.[3]

A further prophecy of judgement
1.29–31

The final verses of the chapter read like an addition from a later time. There is no introductory formula, and the vocabulary and substance are different from what appears in the rest of the chapter. This may indicate the work of an editor who knew the tragic history of the nation and who wanted to match the prophecy to the fulfilment. The sin of which those addressed are guilty is not social injustice but syncretistic worship (but see Introduction, pp. xxiif.). The attack is on two fronts. What the false gods offered appeared attractive, but it offended against the traditional, austere morality of Yahweh's people. And those gods could not deliver what they promised anyway; for they were more vulnerable than their worshippers.

1.29   *sacred oaks, garden-shrines* – both indicate elements in the Canaanite fertility cult. There is another pun here, because *oaks* and 'gods' are very similar in Hebrew.

1.30   A nice example of carrying the war into the enemy camp. The tree that figures in your cult is deciduous; in full leaf it is glorious, but, as the summer goes by, the leaves wither and fall. Not a very good argument, perhaps, for, though the tree appeared to die at the end of the summer, it sprang to life again in the spring and was thus an apt symbol of the dying and rising of the seasons and of the gods associated with them. The *garden without water* is a more successful image, for the flowers soon shrivel and die under the Mediterranean sun and the garden becomes grey dust.

1.31   Another weakness of the supposedly sacred tree was its

---

[3] The supposed last words of Heinrich Heine, nineteenth-century German poet and author, who never was anything of a theologian.

inflammability. Fires at the end of the summer are a terrible threat in hot countries. A forest can disappear in a few hours. *tow* – some kind of tinder that easily catches fire. *what is made from it* – the Heb. is not entirely clear at this point, and various suggestions are made by commentators to tidy it up. REB is as good as any and it makes a telling point: 'even supposedly sacred trees burn, and idols, made from trees, burn too.' The poor god and his sacred tree go up in smoke together and there is no one to save them. A similar attack on idols, at greater length, is found in 44.10–20.

The inadequacy of what different people call god is a proper theme for the preacher. Belief is a complex mixture of perceived truth and desire. The prophet was so sure of the former that the latter had no place in his reckoning. Not so his contemporaries. The truth they perceived was confused by desire for a more indulgent god and a more pleasurable service. Wishful thinking was ever the enemy of truth.

All nations turn to Zion
2.1–5

This well-known passage occurs in many lectionaries allied to themes as different as Advent, Christian Unity, and Remembrance Day. It presents a remarkable picture of all the peoples of the world coming up to Zion to learn humbly from Yahweh and to accept his judgements in peace. Micah 4.1–4 contains an almost identical oracle (Micah was a contemporary of Isaiah). Who was the original author? The evidence points in different directions. Micah's is the better version, because his v. 4, omitted from Isaiah, provides the proper climax; but Micah concludes with a formula, 'for the mouth of the Lord has spoken it', which is, perhaps, more characteristic of the Isaiah tradition (see 1.20; 40.5; 58.14; cf. only Micah 4.4). The matter is of no great importance, for an oracle does not necessarily gain in authority if it can boast a clearly identified author. On the contrary, the fact that two editors wished to include it underlines its significance.

The passage is unrelated to what goes before and what comes after, and its theme does not fit well with Isaiah's historical context; it

15

would suit the time of Second Isaiah rather better. It is possible that we have here, not so much an oracle, as a psalm. There is a fairly obvious group of 'Songs of Zion' in the Psalter (24; 46; 48; 76; 87; etc.); they represent affirmations of faith rather than precise prophecies. This passage represents the pinnacle of Zion theology; if it does belong to the First Isaiah, then it must surely come late in his life, after he had witnessed the deliverances of 735 and 701 and become convinced that Zion had a unique place in the plan for the fulfilment of the divine promises.

On balance, the best explanation is that the oracle was born out of the Zion theme, as it developed both in the thought of the First Isaiah and in cultic celebration, but actually composed amidst the hopes of the late exilic period.

2.1 Already we have another heading much like 1.1; again it is not clear over which oracles the heading extends. *message* in Heb. is simply 'word', a word that Isaiah 'saw'. REB distinguishes having a vision in 1.1 from receiving a message in a vision in 2.1; the difference is slight in Heb. and theologically there is no difference at all.

2.2 *In days to come* – the time reference is vague. There are no hints of when the climax of history will be reached, as there were in later apocalyptic writing. *the mountain of the Lord's house* – an ungainly phrase made by joining two common phrases, 'mountain of the Lord' and 'house of the Lord' together. Mountains are important in Hebrew religious imagery. Yahweh revealed himself to Israel on a mountain, and in Canaanite mythology a mountain in the north, secure against the floods of chaos, was the abode of the gods. Zion combines elements of both, but challenges the Canaanite concept by affirmations such as we find here and in the 'Songs of Zion'. *set over, raised high* – these terms are best understood as a strong metaphor rather than as a prophecy of a new cosmology. *all the nations* – the Heb. word is *gôyîm*, the term that later meant 'gentiles'. Universalism of this kind belongs to the Isaiah tradition, but there is real doubt whether it began in the eighth century BCE. It is easier to place such a vision in the Persian period, when there was some kind of religious freedom, than in the years when Assyria was mercilessly pillaging the lands around Judah.

2.3 *go up* – the procession up the slopes of Mount Zion was an important part of Hebrew worship, as many psalms testify, but, for many country dwelling Hebrews, the procession began far away when they left their homes to *go up* to Jerusalem. A huge composite procession is indicated. *ways, paths* – these words are used frequently as an image for the will of Yahweh. In the unmapped and dangerous terrain in which the Hebrews lived, *ways* and *paths* provided a certain security and so gave grounds for confidence. The use of this image suggests that Yahweh's commandments provided his people with a secure route from life to death through a world that was often hostile and threatening. Note that the root meaning of the Heb. word for sin is 'erring from the path'. *instruction* – *ṭôrâ*, see note on 1.10. The fact that the only reliable teaching, for all nations, emanates from *Jerusalem* means, of course, that Yahweh is the only reliable God. It also implies that divine instruction was mediated in the temple cult, in which both priest and prophet had a part.

2.4 In the age of blessedness, the primary factor will be justice between the nations. Once a fair *arbiter* has been recognized, weapons will be unnecessary. The temple was a place where people could seek settlement for disputes and answers to searching questions (see Deut. 17.8–13). Almost certainly this picture of the glorious future contains no reference to a messianic figure, though it is just possible that the word *arbiter* implies such a ruler laying down the law under Yahweh. This illustrates an important, but frequently overlooked, fact, that the future hopes of the OT writers do not form a consistent pattern. They represent flashes of insight, not a full scenario. The attempts, and there have been many, to make a coherent picture out of these flashes of insight owe more to the imagination of the modern authors than to the text itself. *mattocks* – probably a better translation than the traditional 'ploughshares'. The Heb. word is rare, but it seems to have meant a tool that needed sharpening. For centuries these vivid lines have been used to represent mankind's longing for peace and they have acquired a meaning far greater than any author intended. The more accurate, modern translations destroy the rhythm and the associations. Is it worth it? There is no easy answer.

2.5 A rather flat end to a stirring oracle, and yet an essential one. Glorious visions of the future are simply self-indulgent if they do not determine present behaviour.

This oracle can be misunderstood. Superficially it can be seen as a piece of Hebrew triumphalism, brazenly supposing, as all expressions of nationalist triumphalism do, that other nations will come to see that they have been wrong. But on the deepest level the oracle transcends nationalism. The God of Jacob is not Israel's possession, but the One, True, Holy God, who upholds all creation, on whom all peoples depend, from whom all truth and faith derive, and to whom all worship is due. Peace is not made by errant humans contriving schemes, even co-operative schemes, for their own advantage. Peace can rest only on common recognition of the ultimate and transcendent truth which demands absolute loyalty. So common worship and common obedience are the key. This, of course, is idealistic, but idealism has a proper place in theology and it is sad that it is commonly put down as 'soft-headed'. So-called realism, which means limiting one's hopes to what can be envisaged and fulfilled, more or less at once, fails to do justice to the biblical vision and fails to allow space for the divine surprise. Moreover, realistic programmes must be judged against ultimate ideals; otherwise their goals will be reduced to the level of expediency.

Against idolatry
2.6–11

In this oracle and the next one we seem to have two oracles that belong together; the same two subjects, idolatry and the day of Yahweh, run through both. The text is rather mixed up, but this does not prevent the expression of a powerful doctrine of God.

2.6   The structure of the verse is awkward. *you* can only mean Yahweh, but the imperatives in v. 10 are addressed to the people; everything in between 6a and 10 is a description of the people in the third person. The picture in 6b–9 is not of a people miserably abandoned by Yahweh, but of a people quite happily abandoning him. The only way to improve the sense is to emend or rearrange the text, and unfortunately there is no obvious and agreed way of doing that.

2.7   The verse describes a land enjoying great prosperity, which could apply to Judah only in the period before the Assyrians became a threat (cf. 1.10f.).

2.8 The wealth was the result of trade, and trade meant familiarity with and obligations to neighbouring nations. Religion was an integral part of social and even commercial life, so syncretistic practices were the almost inevitable consequence of these contacts. *idols* – there are various words for 'idol' in Heb. The one used here is very useful to the prophet because it derives from a word suggesting worthlessness and yet it is similar to the word for a god. It makes a nice pun.

Throughout Isaiah the argument is pressed that idols do not deserve worship from human beings because human beings made them (2.20; 40.19f.; 44.9–17; 46.6f.). Idolatry was not quite as unsophisticated as we are inclined to suppose. If someone made an idol, he was not creating a new god, but giving extended existence to a god already supposed to exist. This idea of fluid and multiple manifestation is present, weakly or strongly, in most cultures, including our own. A portrait of the queen in a foreign embassy is not just a piece of coloured cardboard; it is a manifestation of her theoretical presence and real authority. This is why some Christians are nervous about idol figures brought back from abroad. Of course the concept depends upon the reality of the original. Isaiah, with brilliant vision, sweeps the fears aside. The supposed god is nothing and all the copies of it are copies of nothing!

2.9 The conclusion of this part of the oracle is that the prosperity is hollow; a great humiliation awaits the nation, and not only the nation but all mankind. Perhaps a natural disaster rather than an invading army is indicated. REB omits a difficult phrase; see marg. A similar refrain occurs in v. 17.

2.10 A peremptory command to go out and hide in the rocks away from a disaster, identified with the divine *presence*, that Yahweh will bring upon the world. It is not clear here what kind of catastrophe is envisaged. Flight would be the natural response both to an invader and an earthquake. Evidently the blow has not yet fallen. *dread presence, splendour of his majesty* – these words, repeated in vv. 19 and 21, testify to the profound doctrine of God that Isaiah presents. God is unutterably good, but not in the easy-going way of sentimental

19

piety. His goodness is awe-inspiring, holy, righteous; hence the urge to hide.

2.11 When the disaster strikes, proud human beings will be brought down, but Yahweh will be exalted; for the event will reveal the true state of affairs. Such a revelation can only add to human humiliation and divine majesty. *on that day* is another link between vv. 6–11 and 12–22, for the latter is all about the coming day of doom. The idea of an appointed day when Yahweh will intervene to settle all scores is common in prophecy.

The passage may be difficult, but the majesty of Yahweh, the utter hollowness of supposed rivals, and the helplessness of the human race all find expression in it.

The day of doom
2.12–22

The first six verses prophesy a day of doom on all human pride. Throughout the passage the proud are described in impressive images drawn from both nature and culture. The precise form that the divine action will take is never made clear, but it seems to involve a universal catastrophe. If there are righteous people in the nation, they will apparently share the fate of the unrighteous. Much is said in the prophetic books about social injustice, false worship and moral excesses; here we concentrate on the fundamental sin of arrogance before God.

2.12 *high and lifted up* – the Heb. reads, 'lifted up and it shall become low', which rather clumsily anticipates the blow that falls in v. 17. The REB translation requires a slightly different reading, but the LXX provides encouragemernt for making the change.

2.13 *cedars of Lebanon* – tall cedars flourished in the mountains of *Lebanon* to the north of the land of Israel. They provide an obvious image for the proud (cf. Judg. 9.15; II Kings 14.9; S. of Sol. 5.15; Isa.

35.2; 60.13). *Bashan* was a fertile area to the north-east of the Sea of Galilee.

2.16 *Tarshish* is probably in Spain; only the largest and tallest ships could reach it (cf. note on 23.1). *vessels* – the meaning of the Heb. is uncertain, hence the strange translations of AV, RV and JB, but a small emendation gives the word for 'ship' or 'vessel'.

2.17 At this point we have left the images behind. The *pride* and the *loftiness* belong to human beings alone. They will be brought down; Yahweh alone will be exalted.

2.18 The futile gods will share in the humiliation.

2.19 See comments on v. 10. The Heb. of 19ab is slightly different from that of 10a, but the sense is the same.

2.20 *On that day* things will seem as they really are. *idols* – see note on v. 8. *dung-beetles* – the Heb. word occurs nowhere else and its meaning has to be guessed from its root, which has to do with digging. It hardly matters. The force of the contemptuous reference is clear even in the uncertainty.

2.21 The Heb. of 21ab is different from both 10a and 19ab, but the sense is the same.

2.22 The verse looks like an addition, a prudential comment addressed by an editor to all readers of the text. It is missing from the LXX. REB has rearranged the verse to enhance the sense.

This too is a tangled passage, but it includes a fine doctrine of God, majestic in absolute being but also powerful in history, a wise recognition of the human propensity to posture arrogantly before God, strong words about idols, and solemn references to the day when Yahweh will vindicate himself. Perhaps the most significant factor is the concept of Yahweh's activity in history. Isaiah began with a righteous and holy God; he was aware of the sins of his people and the tragedies of their history, and he had no difficulty in seeing the causal relation between these three. The first confronted with the second leads to the third (see Introduction, pp. xxvif., xxixff.).

A prophecy of disorder
3.1–7

The inference from vv. 2f. is that society in Judah is well-ordered and prosperous, but v. 1 affirms that this will not last. The anarchy described is surely terminal, but Judah's downfall did not come until more than a century after Isaiah's death. So either this piece is an exaggeration, or it is an accurate long-term forecast, or, most probably, the prophecy must be dated some time after Isaiah's heyday.

3.1   Again Yahweh is introduced with a sonorous title (cf. 1.9, 24). *prop and stay* – no English phrase can be as effective as the Heb. which uses the same word twice, in masculine and feminine forms, to mean 'support of every kind'. Society will be thrown into chaos so that people may see where true authority lies. A rather prosaic editor, possibly remembering the actual siege of Jerusalem, added the reference to bread and water which is in the Heb. See REB marg.

3.2   This verse and the next list the leading figures of society, whether approved or not. *prophets* are not necessarily the noble figures whose work we revere. There were many prophets who operated for financial gain, and there is every reason to suppose that they were open to corruption. Often they worked in groups in the service of the king (see I Kings 22, Zech. 13.3f. and Jer. 2.8, 26; 5.31, etc.). *diviners* are part of the social scenario (but see Deut. 18.10); their employment is given as one of the sins that brought the northern kingdom to an end (II Kings 17.17f.). *elders* had considerable influence as heads of families in the old, pre-monarchical structure, and some of that influence survived. The omission of king and priest is puzzling.

3.3   *counsellors* were appointed by kings to give advice where the king's own knowledge and experience were lacking; they were thus very influential. *magicians* – the meaning of the word is not certain, but this is the best guess. The practice of magic in the ANE depended on a vast deposit of secret lore, the mastery of which made magicians appear *skilled*. They were not fools and many were not rogues. They practised a serious, but as time has shown, a largely bogus science. *expert enchanters* also carries the sense of serious learning. The offence of these professions was that they challenged Yahweh's autonomy by attempting to provide an alternative way of managing events.

3.4 The first three verses have been in the third person, but Yahweh now speaks in the first person. *youths* – the word covers all ages from infancy to young manhood, but the overtone draws attention to the limitations of the age rather than its potential. The idea of *youths* having authority was shocking because age, experience and wisdom were thought to go together. *as the whim takes them* – the Heb. puts it rather nicely: the boys will rule the people and caprice will rule the boys.

3.5 Once the leaders have been removed, unrestrained greed and aggressiveness will do the rest. *nobodies* is not an ideal translation, nor is *men of rank*; these renderings suggest a contrast simply in terms of social standing, but the Heb. means, 'lightweights towards those of real competence and worth'.

3.6 A graphic description of a society in chaos. One brother appeals to another; the father is presumably dead. The *cloak* is not a sign of authority but simply the outer garment worn in the daytime and used as a blanket at night. The man's good fortune is enough for him to be offered power and responsibility. *our stricken family* – an imaginative translation. The noun is rare – we have only Zeph. 1.3, where there is similar uncertainty, to guide us – and there is no adjective in the Heb.

3.7 The brother speedily repudiates the promotion. Who wants authority in such a situation?

A few years ago a British Prime Minister made the memorable statement, "There is no such thing as society." The Hebrew prophets would have disagreed. The force of this oracle is that the order of society is as much the work of Yahweh as is the order of creation. Yahweh has dealings, not only with the individual, but with the city and the nation. The city and the nation can be obedient or can rebel, can be blessed or punished. Yahweh does not approve of all the kings, counsellors and captains, still less of the magicians and enchanters, but even when society acts wickedly, Yahweh still holds it together until the time when he decrees social breakdown as a punitive measure. The righteousness or unrighteousness of society is thus a proper theme for the preacher who takes the OT seriously.

Jerusalem in dire straits

3.8–12

It is difficult to decide whether this passage is a prophecy looking to the future or the record of a past situation by someone within the Isaiah tradition. Even if it is a prophecy, the date is uncertain; unhappily there were many occasions between the mid-eighth century and the Persian period when the description would have been apt.

3.8   *word* – the Heb. means 'tongue' and it emphasizes the distinction between the word of Yahweh and his prophet, and the shameful word of the sinner. *open rebellion* – the Heb. is difficult, but there is no doubt that an offence against Yahweh's glory is intended.

3.9   *The look on their faces* – the meaning of the first noun is problematic; REB's translation is reasonable, though others take a different line. The implication is that the citizens of Jerusalem were shameless in their sin, looking, not guilty, but pleased with themselves. *like Sodom* – in that most wicked of all cities vice was paraded as normality. *Woe betide them!* – into the description of sinful Jerusalem are now inserted five lines of Deuteronomic teaching, in a form we associate with the wisdom literature, interrupting the flow of condemnation.[4] Their force is that the people of Jerusalem have brought this disaster on themselves. One possible explanation is that the last line of 9 was a prophetic comment, a kind of aside, causing minimum interruption; but the aside then attracted a longer, and later, comment in 10f.

3.10   This verse is hardly relevant to the situation. There are no righteous in sight. More importantly, 10f. deal with the righteous and the unrighteous as individuals, whereas the rest of the passage deals with the people as a corporate entity. The comment, then, is not appropriate in its present setting, but it may have been very appropriate to the reading of the passage in the editor's own day. *Happy* – the REB translation requires a slight alteration to the Heb. text, as the marg. indicates.

---

[4] The wisdom tradition throve in Israel as in most nations of the ANE. In the OT it is represented by Proverbs, Job, Ecclesiastes, and some psalms.

3.12 Several small changes have to be made in the text. It is clear, however, that a distinction is being made between an oppressive ruling class and the people, with whom the prophet identifies, who are oppressed by them. There is no suggestion that the people are righteous, but they receive more sympathetic treatment because they have been wronged. *my people* – both 12a and 12c begin with this term in Heb., making it very emphatic; it is also moving because the prophet identifies himself with the hapless community. *usurers* – the text actually says 'women', but this is a highly improbable reading. Only a slight change of pointing is necessary to give *usurers* which accords with the LXX and other ancient versions. *usurers* operated inevitably in an agrarian society. Crop failure was never equitable in a hilly country where different slopes suffered differently from climate and erosion. So the unfortunate had to borrow from the fortunate, and harsh rates of interest could destroy the borrowers, hence the legislation in Ex. 22.25 and Deut. 23.19f. *those who guide you* – there is something of a pun here because another meaning of this verb has to do with blessing. Guidance should be a blessing; actually it is a bane.

The passage sets out some of the main features on the theological map of the OT: Yahweh's glory and his righteousness against which sinners prevail not at all, the brazen wickedness of Israel, the law of rewards and punishments which undergirds all human activity, the fact that, in a wicked society, the weak suffer most, and the vocation of the prophet to identify with the wicked populace.

Yahweh's judgement on the leaders
3.13–15

Vv. 13–15 represent a court scene in which Yahweh lays an indictment against the leaders of Israel.

3.13 Yahweh appears as the prosecuting counsel, but there is little doubt that he is also the judge. The Heb. has 'peoples' in the plural, but the subject matter shows that the case is directed against Israel and the LXX reads *his people*.

3.14 *The Lord* comes first in the Heb. sentence, which means that special emphasis is given to the word: 'it is the Lord and nobody else'. *elders* – see note on 3.2. *officers* – the captains of 3.3, but the word has a wide range of meanings and is not limited to military rank. *the vineyard* – a powerful image as it stands, but more powerful when it is remembered that *vineyard* is a metaphor for Israel in 5.1–8. The LXX sharpens this point by reading 'my vineyard'. The leaders have plundered Yahweh's people. *the spoils taken from the poor* – 'loot' would be a better word. Spoil taken, more or less legitimately, from a defeated enemy after a battle is usually represented by a different word. This is simple robbery, and robbery within the family, as it were (cf. 3.12).

3.15 *my people* – there is a triple offence : violence, done to their own people, and that people Yahweh's own possession. By stressing the majesty of Yahweh, the formula in 15c, more majestic than ever in the Heb., also stresses the enormity of the sin and the awesome nature of the judgment.

Once again Isaiah is concentrating on social injustice as the crucial sin. Leaders are indicted for the misuse of power. 'Grinding the faces of the poor' has become something of a cliché, but it is no cliché in the Heb. and doubtless it was no empty phrase to the poor of Jerusalem. Exploiting the poor for the benefit of the rich is an offence in any context, but within the confines of *my people*, it is an outrage against the Lord of Hosts.

Judgement on the women of Zion
3.16–26

The rest of the chapter is a long and bitter attack on the wealthy women of Zion. Compare Isa. 32.9–12; Amos 4.1–3; Jer. 44.15–30. It is not to be supposed that women were more sinful than men, or that they had greater responsibility in moral matters. The women condemned here displayed their wealth more ostentatiously. Evidently, in hard times, those used to self-indulgence suffer most – the antithesis of Bunyan's 'He that is down needs fear no fall.' The description of the women suggests a period of prosperity, but the impending doom is hard to link with any period during the life of Isaiah or, indeed, with any occasion before the humbling of Jerusalem in 586 BCE. The prophet may have been looking back on the fate of the women of Samaria in 721, a fate which the women of Zion escaped at that time.

3.16 The description, despite its acid tone, has verisimilitude. *Zion* is not just a name but the place that Yahweh had chosen for his own, so the term is deeply ironic. *give themselves airs* – the main charge is arrogance and ostentation. *wanton glances* implies that the women were proficient in seduction. *jingling feet* – due to jewellery worn on the ankles.

3.17 This is a devastating comment. *smite with baldness* may not be quite accurate; the verb might refer to smiting them with a scab. In either case, visible humiliation is intended. 17b looks lame after 17a and some translators have 'secret parts' instead of *foreheads*. The reading is uncertain, but the sense is clear. Stripping away hair and headdress would be shameful enough to the women in question.

3.18–23 At this point an editor has interrupted a powerful oracle with a list of ornaments that leaves translators bewildered. Many of the terms occur here only and are of uncertain meaning. It matters not; we have already grasped that the women were over-dressed. For a conscientious attempt to unravel the terms, see Kaiser, *Isaiah 1–12*, p. 80.

3.24 This verse describes the reversal of fortunes. It is best to take 24–26 as a prophecy that the women of Zion will suffer the horrors of being carried away as prisoners of war. With great skill the prophet provides a counter to all the marks of elegance the women boasted. *stench of decay* suggests a ruined city littered with corpses and rubbish. The *rope* suggests a column of prisoners tied together to make it easier for their captors to drive them. *baldness* – shaving the head was a part of ancient mourning rites, but in this case we have to think of women stripped of their headgear and perhaps shaven as a mark of humiliation. *loincloth of sacking* – the basic covering of the poorest servant, made from the roughest of cloth. The *branding* of slaves was common in the ANE.

3.25   At this point the form of address changes suddenly from a third person oracle about the women of Zion to a second person address to the city itself. *Zion* is not mentioned by name in the Heb.; we simply have an address to some feminine representative, but *Zion* is clearly intended. The fate of the men is quite consistent with what has gone before. They will die fighting and the women will be carried off as slaves.

3.26   Here there is another change. The city, still not named in Heb., is spoken of in the third person. *gates* – the gates of a city are a most important part of it; by controlling who goes in and who stays out they determine the character of the enclave. Here they are used as a symbol for the whole city, which is itself a symbol of the inhabitants. *stripped bare* – the city is personified as a woman, helpless and humiliated, which is totally appropriate.

Denunciation is a common feature of prophecy. We may shrink from it for reasons of modesty, or fear, or because we prefer a positive message, but the prophet took the view that the holy Yahweh was outraged by human behaviour and that Yahweh's mouthpiece must say so loud and long. Denunciation has a place (cf. Luke 11.37–54), and maybe we need to display more courage, always supposing, of course, that we are not speaking for ourselves. The vehemence of the condemnation may surprise us, but the prophet is dealing with grave sins – none the less grave by virtue of the fact that they were socially acceptable.

The dispossessed woman
4.1

This verse is suspended between two passages. The sense ties it to 3.24–26, but the formula 'on that day' links it to 4.2. It describes a time of great distress when many males have been killed and social forms have broken down. The solidarity of Hebrew society was its great strength, but this verse describes the obverse side. When social forms are disrupted, survivors are ill-equipped to stand on their own feet. Here the women are prepared to forego their normal rights and provide for themselves in order to secure a marriage. The proposition is against all custom, but evidently the once proud women were driven to it by necessity.

4.1   *seven women* – dramatic hyperbole, no doubt. *take hold* – the fact that the women take the initiative is the really shocking detail; they will do so quite strenuously. *bear your name* – accept your authority and gain the social identity that such a connexion confers. *disgrace* and scorn arise from being single, from being childless, but apparently most of all from being socially disconnected. Not to be a member of a family was to be almost an outcast. If 3.24 relates to women taken prisoner, this verse may well describe the fate of those left behind.

Jerusalem cleansed

4.2–6

The phrase *On that day* is the only thing that links 4.1 and 4.2. The tone of the two prophecies is entirely different. Here we have a picture of a holy people living in a purified city. Like 2.2–4, it is an idealized picture of a glorious future for Zion, based not on the current political situation, but on confidence in Yahweh. It seems to have been constructed in two stages: v. 2, then 3–6. As with 2.2–4, there are indications that the passage belongs to a later period in the Isaiah tradition than the eighth century BCE. This is an oracle of ultimate hope based on confidence in Yahweh's concern for his people and his intention to redeem them.

4.2   *plant* – in later times this term was used as a designation for the messiah (Jer. 23.5; 33.15; Zech. 3.8); a similar image, using a different word, is found in Isa. 11.1. *glorious* – the word is commonly associated with Yahweh, though kings also enjoy glory. Only in a few cases does it relate to nature. Linking *glorious* to *plant* may imply a messianic reference here. *fruit of the land* – one of the features of the golden age will be a rejuvenated natural order that produces food and drink in such abundance that the inhabitants bask in *splendour* (Isa. 30.23–26; Joel 3.18; Amos 9.13; Mal. 3.11f.). *survivors of Israel* – those who have escaped from some disaster, an Assyrian attack, the Babylonian exile, or possibly some future divine judgment.

4.3 *those who are left* – the Heb. word comes from the same root as the first part of the name Shear-jashub (see 7.3). Isaiah was concerned with surviving remnants and the idea has a significant place in the Isaiah tradition. *in Zion* – the group that would come through the sifting process is defined in three ways, all relative to Jerusalem. Many others would be killed or scattered. It is easy to see a reference to the struggling community which attempted to preserve the identity of Israel after the exile. *decreed* – the Heb. refers to 'everyone that is written among the living in Jerusalem', which suggests a census list. The idea of a list of the righteous is a late one (cf. Dan. 12.1; Mal. 3.16). It belongs to a time when the holiness of the whole people of God seemed scarcely credible and it was necessary, within the general concept of the holy nation, to consider individual virtue. We see the beginnings of this idea in Jer. 31.29f. and Ezek. 18. The fact that the virtuous are called *holy* is surprising in view of Isaiah's usage elsewhere (1.4; 6.3; etc.), but not so surprising in view of the later tendency to use the word *holy* of people and things associated with Yahweh. This verse, therefore, gives a number of indications that the oracle is within the Isaiah tradition, but is from the exilic period or even later.

4.4 *filth* – meaning 'vomit' or 'excrement', which suggests ritual impurity due to syncretism rather than the sins of oppression and vanity recorded in the last chapter (see Ezek. 5.11; 8). *women of Zion* – this shows why the editor placed this oracle here. The awful picture of the previous chapter needed to be set right. Nevertheless the rest of the oracle is about Zion as a whole, not simply the women. Originally, perhaps, there was a singular here, 'daughter of Zion', meaning the city, not the women. This would be a better parallel for *Jerusalem* in the next clause. This recalls 1.8, where the phrase is used in the singular and it is translated simply as *Zion*. To make a link with 3.16–26 the editor had merely to change 'daughter' into a plural so that the sense changed from the city itself to the actual women who lived there. *bloodstains* – there were strict rules for handling blood (see Deut. 12.20–8); otherwise it made everything unclean. *spirit* – a very significant Heb. word. It expresses first the unseen and unpredictable power of the wind and then the unseen and unpredictable power of Yahweh. That power had all kinds of effects, one of which is scorching *judgement*.

4.5 *he will create* – The LXX reads, 'he will come'. In either case the allusion is clear; Yahweh will come upon Zion as he came upon Sinai in smoke and in fire. The fire and smoke of sacrifice are often thought to suggest a link between Zion and Sinai, but here the fire and smoke come from the presence of Yahweh, not from the actions of the worshippers.

4.6 *a cover* – the same word was used in 1.8 for the flimsy shelter of the watchman. Here it is understood in a positive sense as a protection from the elements given by Yahweh. *refuge and shelter* are more substantial constructions.

Whatever denunciations were necessary, the prophets preserved a glowing hope in the faithfulness of Yahweh. The hope lies beyond the purging and cleansing that the situation demanded. The blessings are expressed in material terms because the material world is Yahweh's creation and it is in the material world that he acts; but it is a material world purged by the spirit of judgement. The initiative lies with Yahweh throughout and the end is not simply the protection of his people but the manifestation of his glory on Mount Zion.

The song of the vineyard
5.1–7

This is a song with three stanzas about Yahweh and his vineyard Israel: how he cared for it, how it was unfruitful, and how he would leave it desolate. Vintage songs were an important feature of social life in the ANE, and the passage is a splendid attempt to take over the form of the vintage festival song and turn it into a withering prophecy. It begins as a typical song and becomes increasingly serious until the final explanation and indictment in v. 7. While we have little idea of the date of the composition, we can be reasonably certain that it was first used in Jerusalem when the grape harvest was being celebrated in the autumn festival (Deut. 16.13–15). Israel is described as a vineyard in 3.14 and the image also occurs in 27.2f., Jer. 2.21, 12.10, and Ps. 80.8f. The passage finds a place in most lectionaries.

5.1   If the *I* is Isaiah, then *my beloved* must be Yahweh, but amorous language of that kind is so suggestive of the rites of Baal that commentators shrink from this interpretation. But what is the alternative? Love is mentioned three times in three lines using two different Heb. words, so it can hardly be a mistake. *beloved* cannot reasonably be reduced to 'friend' (see how frequently the word is used in the Song of Songs). It is better to assume that the opening lines belong to a secular song that the prophet has adapted for his own purpose. This is a guess, but not an unreasonable one. After three lines, the amorous terms do not occur again, so there is no need for us to be concerned about the language; the *beloved* is Yahweh and the *vineyard* is Israel.

5.2   This verse tells us a lot about agriculture in the Judaean highlands. Trenching was necessary to control drainage; *stones* were, and are, a permanent nuisance; *a watch-tower* was needed because thieves could easily make off with the the crop (vineyards are still patrolled by armed guards when the fruit is nearly ready); *a wine vat*, cut out of the rock, was used for the first stage of crushing the grapes. V. 5 reveals that hedges and walls were added to protect the vines and to keep out animals. The horticultural terms are difficult to translate with complete confidence, but REB creates the right effect. The whole undertaking was costly, but a vineyard was a long-term investment. *choice red vines* – a single word in Heb. for a highly-prized red grape. *choice grapes* – the Heb. is simply *grapes*; REB supplies the adjective to bring out the sense. *wild grapes* – the word means anything stinking or rotten. So the picture of the fruitful *vineyard* is built up brilliantly for ten lines, but it all comes crashing down in the last evil word.

5.3   The song now takes a serious turn. The inhabitants of Jerusalem are invited to pass judgement on the *vineyard*. As yet they do not know that they are passing judgment on themselves. Nathan's parable of the ewe lamb, which led to David condemn himself, comes to mind (II Sam. 12.1–14). Subtly the person changes. No longer is the prophet singing about the owner; the owner is speaking for himself.

5.4 The premise of the prophetic faith is that Yahweh has done everything possible for Israel's good. This premise undergirds the whole of OT religion, though it is not universally appreciated. See, for example, Ps. 44. But, given the premise, the logic is perfect. It is against all reason that a vineyard planted with high quality vines and carefully tended should produce only bitter fruit. The first question is rhetorical; the answer is clear. The answer to the second is inscrutable; the infidelity of Israel is bewildering and irrational.

5.5 If vv. 3f. represent the judgement, we now move on to the sentence and its execution. In reality no farmer would go to extra trouble to tear up hedges and break down walls in order to punish an unproductive vineyard. He would simply leave it to grow wild. So at this point the oracle begins to take over from the image. Yahweh will not simply withdraw from Israel. He owes it to Israel to teach her a lesson; so there will be a deliberate breaking up operation, as well as letting her *go to waste*.

5.6 The destruction process is intensified. The theme of neglect is continued, but in 6d the owner emerges as the one who controls the clouds, and who will bring about the final desolation by withholding rain. The vineyard thus loses the benefit that even the uncultivated land receives. So, with the greatest subtlety, the identity of the owner is revealed: first the singer's *beloved*, then the hopeful cultivator, then the disappointed owner, then the judge, then the destroyer, then finally the one who commands all nature.

5.7 In one sense this verse is not necessary; artistically the song is complete. But prophets are not simply poets. The thrust of the song has to be set out plainly, aggressively, memorably. *Israel* and *Judah* might mean the northern and southern kingdoms before 721 BCE, but more probably *Israel* here means the holy people in the ideal sense; in which case *Judah* is identified with that *Israel*. That, in turn, will mean that the northern kingdom had already ceased to exist. 7c and d contain two brilliant puns in Heb., for *justice* and *bloodshed* sound very much alike, and so do *righteousness* and *cries of distress*. The last two lines make it clear that, once again, social injustice is the sin that brings Yahweh's judgement on Israel.

No text in the OT sets out more clearly certain essential themes of the prophetic faith. Yahweh chose Israel to be his vineyard, he bestowed infinite care upon her, he had the highest hopes for her. Despite all the attention, Israel failed; the fruit of obedience never appeared. Yahweh is a God of righteousness as well as a God of love; he will not overlook this ingratitude and treachery, Israel will lose her privileges, even that general care that Yahweh bestows upon all nations. It may be said that this theology lacks the theme of redeeming love. Indeed it does, but the book of Isaiah and the prophetic corpus need to be read as a whole.

Six woes
5.8–23

This passage is a series of woes interspersed with prophecies of doom (which may be seen as interruptions) addressed to those who have committed heinous sins, largely of a social kind. 10.1–4 contain another woe, set out in a similar way, and concluding with the same refrain as is found in 5.25ef. This leads many commentators to suppose that originally there were seven woes and that one of them, probably the first, has become detached and transplanted to 10.1–4. There is much to be said for the hypothesis that the woes themselves belong to the ministry of Isaiah. The general tenor of condemnation recalls the oracles of Amos and Hosea and suggests a date in the early part of Isaiah's ministry. The prophecies of doom, however, seem to have been added later, indeed after Jerusalem had fallen to Babylon. In other words, they were written from hindsight.

5.8 *Woe* – a very strong word, though not quite as strong as 'cursed be'. Woes tend to come in series presenting a litany of condemnation (Hab. 2 ; Matt. 23.13–36; Luke 11.42–52; etc.). This verse gives an insight into the tragic process of an agrarian society. The successful, who control the market, buy up the houses and the land of the failures; the failures can do nothing but leave and seek servile work. Some commentators read 8d as part of the punishment, but REB is correct in reckoning it to be part of the offence.

5.9 This verse and the next provide the first prophecy of doom. Something is missing from the Heb. here. We have the first part of 9a but not the second. REB assumes that a word for swearing an oath has slipped out (cf. LXX). The threat is that *great houses* will be reduced to ruins; the large farms will produce almost nothing. An invasion, in which buildings were destroyed and the agricultural process disrupted, seems to be indicated. This is indeed what happened when Jerusalem fell in 586 BCE.

5.10 REB gives approximate modern equivalents to the Heb. terms on the reasonable assumption that, to most readers, the technicalities hardly matter. *Five acres* – the numeral in Heb. is ten and the area probably that which a pair of oxen can plough in a day. As it was probably much smaller than an acre, REB changes ten to *Five. a gallon* – the Heb. *baṯ* is much more than a gallon, indeed about six gallons. *ten bushels* – the Heb. *ḥōmer* was the load an ass could carry; *ten bushels* is not far out. *peck* translates *'êpâ*, which is a tenth of a homer and equal to a *baṯ*. In other words, the crop is a tenth of the seed.

5.11 Drinking early and late, instead of at the evening meal only, shows complete loss of reason and control. Drunkenness was offensive because it involved addiction, foolish behaviour and extravagance. Those who were able to spend all day drinking could do no work, so one assumes they must have been wealthy.

5.12 The carousals were elaborate affairs with musicians contributing to the relaxed atmosphere. *tabors* – percussion instruments held in the hand, like tambourines.[5] The drunkenness and self-indulgence makes these Hebrew revellers blind to the greatest of all realities, the activity of Yahweh in the world around them.

5.13 A second interruption. The verse represents a swift reversal of the situation described in 11f. REB has the future tense in 13a and the present in 13cd, but the whole verse relates to a single disaster. The wealthy would be brought low and the common people would suffer with them. *captivity* – if, as seems probable, the Babylonian captivity is meant, the verse cannot be by Isaiah. That does not mean that an early date for part of the passage must be surrendered. On the contrary, it is to be expected that an eighth-century lament would be

[5] For details of musical instruments, see Ivor H. Jones, 'Musical Instruments in the Bible: The Translation of Technical Terms, I and II' in the *The Bible Translator* 37(1): January 1986, pp.101–16 and 38(1), January 1987, pp. 129–43, and *Music, A Joy for Ever* (London 1989)

adapted to suit later times. *knowledge* is not simply intellectual awareness; it also involves sensitivity, understanding and acceptance. The charge is not that Israel is unaware of Yahweh's existence, but that she has not taken that awareness seriously and acted upon it.

5.14–16   There are good reasons for supposing that these verses are out of place. They represent an expansion of v. 13 and a further interruption of the series of woes.

5.14   *Sheol* is the name given to the abode of the dead. It appears sometimes as a pit or grave, sometimes as a huge cavern beneath the earth, and sometimes figuratively for a dreadful threat. Here the second and third senses dominate. *Sheol* is not to be confused with hell or purgatory. It simply represents the life of the grave, dark, cold, witless, horrific, and inevitable. See note on 14.9.

5.15   This verse is reminiscent of 2.9,11.

5.16   Again the words *judgement* and *righteousness* witness to the fact that it is Yahweh's world. There is no cause for regret if the wicked suffer, for that very suffering affirms that Yahweh's writ runs and no one can interfere with it. See 2.11cd.

5.17   We return to the scene of v. 13, a city just overrun. Animals ranging free invade the enclosures. The Heb. is difficult and translation requires extensive emendation, though the sense is probably correct.

5.18   The third woe contains a clever image. The wicked are as firmly attached to their sins as animals are to their tethers, but of course tethers impede animals. Sin does not liberate, it confines.

5.19   The Heb. has two verbs for *make haste* in 19a, but REB follows an ancient precedent and changes the first of them into the divine name. Some of Isaiah's contemporaries were evidently sceptics (cf. v. 13). They adopt what was, to him, an outrageously insolent attitude to Yahweh. The use of the term, *the Holy One of Israel*, makes it all the more outrageous.

5.20   The fourth *Woe*. Here is the ultimate condition of wickedness, the complete reversal of values. The common word for 'sin' in Heb. means 'missing the mark', but if one missed the mark often enough and with wilful intent, then one declined into a condition of complete, moral perversity. The people described here were not guilty of lapses; they were deeply corrupt.

The doctrine of the universality of sin can be very misleading. If all are sinners and in need of redemption, then all are on much the same level. This is not true. Some struggle with God's help to act righteously; some call evil good and have no desire for righteousness at all. Of course both need radical redemption, but there is a practical and a theological difference between them.

5.21 The fifth *Woe*. This may be a specific reference to the king's counsellors. The verse provides more evidence that the OT puts forward pride as the fundamental sin (cf. 2.12–17).

5.22 The sixth *Woe*. *heroic topers* – lit. 'heroes at drinking wine'; the term is intended to be an aggressive insult, and REB can only be faulted if it appears to introduce a slightly comic overtone. The noun, *gibbôr*, means 'strong and valiant'; it occurs in 9.5 as part of a messianic title. Here it is linked, not with the service of Yahweh, but with the capacity to consume wine.

5.23 This last verse returns to the theme of social justice. We are dealing with people in positions of responsibility who are venal and corrupt. V. 23 would fit better after 20 and 10.1–4 would follow nicely here.

It may seem difficult for a preacher of the gospel to handle a passage that is fundamentally bad news, but the gospel must be put in its proper theological context. For many of our contemporaries the alternative to Christian faith is personal autonomy in life and gentle oblivion in death. What believers call sin is not all that important and the offer of redemption is irrelevant. The prophetic message is that such a view is totally false. Every moment of every day we live under the jurisdiction of an infinitely holy, infinitely gracious Lord. Sins are not peccadilloes but outrages against those who suffer from them, outrages against Yahweh, and personal calamities for the sinner. Judgement is inevitable and divine redemption the only hope. So the gospel message becomes critical. To some extent the argument depends upon the force that we give to the word *Woe*.

It certainly means 'shame' and 'under judgement', but not necessarily 'irretrievably lost'. In the Isaiah tradition God's holiness burns up sinners, but the holiness and righteousness that bring the wicked under judgment may still express itself in grace. Once again, it is necessary to see the OT as a whole and OT and NT together.

The wrath of Yahweh
5.24–30

This passage represents a fierce judgement on Israel or some elements within Israel. There is some doubt about where the verses belong, but there is no need for us to go into the question. The present position is quite apposite because, as we have seen, comments about consequences have been inserted into the Woes. There can be no certainty about date. Verses 26ff. suggest the ruthless eficiency of the Assyrian army, which implies a date in Isaiah's lifetime, but v. 25 suggests the fall of Jerusalem in 586.

5.24   *tongues of fire* – in the hot, rainless summer, fire was a constant hazard; it spread rapidly and was completely uncontrollable; it destroyed everything, both *root* and *buds*. Truly an awesome image of God's judgement. *instruction* – in Heb. *ṭôrâ*; see note on 1.10.

5.25   *the mountains trembled* – imagery of this kind may suggest an actual earthquake in the recent past; or the language may be explained simply as powerful imagery used by people who knew about earthquakes. *corpses lay like refuse* – suggests memory rather than imagination or prophecy. The harshest memory of all was the condition of Jerusalem after its fall in 586. If the verse dates from after that time, the final comment in 25ef is truly dreadful. Not even the fall of Jerusalem, the sack of the temple, the loss of the land are the end. Still Yahweh's anger remains. But what more could happen? In passing one might observe that the notion that religous faith is based on wishful thinking does little to explain sentiments of this kind.

5.26   Yahweh will now exercise his dominion over all the nations upon earth and use one of them, probably Assyria, to punish his own people. The same idea appears in 7.18f. and 10.5f. *hoist a* standard – until the advent of modern means of communication, hoisting a standard was the regular and functional means of mustering an army for war. Yahweh hoists his standard and the nations rally to do his will. *whistle* – a signal that is used to summon flies in 7.18, but it is more likely that it would be used for animals or perhaps slaves, who were trained to obey. Yahweh can *whistle* up nations in the same way. *with all speed* – the compliance of the nations is total.

5.27 There are no incompetent or worn out soldiers in this army.

5.28 The army is all ready for war. *like flint* – presumably tough enough to operate in rocky country where horses often had difficulty (Amos 6.12). *chariot wheels* – chariots had been used in war for centuries, though they came late to Israel, no doubt because, though they could be devastating on the plains, they were less use in hilly country. Nevertheless they were sufficient to inspire fear. *like the whirlwind* indicates that fear. The speed and power of the chariot gave the attacking army the immense advantage of mobility.

5.29 Still more images of the awfulness of the destruction. The roar of the *lion* as it downs its *prey* must have been a terrible sound, well-known to the Hebrews. The prevalence of lions in the area is shown by the fact that there are several Hebrew words for lion. Lions continued to roam in Palestine until mediaeval times. Here the roar is described three times in three lines to force the message home. The fourth line adds the final touch; the carcase is dragged off and no rescuer dares to go after it.

5.30 A verse added because it is also about roaring, not the roaring of lions, but *the roaring of the sea*. 30cd have some resemblance to 8.22, which is also about inescapable doom.

Despite the difficulty with date and context, the passage makes some profound theological points. First, the absurdity of sin. Israel has all the advantages of divine instruction; Yahweh's majesty and power are well-known to her. Yet, against all reason, she chooses to pit her will against his. Secondly, the infinite range of his righteousness. His anger reaches to the full extent of Israel's sin and none of it will be passed over. Thirdly, Yahweh's control of the nations. He is not simply a local deity who might be bribed or cajoled like a small-time judge. He is the God of all nations that are, far beyond the control of any mortal. Fourthly, his righteousness determines the course of history. Events roll on, crushing some and exalting others, but not even the victors are in control. Yahweh directs everything. He may choose Assyria to strike his own people or Babylon to sack his own city. Yahweh is the free sovereign Lord.

The calling of Isaiah
6.1–13

There is wide agreement that a new division, based on Isaiah's own memoirs, begins here. Where the division ends is not so easily determined. Many say 8.18, but REB implies 9.7. REB divides the division into two, 6.1–13 and 7.1–9.7, thus giving immense prominence to this narrative of the prophet's call.

No chapter in Isaiah is better known than this one. It is used on Trinity Sunday and, for obvious reasons, in Ordination services. Theologically it is important because it deals with the divine call. There were all kinds of prophets in OT times, some of them quite disreputable, but, according to the understanding of prophecy that ultimately prevailed in Israel, no true prophet could function unless Yahweh had called him and given him the word. At the same time there is nothing approaching a stock account of the call. Amos refers to the matter in one verse (7.15).; Jeremiah describes an experience as profound as Isaiah's (1.4–10); Ezekiel's account is typically lengthy and abstruse (1–3). Some prophets give no account of their call; in Hosea's case, an account can reasonably be inferred. Isaiah's account is written in the first person singular and we are given the date and the place. There is no reason to question either.

It may seem odd that a passage as fundamental as this should not occur until ch. 6, but the arrangement of the book is the work of editors who have placed this narrative from 742 at the beginning of a division which deals with Isaiah's memoirs, largely relating to the Syro-Ephraimite confederacy of 735. The placing of the material in chs. 1–5 before the memoirs is probably due to the belief that much of those chapters belongs to the period before 735. A more serious problem is that the commission in vv. 8–11 does not adequately describe the scope of Isaiah's ministry, which was not so devoid of hope nor limited to recalcitrant Judah. But, while 1–9a are a description of inward religious experience, 9b–11 and even more 12f. relate to more public matters. We might expect that the record of these public realities would be more specific than that of the inward vision itself.

6.1 *In the year* – the chronology of this period is problematic (see Introduction, p. xx), so precision cannot be guaranteed, but on the scheme followed in this book, the year is 742 BCE. *Uzziah* is also called Azariah, so care must be taken in reading II Kings 14–15 and II Chron. 26. Some have been inclined to see a causal link between the king's death and Isaiah's call: the death was a tragedy that left Judah in need of a prophet. There is some evidence for this in II Chron. 26.1–15, although 26.16–23 and II Kings 15.1–7 are more restrained. It is also contended that the vision was connected with a royal ritual, but this is very controversial. Our firm knowledge of royal rituals in Israel is slight. Moreover, Uzziah was a leper, according to II Chron. 26.21, who could not enter the temple at all. On the whole it is best to suppose that the phrase is used simply to supply a date. There is no reason to doubt, however, that the vision took place when Isaiah was worshipping on a great occasion in the temple. *I saw the* LORD – it is common for prophets to 'hear' the word of the LORD and much less common for them to have visions. However, the book of Isaiah is introduced as a vision in 1.1, and there is no need to infer an important distinction between the two kinds of experience. Both are subjective; it is not to be supposed that anyone else in the temple would have seen or heard anything. Subjective visions are, of course, open to psychological reduction, but we need to watch the logic. It does not follow that, because some 'visions' can be explained as hallucinations, all can be. *seated on a throne* – it is quite reasonable that Isaiah's vision should reveal Yahweh in terms of royal majesty. How else could Yahweh be 'seen' as majestic? *high and exalted* – again the majesty and holiness of Yahweh are expressed in spatial terms. The 'high altars' of our most splendid churches use the same means to express the same point. *the skirt of his robe* – the longer the train, the more noble the person. The Heb. word is more applicable to a priestly robe than a royal one. *the temple* – the actual building was relatively small, only about thirty-five yards by ten. Most of the action took place outside in the open air. Isaiah would not have entered the building, but, from the outside, he would have been able to see through the porch to the screen at the far end which covered the Holy of Holies. That view provides the setting for the vision.

6.2   *Seraphim* – many passages in the OT imply that Yahweh does not reign in solitary state, but is surrounded by attendants and messengers. Not, of course, human attendants and messengers but mythological ones. The *Seraphim* were among these attendants. The root from which the word comes means 'to burn', and what is probably the same word is translated 'fiery serpent' in Num. 21.6

and Deut. 8.15. Their true form can only be imagined, but it hardly matters. If we begin to speculate about the form of the *Seraphim*, we shall soon find ourselves asking what colour Yahweh's robe was, and we shall have lost the sense of awe and mystery. *six wings* – a testimony to the unearthly reality of these beings. *they covered their faces* – in order not to look at Yahweh (cf. Ex. 33.20). *their bodies* – lit. 'their feet', a euphemism for their nakedness.

6.3   *calling to one another* – this rendering clouds the fact that singing in Hebrew worship was antiphonal. Hebrew poetry is constructed on the basis of parallelism, one line being followed by another, balancing line, which stresses and extends the meaning of the first. Two choirs are implied, responding to each other, and passing the meaning backwards and forwards between them. The *Seraphim* sang antiphonally. *Holy, holy, holy* – this is a fundamental word of Heb. theology (see Introduction, p. xxviii). Strictly it applies to Yahweh alone; it refers to his separateness, his uniqueness, his majesty, his power, none of which is capable of description. The fact that it is repeated three times makes it all the more impressive, if that is possible. Those people and things associated with Yahweh may be said to be holy, but only in a derived and secondary sense. Holiness is not the same thing as righteousness, though the will of the *holy* one determines the meaning of righteousness. For *the LORD of Hosts*, see Introduction, pp. xxviif. *the whole earth* – what Yahweh is in himself is manifested in his creation; it therefore receives *glory* and is a witness to his *glory*.

6.4   The most formative event in Israel's religious tradition was the exodus followed by the encounter on Mount Sinai. Yahweh's presence there was signalled by fire, earthquake, and smoke (Ex. 13.21f.; 16.10; 19.16–18; 20.18; 24.15–18; Deut. 4.11; 9.15; etc.). The fact that the traditional Sinai never was a volcano raises interesting questions which cannot be discussed here. Nothing, however, can remove the quasi-volcanic phenomena from the Sinai narrative. In many ways Zion was a re-creation of Sinai within the land of Israel. The fire and smoke of sacrifice appeared to recapitulate the Sinai experience. Inside the house smoke also rose from the altar of incense. It is not surprising that we also read that *the threshold shook*.

6.5   REB has changed the order of the Heb. lines by bringing the last line, *for my own eyes . . .*, into second place. This may make the verse run more smoothly, but it alters the theological thrust. As the Heb. stands, the verse offers two reasons why the prophet is *doomed*. One is that he is *unclean*, the other that he has *seen the King, the* LORD *of Hosts*. On the face of it, the first reason represents a moral and spiritual insight (though see below on *unclean*), the second a more irrational notion of guilt, for the prophet could hardly be blamed for seeing the vision. REB, in effect, reduces the reasons to one. The seeing is the offence; the last two lines simply underline how scandalous the seeing was. In the circumstances it is best to follow the Heb. order, as do RV, NRSV and NEB. *the King* – provides another hint that Yahweh's majesty appeared to Isaiah in royal terms. *unclean lips* – the Heb. word for *unclean* largely concerns ceremonial matters. One could be unclean by contact with a corpse or with a leper or with substances such as menstrual blood. Any contact with idolatry rendered a person unclean. What we would call ethical factors are not excluded, though English translations tend to imply a more ethical spirituality than the original. *lips* – the reference might be to unclean speech or to unclean food; the former is more likely. Speech is a significant index of a person's true nature; speech is a prime element in worship; and it is to speak for Yahweh that the prophet is about to be called. The standards of true worship in Israel are revealed in 1.10–17; by those standards the prophet felt himself unfit either to worship Yahweh or to be his messenger. *among a people* – one may well ask how much of Isaiah's unfitness was personal. There is much evidence to show that OT writers recognized the universality of sin, that is to say, that all people individually fell short of Yahweh's will, but the OT also stresses the notion of solidarity. It is hard for anyone to think of himself as righteous if the whole people among whom he lives is unrighteous. Jeremiah and Ezekiel struggled against a too rigorous application of this principle, but the principle itself is fundamental to biblical faith. There is no doctrine of atonement without it. Isaiah's uncleanness was partly his own, but, to a greater part, the sin of his people.

6.6   *in his hand* – the mythological nature of the *seraphim* is confirmed by the fact that they had hands as well as wings. *a glowing coal . . . from the altar* – there were two altars in the Jerusalem temple, the large one for sacrifice in the open air and the small one for incense in the Holy Place. The place where God appears in Isaiah's vision seems to have been the Holy Place, but the *glowing coal* suggests the outdoor altar with the perpetual fire. Some commentators prefer the translation 'hot stone' (RV marg.) as a more accurate translation of what might be found on the altar of incense, but the vision does not have to be coherent in practical detail.

6.7   The ceremonial element is still prominent. Both the altar and the fire represent purifying agents. The touch is sufficient to remove the impurity. Though there are rites of purification in the OT, there is no parallel to this ritual. Note that the initiative for cleansing comes from the seraph, that is, from Yahweh; the occasion for cleansing is the prophet's confession of sin. *iniquity* – not a particular action but his guilty condition. *wiped out* – the Heb. verb is *kipper*, one of the most important but difficult terms in the field of Hebrew religion. Originally it meant 'to cover'. A sin must be 'covered' so that it is no longer a source of offence. The verb is used regularly to mean 'to make atonement'.

6.8   Phase one of the vision is the awareness of Yahweh, the recognition of sin and the experience of forgiveness; phase two is the commission. There is a logical progression from v. 7 to v. 8, stated in Heb. by the conjunction 'and'. It is better to include it, or even to strengthen it to 'then', as NEB does, than to leave it out, as does REB. *Whom shall I send?* – no mention is made, in the first instance, of where the prophet is to be sent. The voice asks for a messenger sufficiently committed to go anywhere. Most translations follow the Heb. and include the prophet's reply in v. 8; not so REB.

6.9   The prophet, in complete ignorance of the outcome, says, *Send me.* Our century has seen plenty of examples of unquestioning obedience, many of them ending in tragedy. It is almost impossible to conceive of a situation on the human level where one person can morally hand over to another the complete determination of his actions. But with Yahweh complete surrender is the only appropriate response. There can be no negotiated agreement on the terms of a prophetic calling. In this way the holiness of Yahweh is made manifest. The prophet responds and the commission follows. It is in the form of a message to *this people* (not, significantly, 'my people'), a message that has caused much perplexity. Lit. the Heb. says, 'Hear indeed, but do not understand and see indeed, but do not perceive'. Why should a prophet be commissioned to deliver such a message? REB gives part of the answer by getting rid of the imperatives and turning the message into a forecast. Whatever the message, the

people will never understand it, because they are not listening with
their wills. 'There are none so deaf as those who will not hear.' It is
also well to remember that, though we know the date of the vision
itself, we do not know the date of the records, neither Isaiah's
account to his disciples nor the written record of his editors. It is
reasonable to suppose that even the prophet himself is looking back
on the first part of his ministry and judging it to be a failure. In the
next chapter we read of Isaiah trying to persuade Ahaz to put his
trust in Yahweh, about the year 735 BCE. If this incident is typical of
the first decade of his ministry, and the evidence suggests that it is,
then there is every reason for Isaiah to explain his commission in
negative terms. The original commission is recorded, therefore, in
the light of its known practical results. It might be argued that the
commission makes Yahweh appear foolish. Why send a prophet to
people who are determined not to hear? Two answers can be given.
In the first place, given that the people lack understanding, the
commissioning of a prophet, a true witness, who was ignored would
do nothing to dishonour Yahweh. In the second place, the objection
fails to take account of the true nature of the prophetic word. The
word was not simply information delivered for the hearers' con-
venience. It was a concrete expression of the divine will, which
might be followed by an even more concrete expression in the form
of a historical event. The divine intention, the prophetic word, and
the historical event formed a series with a common thrust and a
common identity. This explains why prophets continued to
prophesy when the time for repentance was past. The word must
stand, even though the issue is certain, because the word is a part of
that issue.

6.10   This verse elaborates on v. 9 and shows signs of being a
secondary attempt to explain the harshness of 9cd. Again the Heb. is
in the form of imperatives, as the REB marg. shows; lit. 'make fat the
heart of this people and make heavy their ears and blind their eyes'.
Once again the editor appears to take the view that, if the consequence is that the people do not listen and repent and receive
healing, then the commission should anticipate this. A positive and
hopeful commission would imply that Yahweh intended well but
was frustrated by the people's unbelief and obstinacy; this in turn
would imply that the people determined the course of events and not
Yahweh. *wits* – a neat attempt to translate a Heb. word (actually the
word for 'heart') in terms of sense rather than anatomical precision.

In Heb. the heart is regarded as the seat of the intellect and will, not the emotions.

6.11   Isaiah's question recalls Pss. 79.5 and 89.46 and suggests a plea by the prophet against the bleak commission; but the reply does nothing to brighten the gloom. It is clear that some editing has taken place because Yahweh speaks in v. 11, whereas in v. 12 he is spoken about in the third person. Perhaps a later oracle of Isaiah has been fitted in here to represent Yahweh's reply. Whatever the literary form, the reply is shocking. Only the complete devastation of Israel will bring Isaiah's ministry to an end.

6.12   The situation described did not come into being in Isaiah's lifetime; there were small defeats, but not complete desolation. This can be explained in various ways: the verse involves hyperbole, making the doom worse than it turned out to be; the verse is a long term prophecy; the verse belongs to a time much later than Isaiah, when exile was in prospect; most complicated of all, the oracle was originally milder and accurate, but was later adapted to suit the exilic situation. One of the last two is the most likely.

6.13   It is difficult to determine what part this verse plays in the whole passage. The Heb. is not entirely clear and REB opts for substantial emendation. 13a seem to suggest a surviving remnant, though even that would be destroyed according to the present text. Does the *stump* of the tree suggest a remnant? Somebody thought it did, because the final line is an attempt to end the oracle on a positive note. We have to be careful, however, because the word for *stump* is not a word that Isaiah uses elsewhere for 'remnant', and these last few words are missing from some ancient versions. One factor that must not be overlooked is that, during the period that Isaiah was prophesying in Judah, Samaria was sacked and the northern kingdom destroyed. Vv. 11f. and even 13 might be seen as partly a threat to Judah and partly a description of the fate of Samaria. It remains most likely, however, that 13 is a later addition recognizing Judah as the surviving *tenth*, remembering her chequered history, her defeat by Babylon and her people's exile, and yet affirming that the exile was not the end of the people of God. If this is the case, then someone within the Isaiah tradition managed at last to bring a little light to the gloomy record of Isaiah's commission.

This is a chapter to which preachers often turn, for it is rich in theology. None of the points made in it, however, have any force if they are divorced from Isaiah's conception of *the LORD of Hosts*. Only in the light of the fundamental conviction that *the LORD of Hosts* is *holy* can the rest of the chapter be said to make sense. A true reading centres on the doctrine of God, not on Isaiah and his commission, hence the relevance to Trinity Sunday. Trinity Sunday is the one Sunday in the liturgical year in which the church concentrates on the being of God. The first nine Sundays are about preparation and expectation; from Christmas to Pentecost the theme is the life, death, and resurrection of Jesus; the rest of the year is given to living in the Spirit. Trinity Sunday alone considers the pure theological question of the nature of God. Isa. 6 is the perfect OT lesson, for it engenders that sense of awe that gives to the life of Jesus and the work of the Spirit their true depth and meaning.

At the same time, the passage represents clearly the position of the human being in the presence of holiness. Isaiah bursts out that he is *a man of unclean lips*. But, in our reading, and if human standards are applied, no one in Israel had less reason to react in this way. The text, however, recognizes the solidarity of human sin. Before holiness all are equally unclean. Moreover no one person can escape the uncleanness that belongs to the race as a whole. We all *dwell among* and are part of *a people of unclean lips*.

Isaiah and King Ahaz
7.1–9.7

This is the continuation of the material based on Isaiah's own
memoirs but extended and adapted by later editors. The section
contains some of the most important matter in the whole of the book.

Shear-jashub
7.1–9

The form of this passage is an account in the third person of a
historical incident, but vv. 4–9 are in direct speech, and they look and
sound like an oracle. Probably, therefore, we have here an original
oracle in the first person (that would fit well between 6.1–13 and 8.1–
18), but one that has been worked over and given a new introduction. The introduction is not entirely successful, as we shall see. It
tells us that Isaiah was instructed to go to Ahaz, taking with him his
son, *Shear-jashub*, to deliver a particular message. The words of the
message are what we are calling the oracle. The editor never says that
Isaiah did what he was told, but we must assume that he did.

The occasion is that of the Syro-Ephraimite Confederacy of 735–33
(see Introduction, p. xxi) and the subsequent invasion of Judah.
Rezin of Syria and Pekah of Israel were conspiring against Assyria.
Ahaz, however, was conducting a pro-Assyrian policy (II Kings
16.5–18), so the conspirators aimed to remove him and put an anti-
Assyrian puppet in his place. The annals of Tiglath-Pileser III
indicate that Philistia and Edom were also involved in the revolt
(*ANET*, pp. 282–4). We can understand why Ahaz was afraid. He
was isolated; he was personally in the direct line of fire, for the
confederates wanted to destroy him and not his army; and his one
ally, Assyria, was a long way away.

7.1 The editor informs his readers about the background to the incident. Isaiah's own contemporaries would not need to be informed, so we assume that the editing took place some time after Isaiah's death. The verse is taken almost literally from II Kings 16.5, which indicates that the editor had no first-hand knowledge of the incident. *grandson of Uzziah* – it is not usual to mention grandfathers in establishing the identity of a king, but Uzziah was mentioned in 6.1 to provide a date for the vision, so the reference to him here neatly ties the two chapters together. *Rezin of Aram* – king of Syria, who reigned from 740 to 733. *Pekah* – a usurper who reigned in Samaria from 737 to 732. *marched on Jerusalem* – the verse tells the whole story of the assault, but the following conversation between Isaiah and Ahaz took place before the armies arrived. If Ahaz had known that they would be *unable to reduce it,* his attitude might have been different.

7.2 *it was reported* – another sign that the editor was working many decades after the event. It suggests that Ahaz learnt about the conspiracy just before the armies appeared. In fact, the plotting had been going on for years, and Ahaz had already suffered at the hands of the plotters (II Kings 16.6). *the house of David* – Isaiah had a special interest in *the house of David* and the city of David. This is the most positive way possible of speaking about a very misguided king. *Aramaeans,* that is, the Syrians. *made an alliance* – the Heb. suggests that Syria had 'come to rest' on Ephraim (see note on v. 19). Syria was either physically encamped on Ephraimite territory or was bearing down on Ephraim's leaders psychologically. In either case, Syria is the dominant partner. *the Ephraimites* – a slighting reference to the northern kingdom. The more common name, Israel, had important religious implications which are here avoided, or even denied. *king and people shook* – Ahaz was terrified. According to II Kings 16.7f., he appealed to Assyria at this time. No mention of this appears in this chapter. Isaiah challenges Ahaz, not so much over his actions as over his attitude. King and prophet agreed in opposing the conspiracy, but disagreed in their reasons. Ahaz fearfully put his faith in Assyria, Isaiah confidently put his in Yahweh.

7.3 *Go out* – out of the city to the place where Ahaz was inspecting the city's water supply. Evidently the armies were still some distance away. *Shear-jashub* – the name means 'a remnant will return'. It was a significant name (see 8.18), and we have to consider why it was given to the child some time before this incident, why it had to be carried as an ever-present reminder throughout the child's life, and why the child's presence was especially relevant at this crisis. *Shear-jashub* is not referred to by name again. Some commentators understand 'return' in a moral sense. A godly few would desert the false gods and return to Yahweh (cf. 10.20f.). Others think that the name is a prophecy of doom. A disaster is coming and only a remnant would survive it. Still others take the name as a hopeful prophecy. Whatever the disaster, a remnant would survive to be Yahweh's true people, Israel. To some extent the solution depends upon a more basic question: was Isaiah's conversation with Ahaz in these verses and again in 10–17 primarily threatening or primarily positive? There has been much discussion of this. The most satisfactory answer is that the name was primarily positive, but that a later editor, probably in the exile, knowing that Israel continued to fail and to suffer, adapted the text to make it appear more threatening. It is also possible that Isaiah was speaking on two levels, reassuring in the short term, but also making it clear that Yahweh would continue to purge his people of their wickedness. *the conduit* – fortified cities were commonly built on hills where water was always a problem. Underground conduits were used to get water into the city from wells outside. The one Hezekiah built (II Kings 20.20) some time after this incident is still in place and very impressive. Ahaz' *conduit* was probably much shorter, but, like all conduits, it had to be concealed; otherwise it would provide a means of entrance to the city (cf. II Sam. 5.8). This may have been the very job that the defenders were doing, hence Ahaz' presence. The precise location, mentioned again in II Kings 18.17, is not certain.

7.4 This verse looks like an oracle spoken by Isaiah to Ahaz, but, as it occurs here, it is part of the instruction to Isaiah from Yahweh. The thrust of it is perhaps the most difficult message of all, 'Do nothing, simply trust God'. Ahaz appears as the type of all unbelievers. He did not trust Yahweh; he preferred to rely on himself and his own crude human plans (in this case servility towards Assyria). *the blazing anger* – an editor has got this wrong. Isaiah calls the two kings *smouldering stumps of firewood,* and the point of that image is that the fire has gone out; the smoke lingers, but essentially the fire is dead. The editor has interpreted the fire in terms of the kings' anger and has all but ruined the point. The kings are not to be feared because they are *blazing*; they are to be ignored because they are spent.

Remaliah's son – Pekah is not given a name, a neat way of expressing contempt.

7.5   Syria took the initiative; Syria was nearest to Assyria and had most to gain, but was likely to be, and was, the first to suffer when Assyria decided to act.

7.6   This verse sets out what was happening and makes the editorial summary in v. 1 unnecessary. *break her spirit* – lit. 'intimidate her', so that Ahaz would be deposed. *bring her over . . .* the verb means 'to break up'. What was to be broken up, the territory, the walls of Jerusalem, or the solidarity of the people behind their king? There may have been a sizeable opposition to Ahaz within Judah, which would make him even more insecure. The aim of the rebellious kings was not to destroy Judah, a potential ally, but to remove an uncooperative monarch. *Tabeal's son* – obviously a Syrian puppet. Note again the contemptuous form of reference. The name should mean 'God is good', but it is pointed in the Heb. to mean 'no good'.

7.7   An authoritative statement, but Isaiah provides no evidence. According to OT understanding the prophet spoke Yahweh's word and Yahweh does not need to prove his case. The oracle is good news for Ahaz, <u>if he can accept it</u>.

7.8–9   A difficult pair of verses. REB has changed round the second half of 8 and the first half of 9, which improves things, but the text is still not entirely clear. The general sense is that, at rock bottom, the two hostile nations depend on two fallible men. Ahaz, with Yahweh on his side, has nothing to fear from such feeble opposition. *Within sixty-five years* – prophets rarely specify exact figures, and what use would this information be to Ahaz when the enemy was only a few miles distant? Damascus fell and Rezin and Pekah died within two or three years. Ephraim's demise was only a dozen years away. Efforts to explain the arithmetic are not very convincing. Mistakes do happen with numerals, and there must be some mistake here, though we do not know what it is. *Have firm faith* – fortunately this part of the message is clear. The key lies in the fact that in Heb. the two verbal forms ('believe' and 'be established' in RV) are parts of the same verb. REB tries to preserve the pun.

It is a very theological pun, and it tells us a great deal about faith in the OT. Faith is holding something to be reliable, proving its reliability in action, and thereby gaining its reliability oneself. If you do not hold Yahweh to be reliable, his reliability will not grasp you and make you confident. The verb in question is *'āman*, which gives our word 'amen'. Amen does not mean 'so be it', but 'true, reliable, sound'. When a congregation says 'amen', it affirms that what has been spoken is true and carries their conviction. Ahaz did not say 'amen' to Yahweh; he said 'amen' to Assyria instead. The essence of OT faith was not intellectual reasoning. Isaiah did not invite Ahaz to consider whether Yahweh existed or not. He asked him to take a practical step. The crucial factor is the existential one. What do you hold to be reliable, what are you prepared to stake your life on? This is not simply the crude question of who you think will win, but the more profound one of where you want to place your allegiance, come what may. Ahaz was found wanting because he foolishly trusted Assyria, and because what he hankered after was what Assyria could provide. Isaiah pleaded that he should relax and let Yahweh take control both of the situation and of himself.

Immanuel
7.10–17

This is one of the best known and most interesting narratives in Isaiah. Traditionally it provides a lesson for the Nativity season and it is still used in most lectionaries at some time around Christmas, though *JLG 1* does not use it at all. The four-year lectionary of 1990 (*JLG 2*) reintroduces it for Advent 4 and Christmas Eve.

The passage connects closely with the previous one; the circumstances and the prophet's aim are the same. The speech in vv. 4–9 failed to stir Ahaz, so he is offered a sign to aid his feeble faith. Again the commentators differ over whether the passage is a threat or a promise. Even v. 17, which ought to settle the matter, is teasingly ambiguous. The view taken here is that the passage should be read as a promise. The birth of a child, especially a boy, was always a happy event in Israel. It is a most unsuitable sign for a disaster. The naming of a child was a significant, not to say a prophetic, event.

Awful names were sometimes used for awful circumstances, but Immanuel is a very positive name. It is true that vv. 18–25 have a threatening character, that the good fortune that Ahaz enjoyed did not last long, and that Isaiah is, in general, an astringent prophet. Nevertheless, the present passage makes the best sense if we see it as a positive promise to Ahaz which was later interpreted more austerely and edited to bring it into line with both the tone of vv. 18–25 and the course of subsequent history.

Three children with symbolic names appear in 7.1–8.4, which may have some bearing on the interpretation (cf. Hos. 1.1–9). We never hear whether the prophecy of 7.14 was fulfilled in the way that Isaiah predicted.

7.10 *The LORD spoke* – an editorial formula. Practically, the LORD spoke through Isaiah, at first in the conversation with Ahaz and then in the oracle (vv. 13–17).

7.11 *the LORD your God* – Ahaz is given the benefit of the doubt. As a member of the house of David and Yahweh's son and servant, Yahweh is his God. *a sign* – not really a guarantee of prophetic accuracy, even though some signs in the OT appear as miraculous proofs (e.g. II Kings 20.9). According to Deut. 18.22, the only guarantee of prophecy is the subsequent fulfilment of the word. Most signs, like this one, are ordinary events which appear at the appropriate time (e.g. I Sam. 2.34). To speak generally, a *sign* in the OT is a means whereby some great reality, not immediately and fully apprehensible, is made concrete and accessible in representative form. In this sense sabbath and circumcision are signs of the covenant; they express it, witness to it, actualize it concretely (Ex. 31.13, 17; Gen. 17.11). The sign provided here is the first concrete indication of Yahweh's breaking into history. As the child grows, the deliverance comes nearer, thus showing that 'God is with us'. *whether from Sheol* – not so much a precise statement as an astute way of countering Ahaz' prevarications; 'ask for anything you like!' For *Sheol*, see note on 14.9. Isaiah describes a three-tier universe: *Sheol below*, *heaven above* and the inhabited earth in between. The Heb. means 'heights' rather than *heaven*.

7.12 Ahaz refuses the offer. He is unwilling to trust Yahweh and the last thing he wants is evidence to disturb his mind. Of course he gives another reason for his refusal (see Deut. 6.16), which may well be insincere.

7.13 Here the oracle begins. There are indications that originally the oracle existed apart from the conversation of the previous two verses. The verbs are now in the plural and the piece is framed as a public address to Ahaz and his court. *house of David* – the term reminds Ahaz and his supporters of the true calling of the king of Israel. The point of the speech is that cowardice is addictive. The king begins by disappointing the prophet and the more far-sighted counsellors; in the end he does not mind whom he disappoints. *my God* – not Ahaz' *God* any longer (cf. v. 11).

7.14 *A young woman* – this word occurs eight times in the OT and almost everybody now recognizes that it does not mean 'virgin' but *young woman*. There is a Hebrew word for 'virgin' which Isaiah could have used if he had virginal conception in mind. Some Greek versions translate with a word for *young woman*, but the LXX uses *parthenos*, which definitely means 'virgin'. So the traditional translation derives from the LXX and not the Heb. Matt. 1.23 also quotes the LXX, as NT writers commonly do. To whom was Isaiah referring? Some say the queen; but would the queen be described simply as a *young woman*, and could she be expected to co-operate regarding the name? Some say the prophet's own wife, which would mean that the three names in chs. 7–8 would all refer to his own children. Some say a *woman*, unknown to us. Some say the term is generic, meaning young women in general. The solution suggested below by-passes these suggestions and is consistent with all of them. *is with child, will give birth* – both verbs are participles which means that the tense is indefinite. The saving process, which the child's growth signifies, has already begun. *and call him* – though Hebrew society was patriarchal, mothers sometimes chose their children's names (Gen. 4.25, etc.). *Immanuel* – the name, meaning 'God with us', must indicate confidence and hope. Various attempts are made to understand it as a threat, but none is convincing. In vv. 1–17 Isaiah consistently expects Yahweh to resolve the situation. Only later, when the deliverance of Jerusalem proved to be only a temporary solace, did editors begin to modify the force of the passage and so leave us in confusion.

7.15 This verse and the next reveal the time span of the expected deliverance. They do so in the typically elusive style of prophetic speech. *reject what is bad, choose what is good* – there is much discussion about what age is indicated. The words for *bad* and *good* are common and have a wide range of applications. If ethical distinctions are implied, the child would need to be nine or ten, which is hardly good news for Ahaz, but if a simple distinction between nice and nasty is intended, then little more than a year would suffice. *curds and honey* – curds are made by pressing sour milk until the whey runs out; honey was the chief sweetener in OT cuisine. There has been a long debate over whether this food synbolizes prosperity or privation. REB opts for prosperity. The promised land is described as a land flowing with milk and honey (Ex. 3.8, 17, etc.), and in the ancient world the gods were supposed to eat food of this kind. On the other hand, *curds and honey* are the basic constituents of a survival diet; they imply a time when the varied food of a flourishing agricultural community was not available. This difference of opinion is another expression of the uncertainty among commentators about whether this oracle was good news or bad. REB's interpretation of the two problems posed in this verse is positive in both cases: in a year or so the child will be living on the fat of the land.

We suggest, however, that the argument about whether *curds and honey* are a sign of prosperity or privation is a red herring. The *sign* concerns a baby, and the diet of babies, whether princes or paupers, is much the same. They all go through a *curds and honey* stage. The essential feature of the *sign* is the time process; it concerns a child's growth. Isaiah is predicting the future using an elusive time scale. (The apocalyptic writers were very good at this and frequently constructed series of indeterminate stages before the end.) The birth and growth of the child are a *sign* that God is with Israel. The child's life is depicted in four stages: first, gestation, ending with birth; second, the period of naming, which coincides with breast feeding; third, the period of weaning, when the child is put on sweetened milk; and finally, the period of adult food, at which point the child begins to express likes and dislikes, spitting out some things and gobbling up others. These stages represent the working of Yahweh in Israel's history. At present (stage one) it is real but unseen, but it will steadily become more evident. Before the fourth stage begins, before the child comes to the spitting out stage, the two enemy kings will be ruined. Over all, that means a period of eighteen months or two years, which corresponds with what actually happened. If this interpretation is correct, then the identity of the mother is unimportant. Indeed, there might be many mothers. By the time children, at present in the womb, were given names, the news would be good, and in a wave of optimism, babies would be called *Immanuel*, 'God with us'. A few months after that Rezin and Pekah would meet their doom. The hidden process of salvation is slowly being revealed, and the birth and growth of *Immanuel* are the sign.

7.16 According to REB, the good news has already come in v. 15 and 16 simply adds details. But if 14f. spell out four stages, the good news does not come until 16b. We see here what a difficult art translation is. Almost any translation of a difficult passage presses one solution on the text and excludes others. *the territories* – the Heb. is singular and means 'ground', an odd way of referring to two countries; but no other meaning makes sense.

7.17 This verse gives some encouragement to those who want to see the oracle as a threat. *since Ephraim broke away* refers to the division of the kingdom on Solomon's death in 922 (I Kings 12), one of the blackest events in the history of the people of God. But the language is ambiguous. Read negatively, it means that the days to come will be worse than any since then; read positively, the days to come will be better than any since before the day of division. The one thing that is generally agreed is that an editor added to the Heb. the words, 'the king of Assyria' at the end of the verse but with no grammatical connection to it. REB treats them as a gloss and relegates them to the margin. Surely they are a gloss by someone who wanted to turn the oracle into a prediction of doom, someone who knew that, well as the Syro-Ephraimite Confederacy turned out for Judah in the short term, Assyria continued to be a problem for another century until the fall of Nineveh in 612. There is no better example than this passage to indicate that we must be able to distinguish between the understanding of Isaiah, the readings of later interpreters, and the meaning of the text for our own day.

The question for the preacher is: can this text be used at Christmas, when it is clear that Isaiah was referring to the end of the confederacy around 733 BCE? Matt. 1.23 does violence to Isaiah's sense. Does that mean that Matthew was wrong? R.B.Y. Scott, writing in *The Interpreter's Bible* (vol. 5, pp. 217ff.), three decades ago, rejects what he calls the 'allegorical' interpretation because it divorces the text from its proper historical context; it implies that Isaiah sees the hand of God, not in contemporary happenings, but in an event of the distant future. How would that help Ahaz? Were such thoughts in the minds of the compilers of *JLG 1* when they overturned an ancient tradition and left Isa. 7 out? Scott is equating meaning with the author's intention, which is something over which a modern commentator would hesitate. Texts can take on a life of their own. 'It's a long way to Tipperary' was written as a romantic love-song about a lonely Irishman in London, but it was taken over by the troops in the first world war. They gave it a new meaning appropriate to their circumstances, and their meaning prevailed. To that generation the song had nothing to do with lonely Irishmen in London, all to do with men in the trenches longing for home in Birmingham, Bristol, or wherever. Similarly, if religious communities, Jewish or Christian, read a text in the light of their own experiences and interpret it as their own over a long period, it cannot be said that the new meaning is false. The meaning extrapolated is not the same as the meaning intended, but both must be taken seriously.

For centuries Christians have seen the words of Isaiah as an indication that Yahweh would act for the salvation of his people, and salvation for them has little to do with the temporary relief of Jerusalem in the eighth century BCE; it is centred in Christ. To read the text in the way that Christians do is responsible and justifiable. It would be wrong to suggest that Isaiah intended to refer to the birth of Jesus (here Scott is correct), but right to say that prophetic language about God's salvation can never be said to have a finite meaning (this is the point that Scott misses). A God who saves, saves again and again, and we can use the language of one salvation to celebrate another. The bottom line is that Isa. 7.14 has been 'possessed' by millions of Christians over twenty centuries. The text cannot now be wrested away from them. Evidently the compilers of *JLG 2* took this view.

Jewish writers have used the text in a similar way. Some have argued that the young woman stands for Zion and from Zion the Messiah would one day come forth. Some have supposed that the child was Hezekiah (715–687) who was messianic in the sense that he was an anointed king of David's line, and a good one, though Hezekiah must have been born some years before this incident. So we could go on. But it does not follow that anybody can read anything from a text. The prophets delivered the word of God in real situations. An interpretation by which a faithful community, standing in the prophetic line, extends the meaning in terms of its own context and experience may be said to participate in the authenticity of the original, but the same cannot be said of divergent, unrelated, contradictory or whimsical interpretations. Careful exegesis of the original text is, therefore, necessary to determine what is honest usage and what is not. The original intention of the prophet, the Isaiah tradition, the community's experience, all set limits; but within these limits, the passage can still claim a place in the Christian lectionary. If the omission from *JLG 1* was due to the desire not to mislead, the compilers can be praised for their caution. But not for their consistency, because, in a large measure, the use of the OT in Christian worship rests on how Christians have heard the words, not on what they originally meant.

Four dire threats
7.18–25

This passage consists of two threats of invasion and two prophecies describing the condition of the land afterwards. The picture is so bleak that it must indicate total disaster. The last years of the northern kingdom might provide a background; otherwise the last years of Judah are the best guess, in which case the words are not Isaiah's. The four parts are linked by the use of the formula, 'on that day', an allusion to the divine day of recompense that figures so largely in prophecy (see Introduction, p. xxxi). Even so, the passage may not be homogeneous. Vv. 18–20 are clear that Yahweh is going to act against his people through an invader. Vv. 21–25 mentions neither Yahweh nor an oppressor, simply a state of desolation; these verses are theologically barren, their background unknown.

7.18   V. 17 closed with a reference to a historic day in the past; v. 18 begins with a reference to a similar day in the future. This, together with the *curds and honey* of v. 22, may supply the reason why these verses are tacked on here. *whistle up* – shepherds today *whistle up* dogs; it is said that ANE bee-keepers whistled up swarms of bees. Yahweh whistles up foreign nations, which indicates his authority over them. *flies* and *bees* swarm in hundreds, an ideal image for a hostile army. *Egypt* was nothing like the threat to Israel that Assyria was. If *Egypt* was called into action, we can only guess at the occasion; it may be one of which we know nothing.

7.19   *settle* – the same verb is used in 7.2, where REB translates it 'made an alliance with'. In both cases it denotes political and military pressure. *swarming* is added by REB to make the image more graphic. *camel-thorn and stinkwort* – the former occurs only twice in the OT, the latter only once, so the Heb. terms may have been as strange to the people of the OT as these English terms are to us. One wonders whether 'thorns and bushes' would not have conveyed the sense more effectively.

7.20   The second threat. Shaving was a mark of dishonour (see II Sam. 10.4). *body* – the Heb. says 'the hair of the feet', a euphemism for pubic hair. *razor* – this is a stirring image helped by the fact that the word could also mean sword. *hired on the banks of the Euphrates* – a clumsy phrase which might be a gloss to help readers who were unfamiliar with the history. REB confines to the margin 'with the king of Assyria', which is in the Heb. but certainly a gloss.

7.21   We come now to two prophecies of desolation with nothing to help us in establishing the context. The descriptions might apply to Israel after 721 or Judah after 586. *cow and two ewes* – this seems like a positive statement, but prosperity means flocks and herds; this is subsistence farming.

7.22   *so much milk* – again a positive statement; The Heb. speaks of 'abundance of milk'. Are these two verses then not part of the series of threats? We go on to read that survivors *will eat curds and honey*. See the discussion on 7.15. REB is consistent in seeing this diet as positive in both places, which means that 21f. are inconsistent with the verses around them. Some commentators take the opposite view, that this is the survival diet of the dispossessed. A reasonable solution is that the verses were originally written to describe privation, but as time went on, *curds and honey* acquired a more positive meaning as the Promised Land figured more and more in eschatological hopes. So this prophecy, without regard to the context, was 'turned' by the insertion of the word 'abundance'.

7.23   The final prophecy. *briars and thorns* occur in vv. 23, 24 and 25;

the words recall the ruin of the vineyard (Israel) in 5.6. Enclosures will be destroyed, agriculture will cease, and a more exiguous existence will replace it.

7.24   *bows and arrows* – there is no reference to hunting in the Heb. and other suggested uses for the weapons occur in the commentaries, but REB is surely right in its interpretation.

7.25   REB provides a smooth translation for some awkward Heb. *once under the hoe* – a vast amount of work went into cultivating the hillsides; it has all been lost. *turned loose* – the cattle will be allowed to roam free. Economically this is a step down. Stock that roams wild is not so well fed and is at risk from accident, wild animals and thieves. *oxen, sheep, goats* – a different picture from v. 21, but the sections may have different provenances.

From the the first two verses of this rather obscure passage we can infer two genuinely Isaianic propositions: first, that no nation, least of all the chosen nation, is exempt from Yahweh's righteous demands; and second, that Yahweh controls all nations and might call on any to be the executioner. The second is striking enough, but the first is quite remarkable. It shows how profoundly important righteousness is in this book. No privilege of any kind can provide exemption from this constant demand.

Maher-shalal-hash-baz
8.1–4

This autobiographical passage records an example of what is widely known as 'prophetic symbolism', that is, dramatic action to make a point. It is in two parts, separated in time by perhaps a year: first Isaiah must write a name, a complex and peculiar name, on a tablet and have it witnessed; then, subsequently, he was required to give the name to a son who had not even been conceived when the name was first written down. The name means, 'spoil speeds, prey hastes' (see REB marg.). V. 4 gives the reason for this procedure, and from it we gather that the date is roughly the same as that for ch. 7, when Syria and the northern kingdom were attacking Judah.

8.1 *large writing tablet* – the word used for *tablet* is curious; it is used only here and in Isa. 3.23, where the meaning is even more uncertain. We must infer a tablet, probably of clay, on which a submission was formally made public. *in common script* – (cf. Hab. 2.2) the marg. gives the literal translation of the Heb.; but REB's rendering is supported by most commentators. The script was clearly meant to be readable.

8.2 *I had it witnessed* – presumably so that when the fulfilment arrived, the witnesses would be able to guarantee that the events had indeed been prophesied, that is to say, the events had proceeded from the mind of Yahweh, through the word of the prophet, to the historical fulfilment. *Uriah* – see II Kings 16.10–18; the name is the same in Heb., though AV, RV and even RSV when it was first published unaccountably make them differ slightly. *Zechariah* is too common a name to allow for identification. The naming of the child was a second attempt to convey the message, which implies that the purpose of the action was to create a constant reminder. See the discussion of 'signs' in notes on 7.10–17 and 20.3.

8.3 *my wife* – the Heb. says 'the prophetess', a term applied to Miriam, Deborah, Huldah, and others, but there is no indication that Isaiah's wife was a female prophet. REB takes the noun to mean simply 'a prophet's wife'. *Call him* – this recalls the naming of Hosea's children (Hos. 1.4, 6, 9) and, of course, Shear-jashub (7.3) and Immanuel (7.14).

8.4 This verse makes clear who receives the spoil and who is the prey. The occasion is the Syro-Ephraimite Confederacy of 735–33. The child was named as a dramatic symbol pointing to the outcome. We can only presume that he bore the name, irrelevantly, for the rest of his life. The time scale is reminiscent of 7.16. *Damascus, Samaria* – the capital cities of Syria and the northern kingdom, but note that eleven years elapsed between the fall of one and the spoliation of the other. If the child was born when Damascus fell, he would certainly have been able to say *Father* and *Mother* before the same fate overtook Samaria. Some telescoping of history has been done, either by the prophet or his editors, to simplify the link between prophecy and fulfilment

These verses do not occur in most lectionaries, though they witness to the prophetic conviction that Yahweh concerned himself with the political and military happenings of the day. Openness to the word of Yahweh was (and is) the diplomat's and the politician's greatest need. In this instance Isaiah was proved right. The passage also demonstrates the essential importance of prophetic word and deed. The prophet is not giving information, still less pronouncing an opinion. He is caught up in the process of history and, by his words and actions, helps to carry it forward.

The flood from the Euphrates
8.5–10

Ahaz has appealed to Assyria for help (II Kings 16.7f.). Now the 'help' is on the way. Like the Euphrates in flood, the Assyrian tide is not selective. Judah herself will be overwhelmed together with the nations that at present threaten her. From 8c onwards the oracle takes a different direction.

8.5 *Once again* suggests that this is an additional prophecy in the same general circumstances, perhaps indicating that the prophet is now concerned with Ahaz' foolish and tragic appeal to Assyria.

8.6 *the waters of Shiloah* – a local stream used here to symbolize Jerusalem; possibly the one that Hezekiah later diverted (II Kings 20.20). It may also have played a part in coronation ceremonies (I Kings 1.33–35). *flow softly* – Jerusalem's stream is not a torrent like *Euphrates*, meaning that Jerusalem does not inspire universal fear as does Assyria. The people, and especially the king, have lost faith, not so much in Jerusalem as in Jerusalem's God. So far, so good, but in Heb. the verse finishes with a reference to Rezin and Pekah (see marg.). How these kings are to be brought into the sentence is not at all clear. REB relegates the names to the margin.

8.7   *Euphrates* – the Heb. says 'river', but that word is often used for *Euphrates*. A reference to the king of Assyria is added unnecessarily after *Euphrates* (see marg.). The real contrast is between Jerusalem whose strength is in her God and the military might of Assyria. Unhappily Ahaz chose the wrong one; he will discover that Assyria is a threat and not a protection.

8.8   The account of the Assyrian flood is terrifying. Poor Judah, whose king had actually asked for Assyrian help (II Kings 16.7f.), suffers a terrible punishment. Now suddenly there is a dislocation. The image changes from a flood to a bird, and Judah, drowned in 8b, hears the cry *God is with us* in 8d. Thereafter the prophecy of doom is switched from Judah to other nations. We can only conclude that 8c–10 belong to a different and hopeful oracle, perhaps a poem celebrating Yahweh's presence in Zion.

8.9   *Take note* – REB wisely follows the LXX (see marg.), which requires a small emendation. *distant parts* – a very inclusive term; it reveals that 9f. address a different constituency from 5–8b. The armies of these distant nations will not protect them; they will take arms only to be slaughtered.

8.10   *Devise your plans* – human shrewdness will be no more use than military power since Yahweh protects Israel.

If 8c–10 are part of a cycle of poems celebrating Zion, they must belong to a period, late in Isaiah's life, when Jerusalem had survived attacks from Syria-Ephraim and Sennacherib, or perhaps even later than that, when the Zion tradition was even more firmly founded. There is no need to look for a precise occasion to which the fragment belongs. Patriotic songs arise in precise circumstances, but thereafter are used with general reference (e.g. La Marseillaise). By accident or design the range of these six verses is enormous. They begin with Judah, perhaps even with Ahaz alone, and they end with all nations. Disloyalty and punishment, confidence and protection, are all woven together. In the Isaianic vision Yahweh's concern, like his power, operates on the smallest scale and on the grandest.

Fear Yahweh alone

8.11–15

An autobiographical fragment which seems like an addition to the call narrative of ch. 6. The prophet is charged to fear Yahweh alone while faithless Ephraim and Judah suffer judgement in the form of historical disasters.

8.11 *charged me* – the form of the verb is in doubt here (see marg.), but the sense is fairly secure. The prophet has to hold himself aloof from the ways of his contemporaries, for their judgements are unsound and their behaviour treacherous.

8.12 *alliance* – political and economic alliances usually meant a threat to religious purity; but a small change in the Heb. would read 'holy' instead of *alliance*. 'Call holy' would then parallel *fear, stand in awe,* and *hold sacred.* Both readings make good sense, but REB faithfully stands by the Heb. unemended. *fear* in English has negative overtones, but there is a positive sense of *fear* as the parallel use of *awe* indicates. Both words relate to the proper attitude of the mortal and the fleshly in the presence of the All-Holy One. Worship without *fear* in this sense is no worship at all.

8.14 *snare* – the Heb. reads 'sanctuary' (see marg.). Possibly the verse originally made a double use of the *rock* image. Yahweh is a sanctuary, built on the rock of Zion, for some, and a stumbling block for others. Other commentators, however, support REB's reading. *two houses of Israel* – this reference helps to date the passage, before 721. *inhabitants* – the Heb. is singular, though many ancient versions turn it into a plural. Perhaps it was meant as a direct reference to Ahaz.

Textual difficulties cloud this passage, but serious themes are still evident. The prophet is reminded of the loneliness of the servant of God in a fallen world. This is a price that has to be paid by every faithful witness because the populace rarely applauds divine messages. Their standards are too slack and self-indulgent. The point of separation between prophet and people lies in what they hold sacred. People may choose what they devote their time and their interest to (what they hold sacred), but Yahweh is not one among many options. Yahweh is absolute and inescapable reality. Rejecting him does not mean that one is free of him. If he is not chosen as sanctuary, he will be encountered as snare.

A prophet in the doldrums
8.16–9.1a

These verses bring the autobiographical section, which has continued, with interruptions, since 6.1, to an end. The theme is the prophet's suffering when the nation continues in sin but he is forbidden to prophesy.

8.16   Prophecies were written down by disciples soon after they were delivered, at least in some instances (cf. Jer. 36.1–4). The scroll was rolled up, tied, and sealed; it was then inaccessible until the seal was broken. *instruction* – Heb. *tôrâ*; see note on 1.10. The Heb. that lies behind 16b reads simply *my disciples*, preceded by a preposition, which is but a single letter in Heb. 'Among my disciples' would be a reasonable translation (see NRSV and NEB marg.). REB boldly translates the single letter by seven words, providing a rendering that is much more precise than the original.

8.17   *wait* – Heb. is rich in words for waiting; this one implies a mood of both patience and confidence (cf. Hab. 2.3) *eagerly* has to be supplied to give a more accurate sense. *hiding his face* – Yahweh has determined that he will no longer be available to Israel, not even to his faithful servants.

8.18   The prophet assesses the position. The two children, Shear–jashub and Maher-shalal-hash-baz, remain as living messages, and Isaiah's own name means 'Yahweh saves'. So the signs and the portents are still there. In the fullest sense *the* LORD *of Hosts* does not dwell anywhere (cf. I Kings 8.27), but Zion, described in Deuteronomy as the place Yahweh would choose (Deut. 12.5, 11; 16.2; 26.2), is supremely the place where he encounters his people. Zion was the local Sinai.

8.19   Gods, demons, spirits, etc. were taken for granted as part of the mystery of existence in the ANE, and it is surprising how little evidence there is in the OT of occult practices. When they are mentioned, they are usually condemned (Deut. 18.9–12; Lev. 19.26; I Sam. 28.3; II Kings 17.17; Jer. 14.14). *ghosts* – Heb. 'necromancers', those who reckon to get advice from the dead, like the Witch of Endor (I Sam. 28). *familiar spirits* – 'spirit guides', who supposedly provide information for necromancers. *squeak and gibber* – clear, coherent speech, such as is attributed to the dead Samuel in I Sam. 28.16–9, was not then, and is not now, the *lingua franca* of clairvoyants. *its gods* – The Heb. word for *gods* has a wide range of meanings including semi-divine figures, cultic functionaries (Ex. 21.6), foreign gods (Deut. 31.16), and Yahweh himself. Some translations (RV, NIV) end the speech after *gibber*, and take the next three lines as a righteous, prophetic comment (*gods* is read as meaning Yahweh). NEB/REB reads *gods* as a reference to all these supposed deities (so too in 21) and makes better sense.

8.20   20a is related to 16a where *instruction* and *message* also occur. The prophetic voice is silenced, so the people turn to other forms of guidance, which prove useless. 20bc in REB is a reconstruction based on this interpretation. Other translations take different lines. *no force* – Heb., 'no dawn'; REB is paraphrasing.

8.21f.   REB reads remarkably smoothly, but note the comment in the marg. Translation is impossible without using some imagination. We can only summarize: the people will be hungry and distressed; they will blame their king and their gods; they will look everywhere, but there will be no hope for them.

9.1a   *for there is no escape* . . . is a very difficult line, as the various translations show. REB makes an emendation and translates with freedom.

No passage better illustrates the hard realities of biblical interpretation than this one. It contains profound theology, but we are in danger of losing it because of the natural depredations that affect a text in its passage through time. The previous passage spoke of the prophet's aloofness; here the theme is divine aloofness. Direct punishment in terms of invading armies is by no means the only way in which Yahweh reveals his displeasure. Here he leaves the people to create their own desolation. It is a horrifying picture, perhaps most horrifying to the prophet himself. The prophets think of the word of Yahweh as a great privilege for Israel, no matter how harsh it seemed. Amos paints a stark picture of the land when the word is withheld (Amos 8.11f.). Ezekiel, too, had periods of dumbness when he could not prophesy, when the people were left without a word. Paul's understanding of the wrath of God follows a similar line (Rom. 1.28). But what of the prophet in this awful situation? There is as much agony in silence, when the people need the word, as Jeremiah, for example, found in speaking when the people were deaf (Jer. 20.7–9). The prophet grieves for the people's suffering; he grieves also that he is bound to silence.

An editorial link

9.1b

There is a difficulty with the enumeration of the verses here (see marg.), but no need to go into it as it hardly affects the sense.

9.1b   The text moves from distress and gloom in 8.22 to a great light in 9.2, a transition so sudden that an editor felt obliged to create a link. *Zebulun and Naphtali* were two northern tribes whose territory had been overrun by Assyria at the time of the Syro-Ephraimite Confederacy (II Kings 15.29). *lightly regarded* – there were all kinds of reasons why this should be: envy, because the north was more prosperous; snobbery, because these 'provincial' tribes were so far removed from Jerusalem; religious sentiment, because the northern tribes had set up their own shrines (I Kings 12.25–33). One could conclude that Yahweh thought these territories undeserving (cf. John 1.46). *honour was bestowed* – it is possible to translate this verb to give the opposite meaning, that these tribes were further weighed down, but REB's choice gives the best sense. *Galilee of the Nations* – Galilee had a richer economy and more trading contacts than Judah; consequently it always had a more mixed population. *on the road* – the trade route from Damascus to the Phoenician ports, which ran through northern Galilee.

Northern tribes had been despised in the past (Isaiah himself was among the chief critics), but Yahweh had chosen the whole of Israel for glory and that glory would duly be manifest. It is not clear at what time the editor was writing, but hopes for the restoration of the whole of Israel continued for centuries after the fall of Samaria. In the course of time Matthew (4.12–16) used this verse to explain the residence of Jesus in Galilee; the sense of 9.2–7 was called upon to justify this interpretation of 9.1. So new meanings are born.

The coming king
9.2–7

Here, for the first time, we encounter a passage that can properly be called messianic, though the term 'messiah' does not occur in it. 'Messianic prophecy' has been much misunderstood. What has happened is that 'Christ', the Greek form of 'messiah', was attributed to Jesus as a title in the NT and so, since NT times, Christian interpreters have readily assumed that all OT prophecies of coming kings and coming deliverances were intended to be prophecies of Jesus. This has led to them being called 'messianic'.

This is to argue exactly the wrong way round. 'Messiah' is an OT conception. The word means 'anointed'. Kings were anointed on accession (II Sam. 2.4; 5.3; I Kings 1.39; etc.), and the term 'messiah' is used in the OT almost entirely of kings of Israel or heirs to the throne. Accessions were always exciting times. There was always the hope that the new king would be better than his father. Consequently great hopes attended the ceremony of anointing and fervent longings that the new king would be a proper 'anointed', a true son of David. If disappointment followed, as it usually did, it was still possible to dream of a future paragon, a true messiah, who would set Israel to rights. That is 'messianic prophecy' and, having said that, we have more or less exhausted the meaning of 'messiah' in the OT. Long term forecasts of an individual in the distant future, and, even more, precise forecasts of Jesus himself are not to be found there.

Once Jesus had lived, however, and his life, death and resurrection had been apprehended as the great act of divine salvation to which the OT looked forward, the OT was read in an entirely new light. It was presumed that God had been working through Israel's history and through Israel's prophets and psalmists to prepare for the new day. So all the hopes and longings that were focussed unavailingly in new kings were read in the light of the life of Jesus and found to be 'fulfilled' in him in a way that their authors could never have expected. In Christian usage the category of 'messianic prophecy' was thus greatly expanded. Once again, the way that the text was read proved to have greater influence and authority for Christians than the way that the text was written.

It is easy to argue that this reinterpretation of OT texts is illegitimate, but such a view does not take account of the reader's contribution to the meaning of a text. Christian apologists saw continuity between the prophets and themselves. The hope of the prophets was true hope in Yahweh, though the exact details of the fulfilment were not revealed to them. The apologists reckoned that they were able to enter into and expand that hope because they had seen in their day what the prophets had been unable to see. This gives to OT texts a new meaning, a Christian meaning. This is why 9.2–7 figure again and again in lectionaries for Christmas Eve, Christmas Day and Epiphany. See the discussion on 7.10–17.

The passage is a poem in three stanzas. The first speaks of a great joy that will come suddenly on the people in their darkest moment; the second of the overthrow of an unnamed oppressor; and the third of the ideal prince who will re-establish the throne of David and introduce an era of universal peace. There is a question of whether such a poem could have been proclaimed by Isaiah in the days of Ahaz, or whether its exultant mood and boundless optimism do not belong to the happy and hopeful days when the exile was coming to an end, or to an even later period when messianic hopes, albeit of a very unrealistic kind, were strong. There is a further question of whether the deliverance of v. 4 could relate to the situation in Isaiah's day. These are weighty considerations. The mood is certainly unusual for Isaiah, but several arguments point the other way: Isaiah was a great supporter of the house of David; he was capable of optimistic promises (cf. ch. 7); he could have composed this poem to mark the accession of a king, perhaps Hezekiah, which would explain its idealistic tone; it is clear from the Psalter that poems of this kind were composed to celebrate events in the life of real, not ideal, kings (Pss. 2; 21; 45; 72; 89; 110; 118); and, though Second Isaiah has much to say about a bright future, he makes no mention anywhere of a Davidic king. On balance it seems best to assume that Isaiah is the probable author.

9.2   The fact that the main verbs are in the perfect tense does not mean that the events described had already happened. It is common for prophets to write as if their oracles about the future had already been fulfilled. *The people* is Israel, the chosen people, who have suffered so much at the hands of invaders, particularly the Assyrians. *a great light* – the first of a series of images describing a wonderful deliverance, yet without the precision that would enable us to identify the actual event. *as dark as death* – death meant the darkness of the grave (for Sheol see note on 14.9), to ancient Israelites, so some extreme suffering is indicated.

9.3   This verse is addressed by the prophet to Yahweh. *their joy* – the Heb. reads 'the nation' (see marg.) and the word 'not' occurs immediately afterwards (cf. AV and RV marg.). A slight change to the text gives the REB translation, and an even slighter one gives NRSV. *in your presence* – there were no secular celebrations in Israel; all communal rejoicing took place before Yahweh. Two great occasions for rejoicing were the gathering of the annual harvests, which were marked by regular festivals, and the division of spoil after a victory.

9.4   The suffering was acute; it requires three metaphors *yoke, rod,* and *goad* to express it. *the day of Midian's defeat* – REB adds the word *defeat,* presumably on the assumption that modern readers would otherwise miss the allusion. The Heb. refers simply to 'the day of Midian', when Gideon, with a tiny force, routed the Midianite invaders (Judg. 7).

9.5   This verse shows why the AV, for all its resonant beauty, had to be replaced. REB presents a clear and accurate translation. Those who had received warriors home from battle would recognize the scene. However glorious the victory, there was filthy, bloody clothing to be burnt.

9.6   The *child* is both a symbol of the new day and an essential part of it. A royal birth is always a sign of hope, but is a physical birth implied? When the king acceded to the throne, he became God's son in a special way (see Ps. 2.6f.). Perhaps an accession rather than a birth is implied here. The new monarch would be exceptionally gifted to carry out his task. *symbol of dominion* – nobody can be certain what the Heb. word means, so this is an acceptable, if vague, translation.

The king will bear four titles. There was an Egyptian custom of giving highly flattering throne names to a new pharaoh. A similar custom may have existed in Israel, but, if so, flattery was not necessarily the purpose. Names were often given in a prophetic sense. They indicate hoped for qualities of the person; in this case they represent prophetic promises. Each of the names or titles is composed of two words in Heb. The AV failed to recognize this and put a comma after *Wonderful* and, to make matters worse, George Frideric Handel put an even stronger comma into his setting. The choirs mislead; his name is not *Wonderful*, it is 'a marvel of a counsellor', that is, a supremely wise man. *Mighty Hero* – again the AV is in error translating the Heb. word as 'God'. Like the similar word in 8.19 and 21, the term used has a wide range of meanings including 'man of great power'. This title refers to the king's military prowess (see the note on 10.21). *Eternal Father* – words relating to time are particularly difficult to translate because the Hebrew conception of time was different from our own. There is no suggestion that the prince will live for ever, but his fatherly care for his people will be continuous and unfailing. *Prince of Peace* – as is well known, the Heb. word for *Peace*, *šālôm*, means much more than the absence of war; harmony, contentment, prosperity, are all included.

9.7   *David's throne* – Isaiah, as we have noted, was an enthusiast for the house of David, the city of David, the throne of David, not because these things represented human achievements, but because they were gifts of Yahweh. REB's *bestowed on*, while saying more than the Heb., conveys the right idea. *establish, support* – kings and kingdoms arose with great frequency in the ANE and disappeared almost as frequently. What every kingdom and every royal house needed was security. *justice and righteousness* are words that we have encountered many times already; they are the mark of a realm that wins Yahweh's approval (see notes on 1.17 and 21). A tryanny made secure is not good news, but a kingdom founded on *justice and righteousness* is the best news of all. *for evermore* – again we are not to think of eternity as an infinite abstraction but of an age that continues into the far distant future. The last line is rather pedestrian; an editor tries to strengthen the poem, but achieves nothing. *The zeal* – the word derives from the same root as 'jealous', which has occasioned so much misunderstanding in Ex. 20.5. It refers to the vigour with which Yahweh defends his people and the exclusive claim that he makes upon them.

The Christian reading of these verses has paid too much attention to 6a, hence the use of the passage in Christmas lectionaries, but the theological force is distributed throughout the poem. Even the order of the stanzas is significant. The poem begins with *light* and *joy* and *gladness*. Thanksgiving is the mark of this community. The second stanza deals with the precise reasons for this *gladness*, deliverance from a terrible oppressor. The third stanza recounts the status and dominion of the deliverer, and here there is a theological message in almost every word.

Preachers will seize on the note of thanksgiving. Thanksgiving in Greek is *eucharistia*, the definitive word of Christian worship. However deep the affliction, however great the need, the fact of God's reality and his grace gives cause for thanksgiving. Worship may be earnest, solemn, challenging, moving, or whatever, but if it is not fundamentally eucharistic, it is not truly Christian worship. The *yoke* of the second stanza, physical oppression in the original circumstances, may be read as a symbol for all kinds of oppression, including, though not exclusively, oppression by temptation and sin. Finally, the vast range of the vision is a rebuke to those preachers who limit the scope of divine activity to individual religious experience. The child brings, not individual salvation, but *justice*, *righteousness* and *boundless peace*. In the whole there is not a word about human achievement. The gift of the *Wonderful Counsellor* and the *dominion* and *peace* are all the work of Yahweh.

Prophecies against Israel
9.8–12.6

REB's heading of this section, *Prophecies against Israel*, suggests, on the analogy of *Prophecies against Judah* (1.1–5.30), a series of oracles against the northern kingdom. Closer inspection, however, reveals that this applies only to the first passage and to one or two fragments. If Israel does mean the northern kingdom, a title, applicable to the first passage, is being used as an umbrella for all the rest. It is possible that Israel here does not mean the northern kingdom but the people of God as a religious community.[1] If that is the case, the analogy with the heading of 1.1–5.30 is false. There is also a difficulty with the word 'against'. Though several oracles are against Assyria, others, which address the chosen community, are hopeful in tone. The NEB heading, *Prophecies addressed to Israel*, might be defended more easily, because all prophecies bear, directly or obliquely, on Israel, but this heading was rejected in favour of the present form. The heading remains a puzzle.

Judgement on the northern kingdom and a message for Judah
9.8–10.4

This passage describes a horrific desolation and attributes it to the punitive actions of Yahweh. The historical setting is the last years of the northern kingdom, when decency and order had completely broken down. The passage is in the form of a poem in four stanzas, each one concluding with an ominous refrain (12cd, 17ef, 21; 10.4cd). This same refrain occurs in 5.25 (see above on 5.24–30). NEB actually printed 5.24f. after 10.4, but REB has not followed suit.

9.8 *Jacob* was the patriarchal father of all the tribes and his name

---

[1] See my *Groundwork of Biblical Studies*, p. 126.

indicates the whole nation, not just the north. The same is true of *Israel*. *fall* – the image is of a great weight pressing down on the people. The word of Yahweh is not simply a communication; it is conceived of as an almost physical power.

9.9 The oracle now concentrates on the sins of the northern kingdom.

9.10 An earthquake may provide the background to this verse. Arrogantly the people imagine that they can survive and reverse the judgement. *bricks* made of mud will be replaced by solid stone; *sycomores* will be replaced by taller and more valuable *cedars*. The boast, 'Yahweh may destroy common dwelling-houses, but we will build ourselves palaces', is absurd.

9.11 The Heb. refers to the enemies of Rezin, the Syrian king (see marg.), but Syria is part of the destroying force in v. 12, so REB emends to make the *foes* Israel's foes.

9.12 *Aramaeans* – Syrians, Israel's neighbours to the north-east. *Philistines* lived in the south-west of Palestine. These peoples were Ephraim's allies against Assyria in 733, but they may have been enemies a few years previously when Menahem paid tribute to Assyria (II Kings 15.19f.). Making and breaking alliances was all part of the chaotic diplomacy of the period. The refrain is typical of eighth-century prophecy (see, for example, Amos 1–2).

9.13 The people failed to grasp the inner meaning of the disaster; rebellion against Yahweh involves stupidity as well as sin. Arrogance, folly, and sin belong together in the OT; so too do humility, wisdom, and virtue. *guidance from* is an REB insertion which limits the meaning. The people should have sought Yahweh in every way, submission, obedience, worship.

9.14 Yahweh's response to their arrogance is further punishment. *on one day* – it is impossible to determine when this day might have been. *palm-frond and reed* indicate a social distinction, the high and the lowly.

9.15 An editor, who wished to put down the false prophets of his own generation, slips in his own interpretation of 14b.

9.16   The original interpretation of 14b. As so often in prophecy, the leaders are more guilty; the common people follow their example and so share their judgement.

9.17   The Heb. of 17a reads 'therefore the LORD shall have no joy in their young men', which satisfies most translators. NEB and REB emend the verse to make it more harsh. Maybe REB is pursuing realism: when villages are overrun by a savage enemy, no one is spared. *youths* may refer to soldiers; if Yahweh used war as a punishment, their loss had to be taken for granted. But it is a shock to read that Yahweh intended the slaughter of *the fatherless and widows*, the very groups whose cause he champions in 1.17, 23 and elsewhere. Nevertheless, so wicked is the nation that the punishment must be as harsh as this. *speaking impiety* – the Heb. normally indicates folly, but folly and *impiety* belong together.

9.18   In this verse and the next the wrath of Yahweh is seen as a forest fire. *wicked men* – most translators have 'wickedness', which suits the image better.

9.19   Plantations and settlements in hot countries are at great risk from fire in the dry season, a factor that invading armies exploited. The people of the villages could become fuel if they were not allowed to escape, and *the LORD of Hosts* was responsible! The last line of the verse in Heb. has been transposed by REB to the latter part of v. 20.

9.20   People are greedily eating whatever they can find without being able to satisfy their hunger. *eating his fill* and *devouring* – they eat ravenously what they can, but it is not good food. *his own children's flesh* – The Heb. reads 'the flesh of his arm'; a slight emendation gives 'the flesh of his neighbour' (cf. RSV, NRSV). REB's rendering requires a different emendation. The last line, *and no one spares . . .*, comes from v. 19; it fits better here. The lines in brackets are an editorial insertion drawing attention to the hostility between north and south and forming a rough link between the third stanza and the fourth.

10.1   The fourth stanza marks a change. It is not about judgement in process but judgement in prospect. Unlike the other stanzas, it begins with *Woe betide*. We infer that the stanza was added to turn the whole into a dreadful warning for Judah. The apparatus of justice is being used to oppress the weak for the advantage of the strong. This represents an attack on individuals or a powerful group (as in 1.23 and 3.14), not a blanket condemnation of the whole people, which is in marked contrast to 9.16f.

10.2   Yahweh emerges again as the defender of *the weakest of my people*, that is, the poor of Judah. The tone recalls the bitter denunciations of 1.17, 1.21–23, 3.12–15, and 5.7–23.

10.3   The doom of the northern kingdom was described in 9.8–21 in the third person. Here the wrongdoers of Judah are attacked in the second person. *devastation from afar* implies a foreign army but without precise definition. *your children* – lit. 'your glory'. 'Dignity', 'honour', 'wealth', are all possible translations; the rendering *children* helps to make sense of the next two lines.

10.4   The awful question is: how will you save yourself and your household when Yahweh determines that judgement must begin?

The neglect of this passage by the lectionaries implies that there is little here for the preacher, but many great OT themes appear: the word of Yahweh (v. 1), the folly and pride of human sinners (9f.), Yahweh's control of history (11), his inescapable wrath (12), the stubbornness and blindness that makes repentance difficult (13), the responsibility of leaders (16), the appalling consequences when society loses its moral sense (17), the values of the prophet who regards the national sin with such horror that he reckons the calamity of verses 18–20 to be appropriate, the importance, once again, of social justice (10.1f.), and the inevitability of punishment for the guilty (3f.). The absence of forgiving grace no doubt accounts for the neglect, but see the discussion in the Introduction, pp. xxivff.

The foolish pride of Assyria
10.5–19

The rest of chapter 10 contains oracles and fragments related to Assyria. They have been brought together because of their common subject and it is now difficult to analyse the passage into its original elements. This is not too calamitous because the whole has a vigour that is lost when the parts are separated.

10.5 *The Assyrian!* NEB introduced this translation, doubtless because it did not like 'O' (AV), 'Ho' (RV), or 'Ah' (RSV). The Heb. exclamation is common but untranslateable; it expresses anguish, discontent, even anger. *the rod I wield* – no phrase reveals Isaiah's interpretation of history more clearly. The bare facts were that Assyrian armies swept westward, sacking cities, taking slaves, plundering, and striking terror into the hearts of all around. Why? A secular answer would be that Assyrian war-lords were bent on conquest and saw the opportunity for rich and easy pickings. Isaiah, however, did not believe that Assyrian war-lords made history. *The Assyrian* was the unconscious tool of Yahweh, with no more self-determination than the spear in the soldier's hand. *in my anger* – Isaiah does not hesitate to attribute *anger* to Yahweh, but it is righteous and well-justified *anger*.

10.6 *I send him* – the initiative is with Yahweh, not with Assyria. *godless* – a very strong word, 'profane', 'apostate'. 6b reads literally, 'Against the people of my wrath I command him'. The *nation* must be Israel, retrospectively the northern kingdom, prospectively the south. *pillage and plunder* echo the name of Isaiah's child in 8.1–4, Maher-shalal-hash-baz.

10.7 The Assyrians are intent on plunder for their own reasons; they do not recognize that Yahweh sends them. *this man's purpose* – lit. 'he (emphatic) intends'. *lawless* – lit. 'not so' in both 7a and 7b.

10.8 Vv. 8–11 express the Assyrian monarch's boast. It is an imaginary speech, what the prophet depicts the Assyrian as saying; and it is a masterpiece of irony. *kings* – probably *kings* of conquered nations who were glad enough to ingratiate themselves with their conquerors.

10.9 The date of the passage is probably indicated in vv. 9–11. Damascus and Samaria have been sacked and Jerusalem is under threat. This requires a date after 721, perhaps just before Sennacherib's invasion in 701. The cities appear in a geographical order, not in the order of their fall. *Calno* – a Syrian city conquered in 738. *Carchemish* lies on the Euphrates; a Hittite city, in Assyrian hands since 717. *Hamath* on the Orontes, mentioned frequently in the OT, marks the northernmost limit of Solomon's empire. *Arpad* near Hamath, fell to Assyria in 720. *Samaria* – capital of the northern kingdom, founded by Omri in 870 and conquered by Assyria in 721. *Damascus* – capital of Syria, conquered by Assyria in 732.

10.10   *idols* – here used as an index of apparent strength, though of course Isaiah knew that they were all useless. *images* – undoubtedly false worship went on in Jerusalem; we see this in Solomon's day (I Kings 11.5–8), and three hundred years later Josiah found a lot to clean up (II Kings 23). The Ten Commandments represent an ideal that was never made actual before the exile. It is possible, however, that Isaiah is deliberately representing the king of Assyria as a theological ignoramus

10.11   *worthless gods* – the king of Assyria shows contempt for Samaria's vain deities; from one point of view the boast is quite reasonable, but if Samaria were true to Israel's God, it would be a different story. Similarly Jerusalem was the city of Yahweh, but that meant nothing to the king, and there is a dark implication that it meant nothing to many of the inhabitants either.

10.12   The speech is interrupted by an editorial summary of the whole passage. The end is anticipated while the boast is still being made.

10.13   The speech continues, though REB does not reintroduce inverted commas. The Assyrian king is being set up for the greatest possible fall. *By my own might* is exactly what he would have said, and precisely what the prophet has denied in 5f. and will deny again in 16. *swept aside the frontiers* – the Assyrians were not good colonisers; they plundered, took slaves, depopulated cities. Then the territories were taken over and the frontiers thereafter had little meaning. The last line of 13 is full of problems (cf. other translations), but the overall sense is clear.

10.14   A graphic, but unusual, image. Birds can do little to defend their nests against human predators, but normally they fly around making a fuss. So devastating was the Assyrian advance, so demoralized the defenders, that they could not even do that. The plunder was there to be taken. This brings the boasting speech to an end.

10.15 In his comment on the speech the prophet returns to the image of v. 5. Tools do not wield men; men wield tools. So the difference between the nations and Yahweh is absolute and he rules them absolutely.

10.16 It is not certain what the relationship of all the verses in this passage is. 16 might be a final comment on 5–15, and 17–19 might be a misplaced oracle against the northern kingdom. We simply cannot know and analysing by guesswork is not very satisfying. Consequently we take the verses together; that is how we read them today. Once the Assyrian army has performed the task allotted to it by Yahweh, the king of Assyria will be struck down. The translation is also daunting. *the king's frame* – a guess; the Heb. means 'fatness' and it is in the plural, which explains RV and NRSV. *on his sturdy frame* – a different Heb. word, but REB continues with the guess. *from head to toe* – this phrase is transferred to this position by REB from v. 18, where it seems out of place. *body* – the Heb. means 'honour' or 'glory'. The translation of the verse is hypothetical. A judgement is clearly intended, but whether we have the description of an actual illness or an image of doom is not certain.

10.17 The Light of Israel – Yahweh is often referred to under images of light (Ps. 27.1; Isa. 60.20; Micah 7.8; etc.). *fire* – see note on 5.24, where fire is an image of judgement. *thorns and briars* – this combination of words occurs also in 5.6, 7.23–25, and 9.18; in every case it refers to the threatened doom of Israel. Such considerations lead scholars to relate vv. 17–19 to northern Israel rather than Assyria. The present position of the verses , however, shows that an editor read them as referring to Assyria, and his view must be taken seriously.

10.18 The forest fire is used again to represent the doom of Assyria. 18b is a puzzle. REB achieves clarity while staying within the bounds of probability.

10.19 *what remain* – the Heb. word 'remnant'; it occurs in the first half of the name Shear-jashub (see 7.3) and three times in vv. 20–23. This must explain why 20–23 were attached to 16–19. The use of this word also provides a reason why some commentators relate these verses to Israel. *record them* – a glimpse of primitive forestry; trees were a valuable resource.

Overall the passage is a good example of prophetic beliefs about Yahweh. He is the LORD of history and determines how the affairs of all the nations will turn out. He takes the initiative in every situation and effortlessly he manipulates the most dreaded nation of the day. Neither the might of Assyria nor the gross ignorance of her king can obstruct him. His anger is righteous and just, but such that every nation, including his chosen, should tremble. The election of Israel is no protection; in her wickedness it brings pain rather than peace. The judgement meted out will be enacted by the most fearsome and, by dreadful irony, the most godless of nations. The passage also underlines the absurdity of human arrogance, exemplified in the hypothetical, but wickedly apt, speech of the king of Assyria. So much might, so much boasting, but to what end? The doom of Assyria is written as clearly as the judgement of Israel.

The fate of the remnant
10.20–23

This passage arises from lengthy reflection on the 'remnant' theme. Some date it in the days of Josiah, others later still. The fact that 20 is in prose suggests that it is an editorial summary rather than part of the oracle itself. When the idea of a remnant was raised in chapter 7, it was not clear whether the main thrust was positive or negative. It is still not clear. Vv. 20f. appear hopeful; vv. 22f. stress that *only* a few will survive. The subject of 'The Remnant' occurs in some lectionaries for the fifth Sunday before Christmas.

10.20 *On that day* – a common prophetic formula referring to a projected catastrophe, but which? If we ask when the idea of a remnant might have come into being, the last years of the northern kingdom appear most likely. Assyria is about to spoil the land of Israel, north and south, but a remnant (Judah and Jerusalem) would survive. There are, however, large gaps in our knowledge of Israel's history, and it is facile to suppose that the verses must belong to the one crisis we know about. Moreover, we have to consider, not when the idea came into being, but when the interpretation found in these verses appeared. *survivors* implies escape from physical calamity. *him who scourged him* – we immediately think of Assyria, on whom Ahaz foolishly relied. *lean on the* LORD – political alliances had religious consequences; to trust another nation was to give credence to her gods. Israel was required to trust Yahweh alone.

10.21 *A remnant will return* – the words in Heb. are the name Shear-jashub exactly. Here they seem to refer to a moral return to Yahweh, which is almost certainly not what the name signified in 7.3. Yahweh is called by one of the titles given to the prince in 9.6 and there translated 'mighty hero'. Here the words are translated *God their strength*. This is puzzling until we remember that the Heb. *'el* has a wide range of meanings, from 'the one and only true God of Israel' to 'a mighty man', and the second word of the pair, *gibbôr*, is used almost entirely of strong men. The designation can, therefore, speak with more than one voice.

10.22 The other sense of *remnant* is now exposed. There will be a disaster to affirm Yahweh's righteousness and only a few will escape. Those looking back on the history of the two kingdoms could see that this was what had happened. Those who survived the slaughter can hardly have been the individually righteous; war follows no such logic. One has to think in terms of solidarity and representation. Israel, as a group, had sinned and was punished in a great calamity; but Israel was also Yahweh's people and was represented in salvation by those who survived. *final destruction* – The emphasis is on the decisiveness and completeness of the doom. *justice* – or 'righteousness', preferred by RV, RSV and NRSV.

10.23 This verse seems to indicate the *final destruction* of Israel, but, if we are to reconcile this with the words about the *remnant* in the previous verse, the phrase must be regarded as hyperbole. This explanation is confirmed by the fact that the Heb. reads, not *the whole land*, but 'the whole earth'.

The idea of the Remnant begins with two observations. First, the righteousness and the unrighteousness of a nation frequently depends upon a small group within it. They give their character to the whole. Secondly, in terms of actual history, after calamities, remnants do survive. Once these observations are coupled with the sense of corporateness in Israel and the fact that the promises of God in the OT relate to his people rather than to individuals, it is easy to see how a remnant comes to be regarded as the true nation. This is a difficult but unavoidable biblical doctrine. Ultimately it points to that most searching of OT notions, the principle of vicarious suffering.

Zion and Assyria
10.24–27

Zion is addressed in terms of encouragement and promise. There is no need to fear; Yahweh will deal with Assyria. Like v. 20, vv. 24–26 are in prose, they are a summary rather than an oracle. The occasion may be the onslaught of 711, though that was not directed against Jerusalem; Sennacherib's venture of 701 seems more suitable.

10.24 Every detail speaks encouragement. The hearers are *My people*; the possessive is especially significant. They are *dwellers in Zion*, and the name *Zion* has its own special ring in Isaiah. Even the reference to the brutal practices of the Assyrians is nicely turned by comparing them with the brutalities of the long since discomfited Egyptians. Egypt's oppression had provided Israel with the most splendid deliverance in her history.

10.25 The second part of the verse is obscure (see marg.), but the message is plainly encouraging.

10.26 Vv. 24f. are represented as Yahweh's own words; 26 is an oracle in the third person (cf. 1.2–17). The direct speech has greater dramatic effect, though the oracle is equally understood as the word of Yahweh. *Midian* – When Gideon saved Israel from the Midianite attack, he captured the two Midianite princes, Oreb and Zeeb, and executed them, the former at a place thereafter known as *the Rock of Oreb* (Judg. 7.25). *the Euphrates* – the Heb. word actually means 'sea', but it can be used of a large river. REB's boldness helps the sense; RV and NRSV are more literal but less clear. *Euphrates* is the nearer of the two rivers of Mesopotamia. Assyria encompassed them both. Nineveh, the capital, was on the Tigris. *Egypt* – a second reference in a short passage is not surprising in view of the absolute centrality of the exodus theme in Hebrew self-consciousness.

10.27 The verse is about freedom from the servitude. If, as it appears, it is an addition, it is an appropriate one. *the burden* refers to the taxes, tributes and other impositions laid on subject peoples by stronger nations.

No one can miss the confidence and hope in this passage. No matter how dark the present circumstances, Yahweh will act decisively for Israel's salvation, as he has acted in the past. The conviction here is no less significant than that represented in the much more frequent oracles of judgement, and indeed the judgement oracles add depth and strength to passages like this. Isaiah cannot be accused of facile optimism. When he speaks of hope, he can be relied on. In general, the OT knows nothing of 'cheap grace', comfort and salvation without judgement.

The account of an invasion
10.28–32

On the basis of content we can hardly call this passage an oracle; it is a frightening description of an army drawing near to Jerusalem. If not an oracle, it is certainly a threat, perhaps the more threatening in that the particularities of the invasion are left to the imagination. It could be that an introduction, or perhaps a conclusion, making these things clear, is missing. Most commentators relate the passage to the Syro-Ephraimite incursion of 735–33; the Assyrian advance of 701 is a possibility, but what is known of Sennacherib's route does not conform with the topographical details here. It is even possible that the verses refer to a traditional route, representing an ever-present fear, rather than a particular invasion.

10.28 *An invader from Rimmon* – these words have been detached from v. 27; they still require an emendation of the Heb., and alternatives such as 'from Samaria' or 'from the north', are possible. *Rimmon* was only fifteen miles to the north. *Aiath*, perhaps the Ai of Josh. 7–8, *Migron*, not located with certainty, and *Michmash* must have been only a few miles apart.

10.29 *Maabarah* – REB reads this as a place name, though the word means 'passage' or 'pass'; there is no known village called *Maabarah*. *Geba* is a little further south than *Michmash*. There is a *Ramah* in the same area. *Gibeah of Saul* – Saul lived in *Gibeah* and made it his capital (I Sam. 10.26; 15.34).

10.30 *Bath-gallim* – the place name is Gallim. The usual translation is 'daughter of Gallim', which can be taken as a personification of the city or a reference to the inhabitants, perhaps even the female inhabitants in view of the imperative that follows. *Laish* – location not certain. *Gibeah* and *Anathoth* are close together, just two or three miles north of Jerusalem; Gallim must be nearby.

10.31 *Madmenah* and *Gebim* cannot be located with certainty.

10.32 *This day* – the poem reads as though the enemy was almost at the gates. Was the prophet using the crisis, even the sense of fear, to induce the inhabitants of Jerusalem to put their trust in Yahweh? Not if this is the Syro-Ephraimite invasion and the author of the poem is Isaiah, for Isaiah's view is that these invaders are not to be feared at all (cf. 7.4). *Nob* – only two miles north of Jerusalem and a place from which an attack on the city might well be launched. Titus made his camp in this area in 70 CE. *he gives the signal to advance* – perhaps, but all the Heb. says is 'he waves his hand' or 'he shakes his fist'. *Zion* – the Heb. has 'Bath-Zion', like 'Bath-gallim', hence the translations 'daughter of Zion'.

The poem builds up to an impressive climax. The army drawing near finally comes up to *Zion* and *Jerusalem*, both potent names in Isaiah. Are we to assume that the most dreadful army will be stayed at this divinely defended bastion? Or must the inhabitants of *Jerusalem* understand that they are not secure if Yahweh chooses to bring them under judgement? The present form of the poem provides no answer.

Down come the tall trees
10.33f.

The previous passage was to some extent an essay in terror. These two verses promise disaster, not to the citizens of Jerusalem, but to those represented under the image of tall trees. The juxtaposition is the work of the editor, balancing the fragments of text so that hope and wholesome fear are both kept alive. Who are the tall trees? In 2.13 the image is used of the proud in Israel, but in this context it can only relate to an army moving against Yahweh's chosen city and its holy mountain, Zion. This must indicate the Assyrians again.

10.33 *tallest, lofty* – it is important that the presumptuous invaders should appear as big as possible by human standards. Only in that way can the overwhelming power of *the LORD of Hosts* be properly demonstrated.

10.34 *with the axe* – lit. 'with iron'. *Lebanon* – see note on 2.13. *its noble trees* – the Heb. is singular and refers to something majestic. REB is right to relate it to the destroyed rather than (as RV) the destroyer.

In chapter 10 Yahweh is the manipulator of foreign armies, the destroyer of unjust nations, both the rigorous inquisitor and the comfort of his people, and the scourge of human arrogance. There is no limit to his range of action, to his power, or to his righteousness.

The messianic king
11.1–5

The editorial link between 10.34 and 11.1 may well be that 10.34 sees the destruction of the tall trees of the arrogant and 11.1 sees the sprouting of a new branch from the true stock. The use of the tree image in the ANE is fascinating. The roots of trees went deep into the earth. As the long, hot summer drew to an end, everything with shallow roots shrivelled. Not so the tree; it might appear to die, but it had the unique capacity to survive the season of drought and come to life in the spring. The tree might be burnt but it would sprout again from its roots; it might be brought down with an axe, but new shoots would appear. It is no wonder that, in many places, the tree was held sacred, nor that it was used as an image of the royal house. All the positive associations were thus subtly applied to the monarchy. The image is used in the prophetic writings, but the tree is not divinized. The rebirth of both nature and the royal house is attributed to the act of Yahweh. Many commentators have doubts about whether this prophecy goes back to Isaiah of Jerusalem. Perhaps the most probable hypothesis is that the basis is Isaianic but that later, particularly exilic, writers have heightened the idealism. Although the passage promises a longed-for prince of the Davidic line who would restore Israel's fortunes in justice and peace, the term 'messiah' does not appear (cf. chapter 9; see also Ps. 72). The passage, right down to v. 10, has a place in almost every lectionary for some Sunday in the pre-Christmas season.

11.1 *branch* – a rare word, though the image of a new shoot springing from an old stock is used elsewhere (Jer. 23.5; 33.15; Zech. 3.8). *the stock of Jesse* – the Davidic ancestry of the royal house. It has been said that this phrase implies that the Davidic dynasty has been cut off, and that, therefore, the prophecy must have an exilic background. This is possible, but not necessary. Every time the king dies, a tree from the root falls; but a shoot from the same stock, a new son of David, takes his place. If this is the basic idea, then it could certainly have been re-used by Jews of the exile.

11.2 *the spirit of the LORD* – see note on 4.4. The term means Yahweh as he is powerfully active in the world. When *the spirit of the LORD* enters into a person, extraordinary things follow (see Judg. 6.34; 14.6, 19; 15.14; and especially I Sam. 16.13) The heightened capacities are not always violent or of short duration. They are called throughout the Bible 'spirits of this or that'. *will rest* suggests a gentler and more permanent relationship than we find with Samson in Judges. Wisdom to us is a natural faculty, improved by experience and careful cultivation. Here it is a divine gift. *the spirit of the LORD* imparts the *spirit of wisdom*. *wisdom and understanding* – particularly important for kings whose decisions had wide and lasting consequences. The words imply, more than shrewdness and decisiveness, a deep comprehension of both the will of Yahweh and the ways of the world. By tradition, Solomon was the king who displayed *wisdom* above all others; he was given a wise and obedient heart, according to the narrative in I Kings 3.4–15. Unfortunately history belies this idyll. *counsel and power* – the practical side of *wisdom and understanding*; the means to make sound decisions and the ability to carry them out. *a spirit of knowledge* – a much wider term than our usage would suggest; to know is to have information, but also to have experience, and to be able to reflect upon it and learn from it; *knowledge* includes the knowledge of God. *fear of the* LORD – the most important gift of all and the root of all the others. Many Christians have difficulty with this concept because *fear* to them is largely a negative concept, and I John 4.18 says that love casts out fear. The OT concept, however, is well-grounded. Yahweh is all-powerful and righteous and just; erring mortals should tremble before him. To deny this is to fall into sentimentality. There is a strong ethical element in OT *fear*; it is not so much fear of consequences, but reverence for the lawgiver who must be obeyed. 'The fear of the Lord' dominates the wisdom tradition in Israel, as Job, Psalms and Proverbs show.

11.3 *judge* – the king was the final court of appeal; he must, therefore, have more insight than judges in inferior courts. Particularly he must be able to recognize the plausible rogue and not *judge* by *outward appearances*. *hearsay* is an unfortunate translation because of its technical meaning in English law. The Heb. means that he will not reach judgements on the basis of what other people tell him; he will be able to make up his own mind.

11.4 *justice* – (cf. Ps. 72.2f). REB prefers this translation to 'righteousness', which is unfortunate, because both the ideas referred to on p. xxviii appear in this line, one in verbal form, the other in the adverbial phrase. It would have been better to carry both ideas through into English, as NRSV does. *the poor* – throughout the Bible the poor are the people that matter. The health of Hebrew society is revealed by how they are treated. The rich will usually get all they want, even in a hopelessly corrupt state, perhaps most of all in a corrupt state, but the fate of *the poor* depends entirely upon the reliability of the judicial system (cf. Ps. 72.12f.) and the extent to which altruism is generally accepted as the normal rule of social behaviour. *decide, judge, defend* – the varied terminology suggests that every conceivable kind of judgement is included, not simply formal judgements in court. *poor* and *humble* are also used to ensure inclusiveness. The former means simply the weak, the helpless; the latter, the afflicted, the oppressed, occasionally the righteous afflicted by the unrighteous. The literal translation of 4c, seen in RV, is not helpful; REB requires two changes in the Heb., but it is a constructive guess. *with his word* – REB is deliberately low key. The Heb. has 'with the breath of his lips', which gives rise to a picture of a Dalek-style being, who could strike down enemies with breath like a laser beam. Never, not in the most imaginative of Jewish tracts, do we find such a picture of the messiah, and we certainly do not find it here. The king's breath (the Heb. is *rûaḥ*, frequently translated 'spirit') goes forth in his *word*, which is very powerful; he can pass final judgement on the wicked and they are put to death; but he remains a king of this earth; filled with gifts of the spirit of Yahweh, but a man, no more.

11.5 The Hebrews thought a lot about clothes as symbols of inner dispositions (Isa. 61.3 etc.). *belt of justice* – lit. 'waist-cloth', the most intimate of garments without which no man could be seen in public, but here used simply for 'belt'. *justice* again is usually rendered 'righteousness'. *truth* – a word that indicates reliability, faithfulness, rather than simple veracity. The root of this word is the well-known *'āman*, from which we get our 'amen' (see note on 7.9). *girdle* – the same word as 'belt', but this time linked with the loins, which carry a much more intimate implication. Righteousness is the belt that binds his clothing together; *truth* is the inner, most personal garment, that he is never without.

The fact that this passage is so regularly used in Christian worship in the Advent season has advantages and disadvantages. Truly the passage can be read in terms of the life of Jesus to great advantage, but we need also to remember that this was, for Israel, a portrait of a real, as well as an ideal, king. The gifts and virtues recounted relate to the practical task of exercising power, administering justice, ruling over the whole far from perfect community. If the passage is always read in a christological way, it will seem blasphemous to apply it to others, to the actions of ministers of the crown, politicians, judges, magistrates, local councillors and union officials. Yet that is a proper application of its meaning, and it would be a thousand pities if the full force of the vision were lost because we have come to relate the words exclusively to Jesus. It is almost incredible that an OT prophet could write in this way when tyrants were everywhere and even moderately competent monarchs were a rarity, but that is the essence of vision.

The renewal of nature

11.6–9

The prophet looks forward to a day in which the harsh elements in nature will disappear and children will be happy and secure. These verses probably do not belong to the same prophecy as 1–5; there are strong reasons for dating them in the post-exilic period. They leave behind the virtues and practicalities of kingship and speak of a renewal of the entire natural order. Such hopes belong to the period when the concrete political situation was even worse than in Isaiah's day, when Israel's oppressors were vastly more powerful than Assyria, and her own rulers feeble and treacherous; this is the period of the great world empires, when it was impossible to suppose that any human son of David could rescue the nation, and when visionaries began to think of supramundane solutions, which might well include a complete change in the operation of the natural world. On any reckoning it is hard to connect the vision of 6–9 with the normal course of things in the present world. The link with the previous verses is constructed on the principle that, if it is possible for Yahweh to give Israel a king who is free from the greed and folly of the common run of kings, it is possible for him to provide animals that are free from the aggression that make them a threat to each other and to the human race. There is a flaw in this logic, however; in fact the theme changes after v. 5 from an idealistic, but not entirely impossible, expectation to a symbolic, but quite unrealistic, vision of a world that could never be. On the whole it seems best to regard 6–9 as an addition to the basic poem made by a post-exilic editor who was able to enter into the Isaianic vision but was unable to believe that the present world could provide the theatre for the fulfilment of all God's promises. Of course the passage raises unanswerable questions, not least, what would happen if all carnivores became vegetarians, but such questions are inappropriate. This is poetry; it sets a tone; it does not supply a practical programme.

11.6 *wolf, leopard, young lion* – the natural order was regarded as largely hostile in ancient Israel, with good reason. The climate could produce blazing sun, scorching winds from the desert, and drought; stony soil and soil erosion hindered agriculture; diseases decimated cattle; snakes, scorpions, carnivorous wild animals abounded. It is not surprising that the writer's hopes centred on a day when these banes would be removed. Other prophetic passages hold out slightly different hopes. In Isa. 35.9, Hos. 2.18 and Ezek. 34.25, wild animals will die out or be banished. The details in these pictures may not be consistent, but they do suggest that it was customary in Israel to look back to a primaeval age, when everything in nature was beneficent (and animals were vegetarian; cf. Gen. 1.29f.), and forward to a day when that beneficence would be restored. *will feed* – the Heb. word is a noun usually used of a sacrificial animal (see marg. and NRSV). REB makes a slight change. *little child* – small boy; in normal life parents had to worry continuously about their children, for the adventurous child was easy prey to the wild animal. Here the child is able *to tend them*, that is, to take charge of them as a shepherd takes charge of the flock.

11.7 *be friends* – the Heb. form comes from a verb meaning 'to graze', but REB, with good reason, makes a small change.

11.8 This verse relates to every mother's constant horror. *infant, young child* – both imply small children; the difference is that the latter has been weaned. *cobra, viper* – the snakes cannot be indentified with absolute certainty, but that hardly matters; the translation simply has to create a sense of dread. *dance* – as the marg. says, the Heb. verb is obscure, but 'his hand' does occur in the text, hence the traditional translation. A child poking his finger into a hole in the ground is a more likely picture than a dance.

11.9 *my holy mountain* – Zion and the city of Jerusalem. The *my* indicates that Yahweh is speaking, but the next line refers to Yahweh in the third person. Such little inconsistencies frequently happen as the prophetic speech is reduced to the written record. 9b occurs again in Hab. 2.14, no doubt quoting this passage. *the land will be filled with the knowledge of the Lord* – a spirit of knowledge was to be given to the king in v. 2; from the king it would flow into the whole of society. In other parts of the prophecy rulers are blamed for leading the people into sin; here we have the reverse.

The questions we like to ask – how, when, and where will this state of affairs come to pass? – are not answered in the OT. But two points of the utmost importance are affirmed here. First, the new day and the good life, like the first creation, are gifts of God; they are not human achievements. Everything depends upon the spirit of

Yahweh resting on the king and the natural order returning to the condition in which it was created. Secondly, the creation is one. Whatever the origin of the two passages, 1–5 and 6–9, an editor brought them together and we now read them as one. The gifts of the spirit for the true monarch are now linked with the new day for the whole creation. Common sense says that this is nonsense. The best of rulers will not affect the behaviour of snakes. But the prophet's faith sees them linked as different aspects of Yahweh's will. And evidence is coming to light to suggest that he was not so far wrong. Many of our ecological problems are caused by the absence of the virtues described in 1–5. Arrogance, greed, aggression, insensitivity, profligacy pollute the rivers and destroy the ozone layer. There will be no new day until the will of the Creator is respected and obeyed; that will requires wisdom and understanding, honesty in judgement, care for the poor and the weak, respect for the created order, all practised in the fear of the Lord.

The restoration of Israel
11.10–16

There seem to be three fragments here, the first two only one verse long. Most commentators allot the fragments to the post-exilic period. There is a slight confusion of themes. The predominant motif is the restoration and re-unification of the two kingdoms, but there are allusions to a gathering of all nations.

11.10 *On that day* – a common opening formula for an oracle about future divine action (cf. 2.11, 17, 20; 3.18; 4.1f.; 5.30). *a scion from the root* – The Heb. speaks only of 'a root'. The similarity between v. 10 and v. 1 is obvious. A later editor has re-used the image to send a message of hope to his contemporaries. He pictures a messianic figure who will appear like a *standard* in battle, a rallying point for all *peoples. the nations* – the word usually indicates non-Israelite peoples. This is a larger vision than 1–5 which put the messianic figure in a domestic context. Here he is a figure on the world stage, one reason why the verse is attributed to the post-exilic period (cf. Zech. 8.23). *will resort* – the Heb. term is commonly used for consulting a deity, either in a disreputable way, as did Saul (I Sam. 28), or in a wholesome way (Deut. 4.29). The king in Jerusalem will be widely recognized as a source of wisdom. *his abode* – the word means 'resting-place'; the temple was the resting-place of the Ark of the Covenant (I Chron. 28.2). The resting-place of the messianic figure is either his palace, with the temple next door, or the whole city of Jerusalem. Royal psalms paint a similar picture of the Hebrew king (e.g. Ps. 72).

11.11 A prose fragment beginning with the same formula as v. 10., which probably accounts for its position here. It is concerned, not with rallying the peoples of the world, but with re-uniting the people of God. *exert his power* – a paraphrase of the Heb. which, as it stands, needs emendation. Taking v. 11 on its own, the *second time* must refer to a *second* deliverance from captivity, that is, a second exodus. Second Isaiah was always ready to compare the release of the Hebrews from captivity in Babylon to the exodus, and it is reasonable to attribute this fragment to him or to someone within the Isaiah tradition who was contemporary with him. This writer had in mind the restoration of the kingdom of Israel to what it was in the time of David, before a series of misfortunes dispersed the people around the world. Taking vv. 10 and 11 together, Yahweh will *exert his power* twice on the great *day*, once to gather the nations (v. 10), and then to gather the dispersed Israelites. *recover* – the verb means 'acquire' or 'possess'. *the remnant* – another key term of the Isaianic theology. The rest of the verse catalogues the places to which the people of God had been scattered; so v. 11 is also linked with v. 12, which is about the gathering of the people of Israel from *the four corners of the earth*. *Assyria* – the big deportation was from the northern kingdom in 721. *Egypt* – some fled to Egypt in 586 taking Jeremiah with them; we learn from the Elephantiné papyri that other Jews had gone down to *Egypt*, probably before the exile. One would expect a mention of Babylon at this point. In theory the Jews of the exile returned home in 516, but in fact a large number remained behind, and in the fifth and fourth centuries BCE the Jewish colony in Babylon was the most important of the scattered communities. Babylonian *Elam* and *Shinar* come into the reckoning, but only after the Egyptian kingdoms have been named, which encourages speculation that the names in the last two lines were added to an oracle concerned only with *Assyria* and *Egypt*. *Pathros* – in Upper Egypt. *Cush* – ancient Nubia, or Ethiopia, an area on the upper Nile. *Elam* – in eastern Mesopotamia. *Shinar* – another name for Babylon. *Hamath* – in Syria; see note on

10.9. *the islands of the sea* – the word *islands* is common in Second Isaiah, but it is never quite clear what it means; 'coasts' may be better. Presumably the term refers to people living around the eastern Mediterranean.

11.12   A third verse that has to do with rallying people; it seems to combine the ideas of both 10 and 11; the standard will attract both the nations and the dispersed of Israel. *dispersed* – 'outcasts' is a more literal translation. *four corners* – a natural term for 'distant parts' where the ambient cosmology implied a flat earth. The phrase suggests 'the whole earth'.

11.13   *Ephraim's jealousy* – the northern kingdom's arrogant attitude towards Judah in the Syro-Ephraimite Confederacy has not been forgotten. It was Ephraim's last military venture. As a nation she went out of history in 721 in a state of enmity towards her kinspeople in the south. This was a wound that needed to be healed. *Ephraim* here might mean those who survived the deportation (see v. 16) or those who were left behind by the Assyrians. In neither case was the hope fulfilled. *enmity* – the Heb. refers to 'enemies of Judah' being cut off, which gives the verse a much broader scope. REB makes a change in the Heb. to limit the verse to the subject of Ephraim–Judah relations.

11.14   The result of restored relations between Ephraim and Judah is an attack on the Philistines and Judah's neighbours in the southeast. This is hardly in accord with 10–13, particularly 10bc and 12a. Fragmentary as they are, vv. 10–13 are concerned with the reunification of Yahweh's people to be Yahweh's people and to send a signal to all other nations that truth and peace can be found in Jerusalem. But in 14 the author is concerned with levelling a few old scores. Nothing better illustrates the true nature of Scripture. It is the word of God conveyed through the minds of human beings. Happily human frailty does not often impede the vision, but occasionally the flesh gets the upper hand and dark feelings find their way into the text.

11.15   One possibility is that vv. 15f. are concerned only with the return from Egypt and Assyria, in which case 15a deals with Egypt, and all the rest deals with the return from Assyria, using exodus imagery. The alternative is to link 15 with the situation of Second

Isaiah, in which case the writer is contemplating the return of the Judahites from the Babylonian exile; he sees it in terms of a new exodus (see note on v. 11). *divide* – the verb means 'utterly destroy', and few agree with NEB/REB's rendering; most commentators follow the LXX and emend to 'dry up'. *the tongue of the Egyptian sea* – the Red Sea, now known as the Gulf of Suez, is shaped like a tongue. Crossing *the Euphrates*, referred to in Heb. as 'the river', hardly called for a miracle of Red Sea proportions, but this was, of course, a poetic vision. *a mighty wind* – cf. Ex. 14.21. *wadis* – rivulets that run in winter but dry out in summer; the fertile crescent abounds with them. *dry-shod* – the Heb. means lit. 'in sandals'; cf. Ex. 14.29, where it is emphasized that the land was dry.

11.16 If v. 15 referred to the return of the Judahites from Babylon, this verse refers to the far more problematic hope of regathering the people deported from Samaria in 721. The need to restore the whole people of God for theological reasons was very strong in the exile (see Ezek. 37.11, 16f., 21f.) and the appeal to the escape from Egypt is the only way that the hope could be sustained. *causeway* – most translators are satisfied with 'highway', but NEB and REB prefer this word, which normally means 'a raised road running through flooded or marshy terrain'. *remnant* here means the descendants of those who survived the conquest of the northern kingdom and the deportation; such descendants would have had to preserve their faith and their national identity through several generations.

The difficulty of working out references must not blind us to the central point of the passage. The fact that more than one person contributed to the vision strengthens rather than weakens its force. The writers look back, not nostalgically, but positively. They see the exodus as a pattern for the future. In the exodus Yahweh called Israel as a single people, and as a single people they were saved. Salvation in the future, therefore, must involve the unity of the people of God. (There is a parallel here with the modern situation; the ecumenical movement is not a hobby for a few broadminded enthusiasts; it is a fundamental principle of the very being of the church.) The centrality of Zion is also evident. The unity of God's people and of all the nations is not just a metaphysical idea; it has a practical and concrete base. The OT is sometimes embarrassingly down to earth. We tend to prefer 'spiritual' solutions to our problems. The OT reminds us that, if we are to be true to the Bible, our thinking must be practical and concrete, not simply theoretical. Finally, the great salvation is not simply for us, the chosen, and our friends. All nations are invited in v. 10. This is only a hint, but it points to a theme in the book of Isaiah (cf. 2.1–4) that is breath-taking in its range.

Psalms of thanksgiving
12.1–6

It is widely agreed that four main types of psalm can be recognized: individual laments, communal laments, individual psalms of thanksgiving, and communal hymns of thanksgiving. (There are, of course, other groupings: royal psalms, songs of Zion, Wisdom psalms, etc.) A study of these types can help in the understanding of prophecy. In this passage we have two psalms of thanksgiving, one individual, one communal. The chapter occurs in many lectionaries as part of the Easter thanksgiving.

12.1 The first line provides the editorial link with the previous chapter (11.10f.); then follows an individual psalm of thanksgiving. *you will say* – the Heb. verb is singular; a typical hearer is being addressed. The theme of divine *anger* is common in the Psalter, and its cessation is the occasion for great thanksgiving (e.g. Ps. 30). The *anger* might result in illness or almost any other kind of misfortune.

12.2 *my deliverer* – occurs at the beginning and at the end of this verse and *deliverance* appears at the end of v. 3. In Heb. they are all the same word, usually rendered 'salvation'. The word has a striking resemblance to the name of Isaiah, which means 'Yahweh saves'. Could the author be making a deliberate pun?[2]

12.3 A communal thanksgiving; the verbs are now plural. As long as it was possible to draw water, life was sustainable; if the well ran dry, disaster was imminent. So the image of drawing water was very potent. Gathering at the well was a social event, just the occasion for a song (cf. Num. 21.16–18). A festival, when water was drawn to celebrate some national event, may be indicated.

[2] Compare, for example, John Donne's 'Hymn to God the Father': Having done that, Thou hast done; I fear no more.

12.4 *invoke him by name* – names had great significance in Israel. To know and use someone's name was to have a certain intimacy. When Yahweh revealed his name (Ex. 3.14; 6.2f.), he was granting Moses and Israel a privilege. *proclaim* – the Heb. says 'cause it to be remembered'. Memory played a large part in Hebrew worship. Remembering divine acts in the past was not simply an intellectual exercise but a means of extending the glory of these actions and rejoicing in them afresh.

12.5 *triumphed* – no details are available of the triumph referred to, but that is the nature of cultic thanksgiving. Liturgy is rarely specific because it is used again and again. So too the worship of the temple was rarely confined to a specific event. Last week's deliverance was seen together with last year's deliverance and all the great deliverances before that, right back to the archetypal deliverance in the exodus. Equally the celebration of the exodus coalesced with all the other subsequent successes, with the result that the meaning of the exodus actually increased as it passed through history. That is what the OT meant by 'remembering'. It is a feature of Jewish worship still. Escape from Egypt and escape from numerous afflictions since unite in the Jewish consciousness to create a sense of universal gratitude. To seek for a particular deliverance that occasioned this psalm is, therefore, to miss the point.

12.6 Greater than the specific victory is the perennial fact that Yahweh is present *in majesty* with those who dwell in Zion. This recalls Immanuel of 7.14.

The relevance of these psalms in particular, and Jewish worship in general, to Christian worship at Easter is of great importance. In one sense the resurrection of Jesus, like the exodus and like the battle of Hastings, is an event of the distant past that is absolutely over and finished. But neither exodus nor Easter can be properly understood in this sense. These events signify in the grand manner the constant activity of God on behalf of his people. Christian history is not one Easter event but a series of Easter events, and the personal history of each Christian is a series of Easter events. The first one is archetypal, revelatory, determinative; the most recent ensures that we are still moving within the ongoing history of salvation to this day.

Prophecies against foreign nations
13.1–23.18

The next eleven chapters consist largely of accusations, threats, taunts, warnings, lamentations, and prophecies of disaster relating to Babylon, Assyria, Moab, Syria, Egypt and other neighbouring nations. Not surprisingly perhaps, the lectionaries reveal little interest; not even the *JLG 2* finds space for any passage from this section. This is to be regretted for at least three reasons. In the first place, the section is not simply an attack upon foreigners. Severe as is the programme of judgement, Israel will not be allowed to escape, thus emphasizing that the righteousness of Yahweh represents an absolute and universal demand. Secondly, the story is not all doom. There are many positive prophecies scattered throughout. Compassion will be shown to Israel (14.1f.) and other nations too will share in the felicity of worshipping Yahweh (17.7; 18.7; 23.17f.). There is a remarkable magnanimity about many of the oracles (15.1–16.14; 21.1–15), surprisingly little gloating, and 19.16–25 contain universal hopes that have no equal elsewhere in the OT. Lastly, and most of all, the issue presented here must be faced. Terrible calamities do happen, arrogance and wickedness still abound, theists believe in a moral ordering of the universe and also maintain that God is absolutely sovereign. In these chapters the book of Isaiah tries to hold these four factors together. We may not be fully satisfied with the result, but we can scarcely claim that we have nothing to learn from the approach.

It is not unusual for prophets to make accusations and threaten doom (see, for example, Amos 1.3–2.6; Jer. 46–51; Ezek. 25–32), a fact that raises interesting questions. Would the rulers of other nations ever hear about these oracles? Would they care? And if the answer to both questions is no, why did the prophets bother? There are three points to be made. First, the prophets were concerned about the relations between other nations and Israel; it was, therefore, necessary to be clear where these nations stood in Yahweh's plan. Secondly, the prophets had a majestic view of Yahweh's sovereignty over all the nations on earth. Their oracles would be deficient if they failed to witness to this fact. Thirdly, the prophets believed that word and event were tied together. This notion is often explained by saying that the prophetic word led inevitably to fulfilment, but it would be more accurate if the explanation were reversed. If Yahweh wills the doom, he will first proclaim the judgement. Whether the word is heeded, or even heard, is of secondary importance; the event first finds expression in the word, the word of the prophet, the word of Yahweh. There are a number of introductory formulae (13.1; 15.1; 17.1; 19.1; 21.1, 11, 13; 22.1; 23.1.), indicating much editorial activity.

Babylon
13.1–22

The first passage in the new section does not, as it stands, come from Isaiah's time. *Babylon, fairest of kingdoms* (v.19), threatened by *the Medes* (v. 17), is about to be overthrown, which points to a time in the sixth century when the Babylonian empire was weakening and the exiled Hebrews were directly interested in her fate. There are, however, hints of a grander eschatological expectation, more easily linked with the style of writing known as apocalyptic than with prophecy, which in turn suggests that the passage is composite.[1] Nevertheless Isaianic themes persist throughout, witnessing to the strength of the Isaiah tradition.

13.1 Some details fit *Babylon* precisely (vv. 17, 19), but most of the chapter is concerned with judgement on all nations (vv. 5, 9, 11, etc.). Either an oracle relating to *Babylon* has been incorporated into a more comprehensive one or *Babylon* is used in the heading as a symbol of nations hostile to Yahweh. *Babylon*, after all, had committed the unique sin of sacking the holy city. Revelation describes Rome, the great enemy, as 'Babylon'. The *oracle* is positively attributed to *Isaiah son of Amoz*, which shows that the editors intended it to be understood as part of the living Isaiah tradition.

13.2 Neither speaker nor audience is revealed. Some commentators try to provide a historical occasion for the gathering of this

[1] For the meaning of the term 'apocalyptic', see the introduction to the section, *The Lord's Judgement* (24.1–27.13)

army, but it is better to accept the limitations of an imprecise text than to manufacture precision where there is none. The *wind-swept height* is the place, visible for miles around, where the army gathers. Nobody knows where *the Nobles' Gate* might be. Attempts to locate it in Babylon have not got very far.

13.3 Yahweh is the speaker. The word for *fighting men* derives from the root meaning 'holy'. However unwelcome the idea may be, war in the OT was a holy matter. Yahweh was a man of war (Ex. 15.3; 17.16); warriors were consecrated for battle (Deut. 23.9–14; I Sam. 21.5); in some cases the total slaughter of the enemy, his households and his cattle was a religious duty (e.g. Josh. 6.17–21; I Sam. 15.3). In this verse unknown armies are called to give effect to Yahweh's fearful judgement.

13.4 The muster of the army takes on new proportions. It becomes *a vast multitude; kingdoms* and *nations* assemble, not on a single hill, but on *mountains* in the plural. It is hard to think of this as a normal historical event; the picture has much in common with the notions of divine intervention which characterize early apocalyptic. The word *host* appears here for an army, which shows that, whatever else may be implied by the title *The LORD of Hosts*, the idea of a Lord of armies cannot be ruled out.

13.5 Conflict on a vast scale. The armies gather from the end of the heavens *to lay the whole earth waste*. It is hard to understand this as a reference to Babylon or any other single nation.

13.6 Similar lines occur in Joel (1.15) and Zephaniah (1.14). The context in those books is a catastrophic divine intervention and the same is probably intended here. *the day of the LORD* – the meaning of this term spans both the historical event and the supra-historical cataclysm. A common term in Isaiah, it does not require the sense of a grand, final intervention, but equally that sense is not excluded. *the Almighty* is one of the more mysterious names for God in the OT; it occurs in Gen.17.1 and frequently in Job.

13.7f. A horrific description of terror and helplessness, but still no precise indication of who will suffer.

13.9 Vv. 9–13 describe divine intervention with cosmic effects; but

14–16 are more familiar and specific. The *wrath* and *fierce anger* are directed against *the earth* and *all the wicked*, which suggests much more than an attack on a single nation. It is hard to think of any human army reducing *the earth to desolation*. This action, therefore, belongs to the supra-historical realm.

13.10   It is just possible to argue that the reference to *The stars, the sun* and *the moon* is simply powerful imagery relating to an earthly event like the fall of a city, but it is more likely that we have here an anticipation of the dreadful end-time, such as is found in some apocalyptic literature. When God at last moves against wicked nations, he will need no armies. He will command the heavenly bodies to cease providing *light*. People of every time and place are dependent on natural light, but the people of the OT were more aware of the fact than we are. The heavenly bodies provided them with light by which to work, warmth, a way of measuring time, and a means of finding direction by day and by night. Darkness, therefore, naturally equates with doom (cf. Amos 5.18, 20; Micah 3.6; Zeph. 1.15; Joel 2.31; etc.).

13.11   11cd reveal the nature of the sin that merits such drastic punishment. Significantly it is not false worship or social injustice; nor is it a sin particularly associated with Babylon. It is *insolent pride* and *ruthless arrogance*, the fundamental human sin, the attempt to claim equality with God and to usurp his functions. Appropriately it meets with the most radical punishment.

13.12   A great purge is implied. The site of *Ophir* is unknown, though it is possible to guess that it was in Arabia and approachable only by ship from the Gulf of Aqabah. Solomon's gold came from Ophir (I Kings 9.28; 10.11; cf. I Kings 22.48; Job 28.16; Ps. 45.9).

13.13   More cosmic disaster reflecting God's *wrath*. The earth, like any other structure, was thought, in the cosmology of the day, to have *foundations. the heavens* rested on mountains that had similar foundations. What is described here comes close to being an act of universal anti-creation.

13.14   The picture changes from barely conceivable cosmic disaster to the all too familiar national calamity. Amidst a scene of widespread chaos survivors rush home to where they think, wrongly, that they will be safe.

13.15f.   A common but horrific scene: the sack of a city. Though vv. 9–13 are about divine action, Yahweh is not mentioned in 14–16; but that hardly allows us to claim that the battering of *babes* and the raping of *wives* did not, in the author's judgement, fall within the divine plan. If 9–13 and 14–16 are separated, the former must be treated as apocalyptic, which in this instance means an imaginative account of the activity of Yahweh, and the latter as the brutal realism of prophecy.

13.17   Here at last we have a clear historical reference. Yahweh will make use of *the Medes* as previously he had made use of the Assyrians (10.5). The Median kingdom, situated to the north of Babylon, was conquered by Cyrus around the year 550 BCE. Cyrus was no destroyer; he absorbed the Medes into his newly established empire and it became the empire of the Medes and Persians. It was actually Cyrus who took Babylon in 539, so the reference here is not strictly accurate, but it surely belongs to the time of Second Isaiah. Threatened nations could sometimes buy off their expansionist neighbours with tribute (see II Kings 16.8), but that relatively agreeable option would not be available for Babylon.

13.18   This verse repeats the sense of 16a. Its first line is difficult to translate, so REB relegates it to the marg. Some lines are probably missing altogether.

13.19   The Babylonian empire impinged on Israel only from 605, when Assyria was finally destroyed, until 539, when Babylon itself fell. From the point of view of this oracle, Babylon still exists, so the oracle is easy to date. The famous hanging gardens, one of the wonders of the ancient world, may provide a reason why Babylon is described as the *fairest of kingdoms*. *Chaldaeans* is used in the OT as another name for the Babylonians. *Sodom and Gomorrah* were symbols of the ultimate sin, the ultimate punishment (see Gen. 19 and Isa. 1.9).

13.20   The last three verses read like a curse formula, poetic and repetitive. They were composed before Babylon fell, and even allowing for prophetic hyperbole, they are wide of the mark. Babylon was not sacked when it was taken by Cyrus and the population, including many Jews, remained there for generations. The word *Arab* is used in the OT for any dweller in the desert.

13.21 It is not easy to define the creatures correctly, but that hardly matters. The list of new occupants implies the utter forsakenness of the site. The most interesting term is *he-goat*. AV and RV render this as 'satyr', a mythical deity with both human and animal features. Poetically, if in no other way, AV and RV are right; the fact that the animals that take over the ruined city include some never seen or comprehended emphasizes the desolation (see Isa. 34.14).

13.22 There is nice sense of irony here: *jackals will occupy her mansions* and *wolves her luxurious palaces*. The last two lines make dating even easier. Unless the prophecy is incorrect in every way, the date must be between 550, when it became clear that a new champion had arrived and 539, when the city fell. This argument applies only to these few verses; the date of whole passage remains problematic.

Yahweh's *blazing anger* (v. 13) is seen here both in historical event and end-time horror. No passage puts the theological issues involved more clearly. They are discussed in the Introduction, pp. xxivff.

A taunt-song over Babylon
14.1–23

The core of this passage is vv. 4b–21, an ironic lament for the overthrow of an unidentified ruler. The song has been given a prose introduction (3–4a) and a prose conclusion (22f.), both of which name *Babylon* and so focus the lament on that kingdom. Vv. 1f. thus stand between two oracles relating to Babylon; they describe how Israel will fare when Babylon is brought low.

So much for the present form of the text, but what of the taunt-song itself? The details do not indicate which nation is being mocked. The song might belong to Isaiah's period and indeed to Isaiah himself, for it is a brilliant piece of mockery; if so, it would celebrate the downfall of an Assyrian king, perhaps Sargon or Sennacherib. In that case, a later editor subsequently reissued it with a beginning and ending that linked it with Babylon. There is nothing unusual in that. Later editors showed their reverence for prophetic texts, not by preserving them unaltered, but by taking them over and reading them in the light of their own circumstances. This is probably the best explanation. If the original applied to Babylon, Isaiah can hardly have been the author, for Babylon did not tread *nations underfoot with relentless persecution* (v. 6) in his day.

14.1 Vv. 1f. indicate how Israel will fare when Babylon collapses. The tone and content of these verses are remniscent of Second Isaiah. Yahweh, who has shown his power in judgement, will now *show compassion*. The use of the term *Jacob* for Israel is common in the prophets, particularly in Second Isaiah. Yahweh's *choice* of Israel is the great theme of her religion; many passages trace it back to the captivity in Egypt (Hos. 11.1; Ex. 19.5; Deut. 7.6–8). *once again* indicates that the judgement expressed in the fall of Jerusalem and the exile suspended Israel's election; but now the period of punishment is over (Isa. 40.2) and the choice will be renewed. *He will resettle them* – as Israel understood her history, the first settlement was the work of Yahweh (Ex. 15.17; Josh. 3.10; Ps. 44.2f.). *their native soil* – the land of Yahweh's promise (Gen. 15.18; Deut. 19.8). The reference to *aliens* recalls a feature of life after the return (see Isa. 56.3–6). So these few words may have been inserted even later than the rest of vv. 1f. The *aliens* were settlers from other nations who had an acknowledged place in Hebrew society (Ex. 12.48f.; 20.10; Deut. 1.16; 16.11). They will *attach themselves* to the community, that is, become proselytes, a phenomenon hardly envisaged during the exile, but familiar to the post-exilic community (Zech. 8.23).

14.2 Evidently there was some fantasizing among the exiles on how the return would take place. It was not enough that they would be allowed to go home; there must be a dramatic reversal of roles. *Nations* – unnamed, but presumably those who had oppressed them. Israel will *take them over* – 'possess them as property' (cf. Isa. 45.14–17; 49.2f.). The verse does not reveal a very exalted hope, but doubtless it catches the mood of the captives.

14.3 We come now to the introduction to the taunt-song. Once again we have a reference to a future *day* when Yahweh will act. Unlike the author of 13.9–13, this editor saw it as a day of relief. *the* *cruel servitude* – an attempt to strike an analogy with slavery in and escape from Egypt (Ex. 1.14, etc.).

14.4 The *taunt-song* has the form and rhythm of a dirge (cf. II Sam. 1 and Isa. 1.21), but it is a dirge expressing exultation. *the king of Babylon* must be Nabonidus (555–39), who lost the kingdom.

14.5 For *the rod* as an instrument of persecution, see Isa. 9.4 and 10.5. *wicked* and *rulers* – the plural indicates that the taunt-song is not concerned with a single king but with an empire.

14.6 This verse would not apply to Nabonidus, but would be apt for some of his predecessors, particularly Nebuchadnezzar (605–562), who took Jerusalem.

14.7 The whole world – the small nations who suffered as v. 6 describes. The *cries of joy* would fit the period of Second Isaiah (cf. 44.23; 49.13; 54.1; 55.12).

14.8 Lebanon – a majestic feature of ancient Palestine (see note on 2.13). The forests supplied timber for the building schemes of Near Eastern potentates (I Kings 5.6–14). But there is also a figurative sense. The exploitation of the forests symbolizes the exploitation of the peoples.

14.9 The next three verses describe, with intense irony, the arrival of the hated monarch in the land of the dead. *Sheol* is the destination of all living beings, according to the OT, but existence in Sheol is of such low quality that it can hardly be called survival. The idea of Sheol seems to derive from the notion of life in the tomb. It is dark and silent, a place of worms and corruption, a place from which there is no return (Job 7.9; 10.21; Pss. 94.17; 115.17); a place where there was no joy, no memory, where one is not remembered by God, nor able to worship him (Pss. 6.5; 30.9; 88.5,10–12; 115.17; Isa. 38.18). The picture is not entirely consistent At times *Sheol* appears as a deep, dark cavern where the dead continue their witless existence; at times it implies personal dissolution. For most of the OT, Sheol is literally 'a dead end'; one's best hope was to keep away from it for as long as possible. Resurrection from Sheol is a late idea and appears in only a few references (see on Isa. 25.8 and 26.19). The word is impossible to translate because the concept is so foreign. Corruption in the grave is a familiar idea, but we rarely think of the solidarity of the dead in a cavernous, underground kingdom. The classical Hades or underworld is as near as we can get. AV was seriously wrong in rendering it 'Hell'; the same error still causes problems in the Apostles' Creed. *Sheol* is personified in this verse. *astir* – heavily ironic because that, of course, is what the dead cannot be. The Heb. word for *dead* means 'shades', that is, those who have only the life of the grave. The one thing the dead do have is their identity; the corpse is still the corpse of a particular individual. So the *kings* remain kings in death; they may even have better tombs than commoners, but the reference to their *thrones* is sarcasm.

14.10 The normal style of greeting a monarch was to extol his power, hence the malicious pleasure in this reversal.

14.11 REB follows the DSS rather than the MT (see marg.), so that the monarch confronts those he has slain. NRSV follows the MT making the king's musicians serenade him to Sheol. Both are powerful. In 11cd the luxury of the royal bed is compared with the grave where *maggots* and *worms* provide the coverings.

14.12 The mockery continues. The king is likened to a celestial body that tried to mount up to the highest place in the heavens only to be thrown down and humiliated. Ezek. 28.11–19 seems to allude to a similar story in passing judgement on the king of Tyre and the enigmatic words of Luke 10.18 point in the same direction. The Greeks had a word, *hubris*, for this kind of pride; *hubris* often led to retribution (Greek, *Nemesis*, the proper name of the goddess of retribution). The king, therefore, has not merely overreached himself, and paid the cost; he is also identified with the archetypal figure of arrogant presumption. *Bright morning star* – lit. 'shining one, son of the dawn'. The Latin translation of 'shining one' is *lucifer*, which explains why that name is sometimes given to Satan.

14.13 *the heavens* were thought to be arranged in tiers which meant that there was a highest heaven (I Kings 8.27). This was no place for minor planets or minor deities. As elsewhere in Isaiah, the basic sin is arrogance (cf. 2.11–17; 5.14f.). Canaanite gods assembled on a mountain in the far north, where Baal had his palace (cf. Ps. 48.2).

14.14 *the Most High* – the highest deity in the pantheon. The title, though used of Yahweh (Pss. 7.17; 9.2 etc.), is probably of Canaanite origin.

14.15 So much for the boasting; now comes the crash. From the highest heaven of his ambitions he is brought down to *Sheol* and *the depths of the abyss*.

14.16 *Those who see you* – the inhabitants of Sheol, though one or two lines in the next few verses suggest that the action is taking place on earth. This device enables the author to make use of the atmosphere of both the underworld and the battlefield. The three verbs, *see, stare* and *gaze*, build up the tension. The observers, whether on earth or in Sheol, express their astonishment that so lofty a destroyer could be so humiliated.

14.17 The three clauses imply a particular monarch, but the author also strikes at all unjust conquerors.

14.18 This is the normal fate of kings, not hopeful or cheering, but decent and orderly, and not without dignity.

14.19 This king, however, had no burial. Because there was no life beyond the grave in the perception of ancient Israel, final rites were especially important. To be denied decent burial was a last, horrific insult (cf. I Kings 14.11; 21.23f.; II Kings 9.30–37; Jer. 22.19). *carrion* is a guess to improve a line that is not clear.

14.20 The verse indicates a particular king but does not help us to identify him. REB applies the last five lines of the song (20d and 21) to the king and his family. Other translations make the conclusion into a condemnation of all evil monarchs.

14.21 The sons were reckoned to share in the father's guilt (cf. II Sam. 21.8f, but see Deut. 24.16). The slaughter of the sons would cut off the dynasty, confound its expansionist policies, and ensure that the king was never honoured again. Further, the king would be denied the only immortality that the Hebrews conceived of, that is, continuation through children who would bear the name and the likeness for years to come. Absalom's pathetic act in II Sam. 18.18 illustrates this.

14.22 We now come to the prose ending added by an editor to confirm the application of the song to Babylon. The words, attributed to Yahweh, extend the fate of the dynasty to the whole kingdom. The most radical destruction is envisaged. The loss of *name*, *offspring*, and *posterity* echoes the fate of the king himself.

14.23 The city will be so reduced that creatures of the wild will be the only inhabitants. Translators vary in their rendering of this bird or animal. Determining the exact species is less important than establishing the sense of utter wildness. *the besom of destruction* is an unusual but potent image. With the final formula the passage against Babylon beginning in 13.1 is concluded.

Despite the undeniable touch of venom, the rather worldly expectations of v. 2, and the absence of any belief in a positive after life, this vigorous passage spells out some of the essentials of biblical faith. On one side, physical power and brutal conquest lead to boundless arrogance, the ultimate human folly, and the end of that is complete humiliation in Sheol. On the other, the pain and the suffering of the chosen calls forth divine compassion. Here, at least, the meek inherit the earth.

The doom of Assyria
14.24–27

In this short passage Yahweh promises to overthrow Assyria. The period of Assyrian oppression extended through Isaiah's lifetime and many of his oracles (particularly ch. 10) relate to her. Though there is every reason to see his hand in these verses , the passage expands to allude to events and ideas of a later period.

14.24 It is not unusual for Yahweh to swear oaths in the prophetic literature (see Amos 4.2; 6.8; 8.7). *As I purposed* – according to 10.5, Yahweh planned to use Assyria to punish Israel, but then to ensure that the conquering power sufferred its own just humiliation.

14.25 Assyria was discomfited in Israel in 701, when Sennacherib had to retreat, but the yoke was not lifted entirely until the fall of

Nineveh in 612. The editor has linked these two events; the deliverance of God's people and God's city was a sign of the deliverance of all peoples and nations. The language of 25cd recalls 9.4 and 10.27.

14.26 The events with which Isaiah was concerned are seen as the first part of a plan to include *the whole world*. It is consistent with the Isaiah tradition that Yahweh should care for Israel first and then for the world.

14.27 The foundation stone of the Isaianic theology. Despite immediate appearances, Yahweh has a plan and no power on earth can frustrate it.

A God without power or a God without purpose is no God at all. The writers of the OT were as familiar with the pain and confusion of international affairs as we are, but they believed firmly in the divine power and the divine plan. This is a part of the challenge that the book of Isaiah makes to us.

Warning to Philistia
14.28–32

A difficult oracle, even though it can reasonably be attributed to Isaiah.

14.28 The year of Ahaz' death cannot be established with certainty, but on the system we follow it is 715. The unusual phraseology suggests that the formula was added by an editor.

14.29 An enemy of the Philistines has just died. This cannot be Ahaz, who was no threat to the Philistines. From vv. 30–32 we gather that the enemy also frightened Israel. An Assyrian king must be indicated, either Tiglath-Pileser III, who died in 727, or Shalmaneser V, who died in 722. The death is no cause for rejoicing for worse was to come; the Assyrian threat would grow stronger. *snake, viper* and *flying serpent* represent escalation. The first relates to all snakes, the second to a particularly poisonous one, and the third to a mythical monster.

14.30 There seems to be an abrupt change here from a threat to an expression of confidence. It may be that there has been some displacement. As it stands the sense is that, while the Philistines will be vulnerable, even the poorest among Yahweh's people will be secure (cf. 10.2; 11.4).

14.31 *the gate* was the place for wailing; it was the normal place of assembly and the place where the enemy would burst in. The *formidable foe* must be Assyria.

14.32 The reference to *envoys* suggests that Philistia had sent to Jerusalem for help. The answer, expressed in terms of Zion theology, is that Israel will have a safe refuge in Yahweh and Philistia must prepare for her fate.

Zion represents total security in a terrifying world. Zion is not for the great and predatory nations; it is for the afflicted among Yahweh's people. This reversal of fortune is a recurring theme throughout the book and, indeed, throughout the whole Bible.

Moab
15.1–16.14

These chapters form a lament over the tragic fate of Moab. They are made up of original units plus comments and insertions. Parts of 15 and 16.7–11 reappear in Jer. 48.29–38, which raises questions about provenance. 16.13 says that Yahweh delivered these words *long ago*, so the present format is the work of an editor who was able to look back on prophecies made before his time. The heartland of Moab was between the Brook Zered and the River Arnon, east of the Dead Sea, but Moabite kings frequently pushed northwards; some of the towns mentioned are a long way north of the Arnon. Moab enjoyed a stormy relationship with Israel. According to Judg. 11.17 Moab refused free passage to the Hebrews on their way to the Promised Land and Num. 22 contains the colourful story of Balak, the king of Moab, hiring a professional, Balaam, to put a curse on Israel. There is a gruesome story in Judg. 3 of the murder of Eglon, king of Moab, by Ehud, the judge. David subdued the Moabites, brutally it seems (II

Sam. 8.2), but they regained their freedom until they suffered again at the hands of Omri. II Kings 3 recounts a crushing victory of Israel and Judah over Moab, though it is well to remember that the Moabite Stone, describing what must be the same war, celebrates a Moabite victory. The Deuteronomic laws barred Moabites from the assembly of Israel (Deut. 23.3), though, on the positive side, Ruth, who is recorded as the great-grandmother of David (Ruth 4.13–21), was a Moabitess. The present oracle does not gloat, but even shows signs of sympathy for the sufferings of this ancient enemy.

15.1 It is not clear whether the oracle is an anticipation of Moab's doom or a description of what has already happened; there may be elements of both. *the night* – attacks at night were especially horrific. *Ar* is in the centre of Moab, near *Kir*, or Kir-hareseth, the capital.

15.2 The next few verses describe the reaction of the people to the onslaught. *Dibon* is an important city just north of the Arnon. The local shrine would be dedicated to the Moabite god, Chemosh. *Nebo* is both a mountain and a city; *Medeba* is near them, about twenty miles north of the Arnon.

15.3 Different cultures handle extreme emotions in different ways. These ancient peoples had little use for the reticence which is supposedly the British style. Grief is all-enveloping; so it determined dress, public behaviour, indeed everything.

15.4 *Heshbon* – near Mount Nebo, a mile or two from *Elealeh*. The site of *Jahaz* is uncertain.

15.5 The author feels sympathy for hapless Moab. The *fugitives* are escaping to the south, for *Zoar* is at the southern tip of the Dead Sea. The other three places mentioned, *Eglath-shelishiyah*, *Luhith*, and *Horonaim* cannot be located with certainty. The text is difficult, but the picture of a group of desperate refugees is clear and moving.

15.6 We infer that *The waters of Nimrim* were a verdant area at the south-eastern corner of the Dead Sea. It is hard to imagine that the enemy was responsible for its desolation, so the verse must be a poetic symbol of Moab's sufferings.

15.7 *the wadi Arabim* is usually translated 'the brook of the willows';

here *Arabim* is taken as place name. It may refer to the Brook Zered, Moab's southern boundary. A *wadi* is a seasonal stream, flowing in winter, dry in summer.

15.8 The location of *Eglaim* and *Beer-elim* is uncertain.

15.9 The Heb. refers to Dimon, not *Dibon*, and even if *Dibon* is correct, that town is not located on a stream. The verse strikes a dissonant note. Previously the attitude was sympathetic; here there is a threat of more trouble to come. *Admah* may not be a place name; it could mean simply 'land' or 'ground'.

16.1 There is now an intermission; the lament does not begin again until v. 7. Vv. 1–4b describe an appeal to Israel, backed up by *a present of lambs*, to help Moab in her plight. The present is sent from *Sela*, a city in Edomite territory, formerly but wrongly identified with Petra, via *the wilderness* south of the Dead Sea, *to the mount of Zion*. Any present would be sent to the king, but *the mount of Zion* is more graphic, contrasting the panic in Moab with the security of Yahweh's chosen city. For a precedent see II Kings 3.4, where Mesha, king of Moab, sent a tribute of lambs to Ahab, king of northern Israel (869–50).

16.2 The plight of the women refugees. Crossing the Arnon gorge was a dangerous point in the flight.

16.3 The words of the Moabite rulers, asking urgently for asylum. Note that the sun, usually regarded (at least by us) as beneficent, is here an image for the destroyer. What the Moabites need is shade.

16.4 Some resident aliens had security and certain rights in Israel (Deut. 1.16; 5.14; 10.18f.; etc.); other groups remained permanent enemies. This is a request for the privileged status. In 4ab Israel is secure, but 4cd imply that Israel herself is being oppressed. 4c–5 is, therefore, probably an interjection by an editor who in a difficult time was more concerned with Israel's future than with Moab's fate.

16.5 *a trusted throne* is a rather lame translation of the Heb., which makes use of one of the most important words in the language of Hebrew faith, the word *ḥeseḏ*. The word implies trust, loyalty, reliability, persistence, but also affection; it is the word translated 'lovingkindness' in the AV (cf. NEB, NIV and NRSV). *tent* – used as an image of the household, which in this case includes the whole kingdom. *true judge* – this is messianic expectation in its true OT sense. *justice, right* – see Introduction, pp. xxviiif.

16.6 Now comes a surprisingly unsympathetic response to Moab's tale of woe. The tone is different from that of 15.1–8, though perhaps in tune with 15.9. This suggests that the remainder of the lament, vv. 7–11, is to be read as mockery. On the other hand, v. 11 does not read like mockery. There is an easily understood confusion of sentiments here.

16.7 The lament begins again. *prosperous farmers* – the Heb. refers to 'the raisin-cakes' *of Kir-hareseth* and most translators accept this. Raisin-cakes featured in the worship of fertility cults so they are a reasonable symbol of Moab in its false security and false worship. The parallel verse, Jer. 48.31, refers to 'men' rather than 'raisin-cakes'. *Kir-hareseth* (see 15.1) means 'city of earthenware'; the use of the full title may be a sly allusion to the capital's fragility.

16.8 Most commentators take the view that *the vineyards* represent the land and *the vines* represent the people. The four towns mentioned in vv. 8f. were under Israelite domination during the time of David's ascendancy. No doubt this added spice to the prophecy of misfortune. *Sibmah* was a little to the west of *Heshbon* (see 15.4). The Moabite 'vines' make *the lords of the nations* drunk, a general comment on Moab's dire influence. The last two lines witness to how widespread their vineyards were.

16.9f. In view of vv. 6f. we must assume that the weeping is not genuine. The irony lies in the fact that traditionally the grape harvest was a time of joy when merry songs were sung. *Jazer* was located on the northernmost limit of Moab. *the shouts of the enemy* will replace *the shouting of the harvesters*.

16.11 *heart, soul* – The Heb. means 'bowels' and 'inward parts'. Translators have to choose words that, though anatomically inaccurate, produce the right effect (see on 6.10).

16.12 Moabite gods will be helpless to interfere with the just

113

processes of history determined by Yahweh. Mocking other nations' gods was a regular feature of prophecy (I Kings 18.27–9; Isa. 44.9–20; 46.1f.).

16.13   The final comment is made by an editor who was aware that the prophecy had been in existence a long time, but remained unfulfilled.

16.14   Fulfilment is at last at hand. The exact measurement is unusual. Prophecy (and, much more, apocalyptic) was given to making forecasts about the future in elusive language. Moab was overrun by Nebuchadnezzar a few years after Jerusalem fell (Josephus, *Antiquities* 10.9.7).

It is not easy for us to embrace the fact that biblical authors also had problems in understanding events, but clear as the Isaianic vision was, it did not produce total illumination in the mind of everyone who shared in it. Here we have a painful historical event seen from different points of view. It elicits sympathy from some and no sympathy at all from others. There is a comment from an optimist who, while not feeling the pain, is sure that it will all come right in the end. The final comment is grim, 'Maybe it hasn't happened yet, but it will!' We must infer from this that personal attitudes cannot be eliminated, even from the authors of Scripture. Reading the mind of God in events, for all that it is the grand concern of the book, is not an exact science. Again and again we return to the proposition that the message of Isaiah can only be fully grasped by reading the book as a whole.

Damascus and Israel
17.1–14

This chapter is made up of a number of fragments, but they have been brought together editorially to create a coherent whole. We shall consider the passage as a whole while still taking note of the origins of the fragments.

17.1   The introductory formula strictly applies only to the first three verses. *Damascus,* the capital of Syria, lay at a confluence of trade routes just over a hundred miles north-east of Samaria, and that same distance nearer to the seat of Assyrian power. In the volatile politics of the fertile crescent, Syria and Israel were sometimes enemies, sometimes allies.

17.2 The Heb. refers to 'the cities of Aroer' being deserted (see marg.), but Aroer was a Moabite city, so the sense is not good. REB follows the reading of the LXX here and translates it freely. Ruined cities, overgrown with weeds and reclaimed by animals, were a familiar sight in the ancient world. They make a powerful image, but the fate described never overtook Damascus. Syria lost her independence in 732, but Damascus was made capital of an Assyrian province. This suggests that we have here a genuine prophecy going back to Isaiah's time and not a reflexion after the event.

17.3 The thrust of 3abc, is that Damascus and the northern kingdom of Israel will suffer calamity together. This points to the period of the Syro-Ephraimite confederacy (see Introduction, p.xxi and notes on ch. 7). The *fortified city* would be Samaria, the northern capital, built and fortified by Omri in 870, and taken by Assyria in 721. *remnant* – here used negatively. *Aram* – another name for Syria. The final formula implies that vv. 1–3 were once a prophecy standing on their own.

17.4 *On that day* makes the connection between 1–3 and 4–6 easy. Damascus is now forgotten and the text concentrates on Israel. *Jacob,* also called Israel (Gen. 32.28), the father of the patriarchs, provides another name for the northern kingdom. Vv. 4–6 employ three images, this one is of a person with a wasting disease.

17.5 The second image is of a field attacked by *the reaper.* The verb *gathers* has violent overtones; it can also mean 'destroy'. *gleans* – the romantic picture of gleaning, derived from the story of Ruth and Boaz, needs revision. Gleaners were hungry scavengers who made sure they left nothing. *Rephaim* – a valley just south of Jerusalem.

17.6 Deut. 24.20 lays down the rule for picking olives; no doubt there were farmers, with no sympathy for the poor, who beat the trees vigorously to make sure that the *gleanings* were mean. The image suggests a devastation for Israel leaving little behind. A similar ending formula confirms the editorial link between 4–6 and 1–3.

17.7 By virtue of the present juxtaposition 7f. helps to interpret 1–6. The doom will not be unrelieved because another side of judgement is repentance. This reveals how important editing can be. *all* – the Heb. reads 'a man'; in the present context probably a northern Israelite. The local cult will collapse and 'the man' will worship Yahweh. *their Maker* – an unusual designation for Yahweh, but one that fits well with the argument of the next verse.

17.8 This verse is entirely apposite, but it conceals a historical problem. In the Baal cult *altars* were scattered about all over the country, whereas Deut. 12.13f. required a single altar for Israel at Jerusalem. This law of the single sanctuary, however, was not promulgated until the time of Josiah (640–609); in earlier decades the notion may have had currency among groups of loyal Yahwists, but one may doubt how far the idea had spread among ordinary Israelite farmers. Nevertheless post-exilic writers tend to explain the exile as a punishment for this kind of error. Historically speaking, then, this verse was probably written after the fall of Jerusalem. But structurally it fits in happily here. Idols are not mentioned, but *their own handiwork* is an allusion to a regular way of pouring scorn on them; the classic example is found in Isa. 44.9–20 and 46.1f. The *sacred poles* were cult objects, erected at Baal sanctuaries to symbolize the female deity. The Heb. word for them (*'ašērîm*) is sometimes not translated but reproduced as Asherim (RV, RSV). The singular form, Asherah, was also the name of a goddess, the consort of the father god El.

17.9 *On that day* – the formula is the same as in v. 7, but the note of doom returns. *the Hivites and the Amorites* were tribes that the Hebrew settlers encountered (see Josh. 9.1f.). They were idolaters and their cities were duly sacked. Idolatrous Israelites would fare no better.

17.10 *You forgot* – the verb is a feminine singular, which means that the accusation is addressed to a city or a people personified as a woman. Because of the context, we read it as an accusation against the northern kingdom, though it would be equally applicable to pre-exilic Judah. *rock* is a common image, almost a title, for Yahweh (Deut. 32.4,31; Pss. 18.2,31; 19.14; 31.3 etc.). *your gardens* appears to be a reference to a common practice in fertility cults: seeds were sown to grow up quickly and then wither as the seasons progressed. This process mirrored the supposed life of the god who lived and died with the seasons (see Introduction, pp. xxf.). *Adonis* is the name for the Greek god who functioned in the same way as did Baal and Tammuz in different parts of the fertile crescent. The Heb. does not actually name him but uses a word for pleasantness (hence NRSV), but there are sound reasons for supposing that the term indicated a particular god.

17.11   The prophetic logic is unanswerable: why worship a god of fertility when growth is followed by decay?

17.12   Doom, penitence, accusation now lead to promise and hope. The question may be asked whether originally vv. 12-14 represented a prophetic promise of a particular deliverance in the future, an editorial account of such a deliverance in the past, or a more general promise of deliverance from final disaster in apocalyptic terms. In the present context they follow the line of Isaiah's confident response to the Assyrian threat, but other hints and allusions are discernible. The suddenness of the enemy's disappearance in v. 13 recalls Sennacherib's hasty departure from Jerusalem in 701 (II Kings 19.35; Isa. 37.36). *Listen* translates a short word of exclamation that occurs in 5.8, 11, 18, 10.5, and 18.1. REB treats it in different ways according to context. *vast forces* – rather 'many peoples'; the Assyrian army was made up of conscripts from many subject peoples. In the background there is also the idea of a mythical army taking the field against God's people in the last days. For example, *the roar of mighty waters* suggests the victory of Yahweh over the waters of chaos, hinted at in some versions of the creation myth (Job 38.11; Ps. 104.6–9; Prov. 8.29; Jer. 5.22, but not Gen. 1).

17.13   *rebuke* – a powerful word in Heb. The humiliation of the armies is immediate, dramatic, and apparently effortless, which again suggests an ideal conflict beyond the historical one. The final line refers to something that whirls in the wind; it hardly matters whether it is translated 'dust' (RV, NRSV) or *thistledown*.

17.14   *before morning* recalls II Kings 19.35 and Isa. 37.36, which stress the discovery in the morning that the cause of the terror was gone. This suggests that, whenever and for whatever reason this fragment was composed, the disaster suffered by Sennacherib before Jerusalem was in the author's mind. So the promise of doom on guilty cities concludes with the *plunderers* themselves discomfited. Yahweh's righteous control of the human scene pervades the whole.

Though undoubtedly made up of many fragments this passage draws together theological notions that are remarkably coherent. Israel, when obedient, may be greatly privileged, but Israel, disobedient and disowned, suffers the same fate as Damascus. Election does not compromise the rule of justice. Beyond that, worldly glory is short-lived, judgement awaits the proud, false worship is both futile and outrageous, history is in Yahweh's hands and he will protect and punish as he chooses. This coherence is an impressive testimony to the integrity of the Isaiah tradition.

Envoys from Ethiopia
18.1–7

Chapters 18–20 comprise a cluster of separate units concerning Egypt. In ch. 18 envoys have come to Jerusalem from the land of Cush, also known as Ethiopia, whose kings dominated Egypt in the latter half of the eighth century. Their purpose, though not entirely clear, was probably to secure Judah's co-operation in a rebellion against Assyria. The most probable date is 711, when Philistia and Egypt formed an anti-Assyrian alliance (see Isa. 20). At that time Hezekiah managed not to be involved and the conspiracy was harshly put down. An alternative is 705–701, when some similar disaffection gave rise to Sennacherib's punitive mission which faltered at the gates of Jerusalem. The fine language and the theology suggest that Isaiah himself may well be the author.

18.1   *ships* – the Heb. word is rare. RV, RSV, NRSV, JB, NIV prefer to take it as a reference to the noise made by wings. NEB and REB follow the LXX. *Cush* is a Heb. name; Ethiopia the Greek and Roman one. *Cush* is not to be identified with the modern Ethiopia but rather with the Sudan. *beyond the rivers* refers to tributaries of the Nile in the far south.

18.2   The Heb. says the envoys travel by sea but REB and NRSV render 'sea' as *the Nile*; evidently Thor Heyerdahl had not convinced the translators that *vessels of reed*, made of rushes and used for fishing on the Nile, could have ventured into the Mediterranean. The rest of the verse is diplomatic flattery. *Go* means 'go back to Cush' and the *messengers* are the *envoys*. The *people tall and smooth-skinned* are the Africans of Cush.

18.3   This verse is far from clear and it may be an interpolation. It refers to the moment when a rebellion is declared, but when and by whom is not certain. *All you inhabitants of the world* reveals how widespread Assyrian power was.

18.4   There is a sudden change. Yahweh reveals his word to the prophet; it is expressed vividly but imprecisely in agricultural imagery. *I shall look on and do nothing* – a theological notion, unwelcome to Isaiah's contemporaries, but quite acceptable to Isaiah. Yahweh does not take sides in these alliances. His resolution of the circumstances will not be affected by human initiatives. *heat, dew* – Yahweh is present and powerful but inactive. 'Storm' and 'wind' would have given a very different picture.

18.5   Fruitless *branches* of vines were cut out before the harvest. Older commentators took the view that these branches represented the Assyrians, but a closer look shows that the branches are the meddlesome allies who try to accelerate God's purposes.

18.6   The language becomes more direct. The rebels and their homes will be laid waste.

18.7   An addition by an editor to change the thrust from threat to promise. Ethiopia will come to worship on Mount Zion. The editor quotes v. 2 in order to key the comment into the text. His *At that time* refers to a glorious future when Yahweh's *name* would be honoured the world over (cf. Isa. 45.14; 60.1–3; 66.18–24; Zech. 8.23). The reference to *Zion* recalls a typically Isaianic theme (cf. 2.2–4).

The confidence of the final redactor is astounding. The nation concerned is *dreaded far and near* and Yahweh's policy is to *look on and do nothing*. Nevertheless Yahweh will triumph and the dreaded nation will bring tribute to Mount Zion. This is typical of OT faith and illustrates the doctrine of God that runs through the Isaiah tradition.

The doom of Egypt
19.1–15

Verses 1–4 promise a divine assault on Egypt resulting in civil war, social breakdown, and conquest; 5–10 promise natural disasters; and 11–15 consist of mocking comment. If the passage is a unity and Isaiah is the author – the representation of Yahweh as the Lord of all nations is entirely consistent with his theology – we can be reasonably sure the date is the period immediately after the fall of Samaria in 721. Sargon of Assyria was active in the west at this time and his inscriptions claim a victory over Egypt.

19.1   There is nothing strange in Yahweh *riding swiftly on a cloud* (cf. Deut. 33.26; II Sam. 22.11; Pss. 18.10–12; 68.33; 104.3). Clouds, especially storm clouds, suggest unpredictable and uncontrollable power; clouds belong to the heavens, the unapproachable realm that overrides the whole earth. The imagery was not limited to Yahwism. There was a Syrian god of the storms called Hadad, closely allied to the Canaanite Baal. Just how Yahweh *descends on Egypt* is not made clear. There is something comic about motionless *idols* quailing; they can do nothing useful, but they can shiver! The word translated *courage* actually means 'heart' (see note on 16.11).

19.2   Vv. 2–4b are a speech by Yahweh declaring what he will do to Egypt. Egypt was a large country divided into many different states and regions, subdued under strong monarchs but restless under weak ones. Civil war was never far away.

19.3   The fact that they will *resort to idols* seems to imply general panic. Saul's visit to a witch when he was in trouble (I Sam. 28) is condemned as an act of wickedness (cf. Isa. 8.19), but Egyptians were not Yahwists and might be expected to resort to their gods in a crisis. From the heavily biassed Yahwist point of view this was pathetic. The panic contrasts well with the Isaianic principle of trusting Yahweh and finding security in reliance on him (cf. 7.4; 30.15).

19.4   The *hard master* cannot be identified. It might be an external invader, even Sargon. It could be an Ethiopian monarch, for Egypt suffered at the hands of the Ethiopian kings in the latter half of the eighth century. 4c suggests that the speech and the prophecy are complete, but the sense continues in the following verses.

19.5 The oracle now predicts natural disasters which cannot be the work of a foreign conqueror. The Egyptian economy was dependent on the Nile, and the Nile is not supplied by local rainfall. Every summer heavy rain and melting snow more than a thousand miles away cause the river to flood, and, at the end of the season, a rich alluvial deposit is left behind. The cause of this life-giving phenomenon was not understood in the ancient world and divine interference was easily assumed. The verse suggests a special event because, though the height of the flood varied year by year, the Nile itself never dried up.

19.6 Even watercourses that were normally full all the year round would dry up.

19.7 A difficult verse. *The lotus* – a kind of water-lily, but the rendering is uncertain. JB and NIV prefer 'plants' and NRSV 'bare places'.

19.8 In Egypt fishing was an important industry. Vv. 5–10 reveal more understanding of Egyptian life than do 2–4.

19.9 Making linen from flax was another Egyptian industry (cf. Ex. 9.31).

19.11 The oracle now turns to mockery. REB treats the first half of the verse as an insertion, perhaps a marginal comment that became incorporated in the text. The words are a more prosaic statement of the sense of what follows. *Zoan*, the Greek Tanis, is a city on the north-eastern corner of the Nile delta, near the land of Goshen where the Hebrews were said to be settled (Gen. 47.27; Ex. 8.22). Egypt was famous for its tradition of *wise men*. Not only is this recognized in the Bible (I Kings 4.30; Acts 7.22), but it is now clear that parts of Israel's wisdom writings were dependent on Egyptian texts (see especially Prov. 22. 17–24.22). This makes the mockery of these verses all the more telling.

19.12 The prophet makes a skilful theological point. Earthly wisdom you may have in abundance, but how will that help you to plot the ways of *the LORD of hosts*? As in v. 3, the prophet is judging Egypt by Yahwist standards. The *wise men* of Egypt would hardly make it their business to study the ways of a foreign deity. But, by the prophet's reckoning, that is their greatest folly (cf. Isa. 44.25).

19.13 *Noph*, better known as Memphis, was the capital of Lower, that is northern, Egypt; it was situated on the Nile, just south of where the delta begins to fan out.

19.14 Whatever the wise men think, the folly that has infected the Egyptian leadership is the work of Yahweh. The prophet ascribes to Yahweh total responsibility for the affairs of a foreign country. The graphic language is plainly insulting.

19.15 The second line is almost a quotation from 9.14; we must suppose that it means the same: the high and the lowly, that is, all classes.

Egypt was, of course, the nation of the oppression and the natural target for prophetic mockery. Yahweh will enter on a cloud, derange the affairs of Egypt, deflate the sages, and upset the natural order. All in a day's work for Yahweh. He does not strive or struggle as other gods do; his universal control is effortless.

The conversion of Egypt
19.16–25

Overall this passage represents a complete change of direction from vv. 1–15. There Egypt was threatened and mocked; here Egypt is promised a glorious future. The passage is made up of five prose elements, each introduced by the phrase *When that day comes*. There are no references to indicate their date, or dates, and we need to consider occasions in the history of Hebrew thought when the ideas displayed here might have arisen. Nowhere in the OT is there a more confident statement of the universalist vision. Egypt, Assyria and

Israel will be bound together in the worship of Yahweh! The word 'universalist' must be used with caution. In one sense most Yahwist statements are universalist in that they imply Yahweh's power over all nations (e.g. Ex. 19.4–6). Second Isaiah is universalist in that he envisages the possibility of all nations having a positive share in the divine order (45.22–24; cf. 66.23; see also Isa. 2.2–4; Micah 7.16f., Zeph. 2.11, and 3.9f). But few passages are universalist in the sense that they imply no distinction betweeen Israel and her enemies. Such an idea belongs to the time when Israel's visionaries had turned from the realism and immediacy of the eighth-century prophets to the more distant and idealistic hopes of the post-exilic period.

19.16   The first element continues the threatening tone of vv. 1–15. On the face of it, *When that day comes* refers to the the fulfilment of threats made in 2–10, but, if 16f. are taken with 18–24, they must refer to a more hopeful day when Egypt's humiliation will be the prelude to her salvation.

19.17   In v. 12 the Egyptian sages had not the wit to know what was going to happen; now they will find out. It is hard to think of any normal situation when the *name* of Judah would cause Egypt so much *dismay*, but the passage is not thinking practically. One of the distinctions between prophecy and apocalyptic is that the latter saw no hope in earthly realism and so grounded its hopes in a new kind of transcendental 'realism'. Vv. 16f. show a drift in this direction.

19.18   The second element, though only one verse, presents a number of interesting puzzles. There is a dramatic change of tone; Egypt is now the home of a loyal Yahwist community. The precise number of *cities* and the mention of the name of one of them suggest that this is prophecy after the event. We know that there were Jewish colonies in Egypt from the sixth century onwards, for Jeremiah was taken there after the fall of Jerusalem (Jer. 43.1–7). Jer. 44.1 actually names cities where they settled. *swearing allegiance* suggests Egyptian proselytes rather than true born Israelites, which is in tune with the high hopes of the rest of the chapter. *the language of Canaan* – presumably Hebrew. The name of the city is the greatest puzzle of all, for the ancient sources disagree about it. If REB's reading is correct, Heliopolis (Greek for *City of the Sun*), on the Nile delta is indicated. Altogether the verse is full of unanswered questions, yet its meaning is both clear and breathtaking. Yahweh could and would be worshipped by a faithful community in a foreign land, a land notorious in Hebrew tradition for oppression and synonomous with captivity.

19.19 The longest element, vv. 19–22, prophesies nothing less than the conversion of Egypt to the Yahwist faith and the acceptance of Egypt by Yahweh as a nation under his protection. The *altar dedicated to the* LORD *in the heart of Egypt* occasions surprise, but there is evidence of at least two such altars. The Elephantiné papyri, discovered on an island in the Nile at the beginning of the century, show that a Jewish military colony lived there in the fifth century BCE, and that the colony had its own temple dedicated to Yahu, plainly Yahweh. Less reliable evidence comes from the Jewish historian, Josephus, who writes that, in the second century BCE, the high priest Onias fled from Antiochus Epiphanes and built a temple like Jerusalem in Leontopolis (see *Antiquities* 13.3.1 and *Wars* 1.1.1 and 7.10.2). This second example, even if reliable, is too late to have direct bearing on Isa. 19, but it shows that, despite the categorical statements of Deut. 12, the erection of an alternative place of worship in a foreign land was never entirely unthinkable. Jewish exiles in Babylon went to great pains to foster an altar-less Jewish faith, but the exiles in Egypt may have reacted differently to their religious deprivation; it could be that these verses are an attempt to legitimize a temple and a cult that were already in existence. The *sacred pillar* recalls the sacred pillars of the Baal shrines that, according to Deut. 7.5 it was the duty of the Hebrews to destroy (cf. Deut. 16.22). The use of the word, however, is not confined to the Baal cult. Jacob set up a pillar in Gen. 28.18 as a memorial of a divine revelation (cf. Gen. 35.14; Ex. 24.4; Hos. 3.4).

19.20 The pillar is a *reminder* that *the* LORD *of hosts* had shown his might in delivering his people from Egypt long ago. Now it is the turn of the Egyptians to be oppressed and the prophet, amazingly, has no vindictive feelings. He announces happily that Yahweh *will send a deliverer*.

19.21 Yahweh had made himself known to Pharaoh in the plagues and in the exodus, according to Ex. 7.5; now he will *make himself known* in response to their worship. The pattern of worship and service is the same as that laid down for the chosen people themselves.

19.22 A summary of the whole process described in 16–24; it does not imply further punishment.

19.23 The fourth element is even more extraordinary. *Egypt* was the archetypal oppressor, *Assyria* the most destructive enemy of the pre-exilic period. These two are now to make common cause and the prophet plainly approves. *Assyria* ceased to be important after the fall of Nineveh in 612 BCE, but the name lived on as a code word for a violent enemy. Highways, systematically planned, as distinct from ancient caravan routes, came into being with the Persian empire; this *highway* seems to be more metaphorical than real. It implies a bond between *Egypt* and *Assyria*, both economic and religious.

19.24 In the fifth element three nations, *Israel* and her ancient enemies, will enjoy the divine blessing formerly given to Israel alone. *rank as a third with* means 'share the pre-eminence with', not 'take third place'. The promise that Israel would be *a blessing* to the whole earth appears in Yahweh's promises to Abraham (Gen. 12.3) and regularly elsewhere in the OT.

19.25 There is no distinction between the three expressions of blessing. The designation *my people*, elsewhere Israel's supreme glory (Deut. 4.20; 7.6; Ezek. 36.28; Hos. 2.23; etc.), is here awarded to Egypt. The verses represent a summit in OT theology. In Deuteronomy, the notion of election is coupled with disrespect towards other nations, sometimes descending into outright hostility. In Second Isaiah, Israel has a vocation to be 'a light to the Gentiles' (42.6; 49.6), which implies that other nations will observe Israel's felicity, honour her God, find a small place in his favour, but not gain an equal share in Israel's privileges. Here Israel, *my possession*, has no advantage at all. This is truly remarkable and it is hard to find any period in Israel's history when these sentiments could have been anything more than a visionary's dream.

Studying the prophets requires us to spend a lot of time with oracles of doom, and readers may be led to make hasty judgements about the negative and indeed the barbaric nature of some of them (see the discussion on pp. xxivff.). Here is a reminder that isolated passages do not tell the whole story. Books can only be fully understood as wholes and, more than that, as elements in a complete religious tradition. Certainly there are whoops of joy, even in Isaiah, over the destruction of enemies, but the final vision is of great nations joining together to be a *blessing in the world*. When one remembers how much the people who gave us these books suffered at the hand of oppressors, this vision is almost beyond understanding. It witnesses to a doctrine of God that bears comparison with any that the world has ever seen.

Isaiah parades unclothed
20.1–6

After a series of oracles about other nations, we come to a short biographical piece with a precise date. The occasion is the conspiracy against Assyria in 714–11 BCE. Philistine cities took a leading part, but there were other conspirators, possibly including Hezekiah; they hoped for support from Egypt which was not forthcoming. Assyrian forces came to Ashdod in 711 and sacked it to end the conspiracy. The other conspirators got off lightly. This chapter shows Isaiah's reaction to the event by recounting a dramatic action he carried out at the time. Under divine instruction, he removed his outer garment and his sandals and, in that condition of discomfort and shame, walked about to indicate how captives from Egypt and Cush would appear when they were taken away to Assyria. His purpose was to inspire in the onlookers a reaction of shock and horror and so to underline the painful futility of trusting other nations to save Israel from her enemies. Dramatic actions of this kind are a common feature of pre-exilic prophecy.[2] Many have been unwilling to believe that God instructed Isaiah to do anything as outrageous as walking about without clothes, for the Hebrews regarded nakedness as shameful (Gen. 3.7; 9.22; etc.). Against this it must be argued that the purpose of the act was to produce a horrified reaction. Isaiah was deeply involved in his vocation and he was ready to behave immodestly, if he was so instructed.

20.1   *Ashdod*, one of the five Philistine cities, lying due west of

[2] For a full treatment of this interesting phenomenon, see my *Prophetic Drama in the Old Testament*, London 1990.

Jerusalem and a few miles from the sea, was taken by the Assyrians in 711. Assyrian records say that *Sargon* himself was responsible; evidently he took the credit.

20.2 Yahweh's command is clear but shocking. Isaiah was wearing *sackcloth*, perhaps as an act of penitence on behalf of his people, perhaps because prophets were inclined to wear coarse clothing (Zech. 13.4). To be obliged to appear in public without proper covering was a great humiliation; it was also uncomfortable, for Jerusalem is high enough to experience frost in winter.

20.3 *for three years* – it is hard to believe that Isaiah was naked for three years. Perhaps he appeared naked from time to time over that period; perhaps the language of v. 2 means something less than total nudity; perhaps he appeared naked once or twice only but the *sign and portent* lasted three years; perhaps Isaiah's editor, ignoring practicalities, wanted to stress that Isaiah's witness was constant throughout the conspiracy. Signs and portents in the OT refer to immediately apprehensible realities (in this case a striking action) which witness to the existence of greater realities which are not so apprehensible (often because they are hidden in the future). The presence of one is taken as the proof of the other. The *sign and portent* are directed *to Egypt and Cush*. Although Egypt was always anxious to stir up trouble, she avoided the 711 crisis, and if Isaiah's action was carried out then, it would hardly have pointed to Egypt. Not till around 701 did Assyria threaten, and indeed, defeat Egypt. So either the action belongs to 711, and an editor, concerned about Egypt, changed the reference to give us the present text, or the action took place around 705, when Isaiah was very anxious that Judah should not put her trust in Egypt, in which case the date given in v. 1 is a too precise addition. For *Cush* see note on 18.1.

20.4 There is no evidence that Egyptian prisoners were taken to Assyria after Egypt's defeat in 701. Only in relation to campaigns of later times do Assyrian records refer to *captives*. It may be that Isaiah's action depicted the worst possible scenario, and that, in the event, both Judah and Egypt proved more fortunate than the prophet feared. Defeat was always horrific (cf. Amos 2.16). Prisoners were dragged from their hiding-places, stripped of their valuables, ill-used, and marched away. Little imagination is needed to see why they would have little clothing left.

20.5   The verse displays both historical knowledge and theological acumen. In the OT period, *Egypt* frequently promised help to the smaller nations of the fertile crescent, but rarely fulfilled its promise; and Isaiah's constant assertion was that Yahweh was the only support his people needed.

20.6   The sorrows of the Philistines, *those who dwell along this coast*, are recited to provide the right lesson for Israel. How sad are nations who rely on false allies, and, by implication, how happy is the nation that relies on Yahweh!

Once again Isaiah and his editors make the point that human allies are not to be trusted, that diplomatic cleverness is insufficient, that earthly armies fail. The obverse side of the coin is not displayed here, but we know what it is. Righteousness and fidelity to Yahweh represent the true way.

A vision of doom
21.1–10

Much in this passage is mysterious; it is poetic, not precise. The thrust is found in the terrifying atmosphere that the piece generates. The subject is the fall of Babylon (v. 9). Some commentators attribute the vision to Isaiah himself, but the references to Babylon, Elam and Media would make little sense in his time. Some take the view that the distraught tone is more appropriate to an eschatological calamity, in which case Babylon is a symbol for nations hostile to Yahweh, and the date is post-exilic. But the most probable date is just before the fall of Babylon to Cyrus in 539, which would make it contemporary with Second Isaiah.

21.1   The title is used for atmosphere rather than topography; *The wilderness* is a symbol of desolation. 1bc announces an impending disaster without mentioning where the intelligence comes from, without even saying when or where it will strike. The *storms* are sand-storms, more unpleasant than rain-storms and without any useful purpose. *the Negeb* is the arid waste to the south of Israel. It was a long way from Babylon, but it was the wilderness best known to Israel and, therefore, the origin of its desert symbolism. *Negeb – wilderness – land of terror* – an impressive escalation.

21.2 A grim vision – the prophet displays human sympathy while still calling on Babylon's enemies to *Advance*. *Elam* was a small nation to the east of the Tigris. Never much in its own right, its appearance here is surprising. *Media*, further north in the Zagros mountains, was an empire contemporary with Babylon. Cyrus came from the south of *Elam*, and *Media* was the first nation to fall to him, so it may be that these names are a veiled way of referring to the Persian conqueror.

21.3 The prophet's reaction to the vision could hardly be more extreme. This suggests eschatological disaster, but a better explanation may be that the prophet is acting out the future agonies of the Babylonians, as in ch. 20 he acted out the humiliation of Assyria's captives.

21.4 REB is right to see a break after 4a. 4b introduces a description of the scene. *The evening cool* was the most pleasant part of the day when it was customary to meet, eat and converse.

21.5 A *banquet* has begun for the Babylonian nobility when suddenly they are called to battle. The interruption is reminiscent of Belshazzar's feast in Dan. 5. *burnish your shields* – the verb means 'to anoint'. The process could be part of a pre-battle ritual or it could be functional; much 'armour' was made of leather and needed regular attention.

21.6 The prophet receives an instruction from Yahweh to *post a watchman* to observe the approach of Babylon's enemy. But in v. 8 the watchman seems to be the prophet himself (cf. Hab. 2.1). In a vision, as in a dream, the contradiction is quite comprehensible.

21.7 The verse indicates a large and fully equipped force. The mention of *donkeys* somewhat reduces the tension, but no army could march without a substantial baggage train.

21.8 We move on to a new phase. The prophetic watchman reports what he sees. The Heb. reads 'lion' (RV) rather than *look-out*, but most translators recognize a copyist's error here and make the slight emendation necessary.

21.9 *A voice* calls from nowhere with the tragic news in typical lament form (see II Sam. 1.18ff.; Amos 5.2). Second Isaiah mocks Babylon's idols (Isa. 44.9–20; 46.1f.), but here the tragedy almost arouses sympathy.

21.10 A concluding comment from the prophet. He addresses his *people*, Israel. They have been *trodden out* in the loss of Jerusalem and the exile, but now it is the turn of Babylon to face humiliation.

There is a certain magnanimity here which is rather impressive; no delight in slaughter, nor exultation over the humiliation of an enemy. The author regards the onslaught as necessary (v. 2), but still contemplates it with anguish. The duty of prophecy, harsh as it is at times, does not extinguish human sympathy.

Dumah
21.11f.

These two verses test the ingenuity of commentators, but, truth to tell, they are totally enigmatic. All we can say is is that a conversation piece drawn from urban experience is cited for a purpose unknown. There is a theme link between 1–10 and 11f., but the Heb. words for 'watchman' and 'look-out' are different.

21.11 *Dumah* means 'silence', but it is probably a place name here. There is a *Dumah* in Arabia. On the other hand, the LXX reads, not *Dumah*, but Idumaea, that is, Edom. This is consistent with the reference to *Seir*, which is in Edom, to the south-east of the Dead Sea. This is the only reference to Edom in the series of oracles relating to foreign nations in chs. 13–23. Yahweh sets forth from *Seir* in Judg. 5.4 (cf. Deut. 33.2), but, if that fact is relevant, it is hard to see how. Yahweh is not the speaker; some townsman asks the watchman how much of the night remains.

21.12 The watchman's answer, as it stands, is a vacuous statement, hardly requiring a watchman's special knowledge. It is just possible to render the Heb., 'Morning comes, though it is still night'. This has more point, even theological force (cf. Ps. 30.5), and it makes better sense of 12c, but it is not the obvious rendering of the Heb.

Trouble in Arabia
21.13–15

This fragment is a humanitarian plea to help fugitives fleeing from a battle. The details cannot be fixed.

21.13 The title, missing from the LXX, probably refers to a desert place rather than a people (NRSV). *Dedan* was a settlement deep in the Arabian desert, some four hundred miles south and east of Jerusalem. Its merchants appear in Ezekiel (27.15, 20; 38.13). REB implies that camping *in the scrub* was normal practice for the *caravans*, but it is possible that the caravans are instructed to camp off the main route for safety's sake.

21.14 The war has created *fugitives* and in the desert problems of food and drink are intensified. The *thirsty* must be those fleeing from the battle, so the notion that the Dedanite caravans are themselves in need is wrong. Rather the caravans are charged to help *the fugitives* (as REB). *Tema* is a desert city, some eighty miles north of Dedan.

21.15 The terrible picture of defeat and pursuit by the well-armed victors, coupled with the risk of death from thirst, conjures up feelings of horror and sympathy.

Trouble for Kedar
21.16f.

The atmosphere of this brief oracle is different from that of the previous two. Here is a concise oracle of doom, pronounced without regret. It has a formal beginning and a formal conclusion. Though the subject matter is clear, there are few clues about date.

21.16   The speaker is a prophet, but we cannot be sure that it was Isaiah. The DSS has 'three years' rather than *a year*, perhaps because the term of a hired labourer would be longer than a single year (see 16.14). *Kedar* was an area in the north of Arabia, the home of a powerful tribe, rich in flocks (Isa. 60.7; Ezek. 27.21).

21.17   The theological point must not be missed. The fact that Yahweh *has spoken* is more significant than anything armies can do. Battles, sieges, skirmishes, and other kinds of slaughter were regular occurrences. Fear was a constant fact of everyday life and no nation suffered more than Israel. Yet the oracle is almost serene. Such unruffled confidence in an insecure world, where armies were always on the march, is very impressive.

The tragedy of Jerusalem
22.1–14

In the midst of oracles relating to foreign nations comes this piece addressed to Judah. It is a poem, with prose interjections, beginning and concluding with prophetic formulae. There are some inconsistencies which are hard to sort out. V. 4 speaks of *the ruin of my people* and the despair of the prophet, v. 5 of a divinely ordained *day of tumult*, but in v. 13 the people are giving themselves up to *joy and merrymaking*. Moreover some verses suggest that calamity has been averted, others that it has taken place. The best hypothesis is that this is an oracle from Isaiah's own day, probably delivered by Isaiah, relating to an occasion when Jerusalem enjoyed a deliverance beyond her deserts, but an oracle that was later adapted to an occasion when the city suffered complete devastation.

22.1   'The Valley of Vision' is an enigmatic title, and the fact that it reappears in v. 5 does nothing to help. The prophet is shocked and indignant at the reaction of the inhabitants of Jerusalem to what has happened. They have *climbed up on the roofs* to celebrate. In small, fortified towns the streets were too narrow and the open spaces too small for large concourses. On *the roofs*, however, where people customarily sat at leisure, it was possible to see and communicate with others and form with them a large, excited (and insensitive) mass. If we suppose that the occasion was the deliverance of 701, the situation becomes fairly clear. According to Assyrian records, Sennacherib had dealt savagely with Philistia and with Egypt and then devastated Judah and humiliated Hezekiah. Hezekiah himself had to pay a substantial tribute. That this was not simply Assyrian boasting is shown by the account in II Kings 18.13–19.37 and Isa. 36–7 (see Introduction, p. xxii). The OT record concentrates on the fact that Jerusalem was saved, but there is no concealing the extent of the loss. How should the people of Jerusalem react? Evidently they thought it was time for a big party. Isaiah thought it was time for shame and repentance.

22.2 The city is in a state of great excitement, but REB, almost alone among modern translations, fails to register that the excitement was expressed in revelling. *tumult, ferment* and *uproar* suggest riot and civil unrest, but the words translated *filled with uproar* mean 'a city exultant', which affects the way the other words are understood. The mood is made more clear in v. 13. The prophet protests that those who died did not die bravely defending the City of David, but shamefully in flight.

22.3 The *flight* was led by *commanders*, who should have been rallying the troops for defence.

22.4 The prophet asks to be left alone to lament the disaster. *the ruin of my people* would be equally appropriate at the fall of Jerusalem in 586, but Sennacherib's inroads were ruinous enough.

22.5 Vv. 5–11 are difficult to relate to 701 but fit the tragedy of 586 more easily. This verse looks to the future. It announces that Yahweh, introduced with a majestic title (cf. v. 12), has decided to punish Judah. There will be *a day of tumult* (see Introduction, p. xxxi). The verse is a deliberate echo of v. 2 where all the hubbub was positive; here it is the opposite. The *cries among the mountains* indicate the slaughter before the invading armies reach Jerusalem.

22.6 We return to prophetic verse, the point of view changes, and the prophet looks back on the disaster. *Elam* was located at the east end of the fertile crescent. REB has made a slight emendation to the Heb. to produce *chariots of Aram. Kir* (not the Kir-hareseth of 16.7, 11) was the place of origin of the Syrians (Amos 9.7) and we assume that it was a country in Mesopotamia. It is reasonable to suppose that troops from these areas marched with Nebuchadnezzar.

22.7 This verse describes what happened when Jerusalem was put under siege. The chariots followed the roads at the bottom of the valleys, Kidron, which runs north to south on the east side, and Hinnom, which runs round the south. In this way the city was invested with troops well clear of the defenders' weaponry. Then the cavalry attacked specific points, of which the gates were the most obvious.

22.8 The verb in 8a is active and could be translated, 'he uncovered Judah's defence', suggesting divine action (see NRSV), but REB sees no explicit theological statement here. The next few lines describe preparations for a siege. They were written by someone who knew what happened. Solomon built *the House of the Forest*, so called because of its cedar pillars (I Kings 7.2; 10.17). It was used as an armoury.

22.9 The translation here is a problem (see marg.), but clearly the verse refers to defence preparations. Water was the chief problem for besieged cities, particularly if, like Jerusalem, they were located on hills. Through the centuries the defenders of Jerusalem adopted various devices to bring in water from the spring of Gihon which was outside the city wall to the east. Hezekiah's tunnel (II Kings 20.20) is best known, because tourists can still walk through it, but there were others (cf. II Sam. 5.8.). The water was stored in pools and cisterns.

22.10 A typical pre-battle scene. Houses near the wall, or between the walls, prevented free movement of the defenders. The buildings were removed and the rubble used to strengthen weak points.

22.11 The best defended cities had a double wall so that attackers who succeeded in scaling the first could be dealt with before they could run riot. Flooding the space between them was also a useful option. The prophetic accusation is that the defenders had been too self-reliant; they had failed to submit themselves to the God who alone could defend the city (cf. Ps. 127.1). 8b–11a looks like an insertion to describe what they *did* do, in order to highlight what they did not. But the attempt is ham-fisted. All the details suggest prudent, military thinking, whereas the point is that these preparations, unattended by divine service, were arrogance and folly. Hezekiah was not so foolish according to II Kings 19.15–20, though the accusation is credible in relation to the affairs of 586. Jerusalem in 11bc is not so much the city of David as the city of Yahweh.

22.12 Here we return to the original theme of vv. 1–4 and probably to the event of 701. The prophet looks to the recent past, to the day when Judah suffered a serious loss and Yahweh called for signs of corporate grief. The prophet does not take the view that outward signs are unimportant, rather that they are real indicators of penitence. In grief, bright appearance, personal comfort, and even wellbeing were deliberately abandoned.

22.13 The *killing of cattle* for celebration was commonly associated with peace offerings in the temple, but not so here. Here the high life is linked with a hedonistic, if not nihilistic, proverb that, in one form or another, is found in ancient Egypt, in Greek and Roman culture (cf. I Cor. 15.32), in mediaeval songs, in Elizabethan lyrics, to say nothing of the modern pop scene. It is the antithesis of the Hebrew belief that present and future were ruled by Yahweh's will.

22.14 We have more literary formulae here than we need, one at the beginning of 14, one at the end, and another in 15a beginning the next passage. 14a seems like an unnecessary insertion to strengthen the prophecy of doom. The force of the verse is, 'Moral considerations rule; you will never escape from your evil deeds.' *you will die*, that is, suffer an early death. The Hebrews of this period had no doctrine of heaven and hell. All who died, good and bad alike, went to Sheol (see note on 14.9). To die young was an unrelieved tragedy, often to be understood as a punishment.

There are two points of the utmost importance in this passage. The first is the loneliness of the man of God. The prophet can see what other people cannot see which, at times, causes him great suffering, for the prophet is not a self-righteous accuser who takes pleasure in his moral superiority. He is one of the people, God's people, who weeps in misery over the people's blindness. All this is very reminiscent of Jeremiah. Secondly, the passage is an outright denial of the cynical dictum, 'God is on the side of the big battalions.' God rules history; therefore military prudence takes second place to obedience and faith. That notion may be commonly put down as wishful thinking, but for Isaiah it was the only realism. See Introduction, p. xxvi.

The disgrace of a steward
22.15–25

There are two complementary prophecies here, 16–18 in verse and 20–23 in prose; they relate to the shortcomings of Shebna and his replacement by Eliakim. V. 15 provides an introduction, v. 19 a bridge between the two, and vv. 24f. an additional comment, perhaps two additional comments, by a later hand or hands. Only rarely did the classical prophets attack individuals, but there are parallels in Amos' attack on Amaziah (Amos 7.14–17) and Jeremiah's on both Pashhur (Jer. 20.1–6) and Hananiah (Jer. 28.15–17). There is, then, no reason to deny that vv. 15–18 are from Isaiah himself. This passage, the only one in the oracles 'against foreign nations' in chs. 13–23 to find its way into a well-known lectionary, appears for the 21st Ordinary Sunday in Cycle A of the Roman Catholic lectionary. When we come to v. 22 we can see why.

22.15   In the Heb. *Shebna* is described as the *steward* who is 'over *the household*', the royal household. REB makes this into a resounding title. In II Kings 18.18 *Shebna* is called a scribe.

22.16   The two questions in 16a imply a confrontation between Isaiah and Shebna on the site of the prestigious tomb. The sense seems to be, 'What have we got here? An imposing tomb. And who have we got here? A mere steward!' Imposing tombs were a means by which potentates could cling to glory after death. The accusation of pretentiousness is spelt out three times, and no other evidence of Shebna's villainy is mentioned. This is enough to bring on him Isaiah's (or Yahweh's) acerbic judgement, though commentators speculate that perhaps Shebna was pro-Egyptian and politically unacceptable to Isaiah; there is no evidence of this.

22.17   REB's *garment* involves a slight emendation, but it produces a strong image of a louse being shaken out of its snug resting-place.

Maybe Shebna's chief sin lay in exploiting the economy for his own ends.

22.18   The image is not entirely clear, but it seems to imply that Shebna will be despatched into exile, there to die, in which case his tomb would prove a monumental mockery. The *chariot of honour* was the company car of ancient Israel. His own *disgrace* would be no bad thing, but it is shameful that he brings disgrace on the royal *household*.

22.19   This verse seems to have been inserted to modify the terms of the preceding oracle and to relate it to what follows. The punishment is not now exile and death but removal *from office*.

22.20   From the point of view of a later editor, the wickedness of such a high official reflected badly on Hezekiah, who was a hero to enthusiasts for the house of David. So we find a change of tone, a change from poetry to prose, a change from prophetic speech to divine speech, and a change of thrust. Shebna is mentioned no more and Eliakim comes on the scene. *Eliakim* was over the household and Shebna's superior in II Kings 18.18. Here he is *my servant*, and the language used of him is more than enough to reassure the faithful monarchists of later times.

22.21   Formally Yahweh is still addressing Shebna. The honours heaped on Eliakim represent an oblique honouring of the house of David. The *robe* and the *sash* are marks of high office. The language is very exalted for a civil servant; the term *father* is used in 9.6 of the messianic figure.

22.22   Carrying *the key* of the *palace* was a great responsibility; it was also a symbol of power, and one wonders whether the latter half of the verse is simply concerned with opening and shutting gates. Matthew takes up the idea with very different force in 16.19, and Rev. 3.7 quotes the verse, assigning the power to the exalted Jesus. If the author of this passage had something similar in mind, his real intentions become clear. He has moved away from Eliakim to the ideal royal figure of the future who would have true authority, including the right to admit to and exclude from the people of God.

22.23   Another verse that, though formally about Eliakim, is more applicable to his overlord. The *father's family* makes more sense if it refers to the royal house. So too the metaphor of the tent-peg held *firmly in place* is more apt if it is understood to express the hopes of Israel for her monarchy.

22.24 The tone changes again. A third person must have read these fine lines and decided that, whatever oblique meaning they had, they might be taken as a prophetic glorification of a steward. So he slowly punctures the balloon inflated in vv. 20–23. He changes the *peg* from a tent-peg that supports the structure to a *peg* on the wall on which menial pots and pans are hung.

22.25 The author of 20–23 may have been looking idealistically beyond the steward to the king, but in this verse the sense has swung round completely. This editor is now concerned strictly and realistically with graft and palace politics. The judgement of *the LORD of hosts* is devastating.

In this passage arrogance and corruption are set beside an idealistic vision of the true office-bearer. Could anything be more topical? No task is nobler than that of ruler of the people, and in the Hebrew tradition the just ruler receives spiritual gifts for his task. But no occupation is more open to the sins of arrogance and corruption. In prayer and in preaching, those who lead worship must return to this theme again and again.

Tyre
23.1–18

The first oracle in the section concerned Babylon (13.1–22), the great empire of the east; the final oracle concerns Phoenicia, the great trading nation of the west. The message in both cases is the same. Wordly power, worldly wealth, worldly schemes and plans come to nothing. History belongs to Yahweh. His righteous demands cannot be evaded; he will punish and he will restore, exactly as he wills and when and where. The present passage is full of difficulties, but REB reads smoothly and convincingly – in the circumstances, a great scholarly accomplishment. The title refers to Tyre alone, but the text also mentions Sidon. Tyre and Sidon were attacked by great armies, Assyrian, Babylonian, Persian, Greek, and the basic oracle here must be a lament over or an anticipation of one of those disasters. Israel had reasons for disapproving of Phoenicia. It was the home of a vigorous cult of Baal, Jezebel hailed from Sidon (I Kings 16.31), and Elijah's stand on Carmel indicates a border dispute as well as a theological confrontation. Neverthless the two nations were trading partners and it is noteworthy that there are no bitter accusations in this passage. Tyre's sin is simply pride (v. 9), but that is sufficient to bring down Yahweh's judgement. The passage should be read in conjunction with Ezek. 26.1–28.24, which is also a condemnation of Tyre.

23.1 *Tyre* – Phoenician port on the eastern Mediterranean coast, some 50 miles north of the valley of Jezreel. *Tarshish* was a distant trading point for Phoenician ships; probably located in Spain. *ships of Tarshish*, which sometimes appear in seas other than the Mediterranean (I Kings 22.48), means large, 'ocean-going' ships, as distinct from fishing-boats and coasters. They make a useful symbol for pride. *Kittim* derives from Kition or Citium, a port on the south coast of Cyprus, founded by the Phoenicians.

23.2 All the inhabitants of the eastern sea-board are invited to join in the lament. *Sidon* – the other great Phoenician port, 25 miles north of Tyre.

23.3 This verse spells out the majesty of Sidon in order to make her fall the more dramatic. *Shihor* must refer to the Nile as in Jer. 2.18, where the word is translated 'Nile'. Though Egypt produced grain, Phoenicia became rich by transporting it.

23.4 *Sidon* is personified as a woman who has lost both her fertility and her children. *the anguish of labour* is meant to indicate a privilege.

23.5 *Egypt* shares the grief of Tyre. The word *anguish* appears again, but this time it has a negative sense.

23.6 The mourners are told to go to *Tarshish*, though it is difficult to see why; perhaps to seek refuge or to observe that the desolation of Tyre affects cities far away (v. 10).

23.7 As in v. 3, past glories are recalled to underline the tragedy. The *bustling city* is presumably Tyre. The antiquity of Tyre and Sidon was a byword; even Josephus allows that the building of Tyre pre-dated the building of the Jerusalem temple by 240 years (*Antiquities* 8.3.1). The Phoenicians founded colonies and developed trade routes all over the Mediterranean and even beyond it.

23.8 Again the glory of Tyre in the past is underlined. The question sounds unanswerable: who could possibly do this to such a magnificent city?

23.9 The question is answered. *The LORD of Hosts* adjuducates on the pretensions of earthly potentates and humbles those who have climbed too high (cf. Ezek. 28.1–10). This is a doctrine that encouraged Israel in the hard times after the exile when great world powers held sway.

23.10 This verse has been largely reconstructed by REB, but the reconstruction is soundly based.

23.11 A bold theological statement in true Isaianic style. There are echoes here of ancient myths in which creator gods subdued sea monsters and made the inhabitable world safe (cf. Pss. 46.1–3, 74.12–7, and 89.9–11). We tend to think of *Canaan* as the land occupied by the Hebrews, but the name belongs properly to Phoenicia and more generally to the whole of the eastern coastline of the Mediterranean.

23.12 Attention turns to the city and people of *Sidon*. *Kittim*, (cf. v. 1), is a more obvious place of refuge than Tarshish (as in v. 6).

23.13 A most difficult verse. There is a gloss in the middle in which an editor points out that the invading force was not Assyria but Babylon (Chaldaea). This suggests the re-use of an earlier prophecy by someone living in or after the Babylonian period. The gloss is inaccurate. Nebuchadnezzar laid siege to Tyre unsuccessfully for thirteen years (Josephus, *Antiquities* 10.11.1).

23.14 This verse is a doublet of a line in v. 1. Happily it helps us to straighten out the text of v. 1. The two verses make an envelope in which the devastating prophecy against Phoenicia is contained.

23.15 The lament ends and the text turns to prophecy. There is wide agreement that these verses are an addition, in fact two additions, 15f. and 17f. The history of Phoenicia went up and down; the land was often overrun, but her ports were valuable and inevitably they came back into use. Hence this contemptuous comment which likens Tyre to an aged prostitute trying to get back her trade. The *seventy years* can hardly be meant as a precise figure. It is a lifespan, meaning that those who saw the destruction will never see the rebirth.

23.16 The tone is that of a tavern song, such as might be sung by sailors who make use of harlots but have little sympathy for them when they cease to be attractive. This sums up the attitude of the editor to neighbouring Phoenicia.

23.17 The second addition is an attempt to re-present the sense of 15f. in a more positive light. This time Tyre does not struggle alone. Yahweh *will turn again* to her. The metaphor of harlotry is preserved but interpreted simply as a profitable trade. Tyre will have her trading partners again.

23.18 This final verse is astonishing. The *profits* of Tyre's trade, which only a line or two before were tainted by the association with prostitution, are now *dedicated to the LORD*. Not only is the harlot image neatly manipulated to give a positive meaning but the contemptuous tone is replaced by one of astounding hope. In the days of Solomon, Hiram gladly supplied the timber for the temple (I Kings 5.1–12); in the last days this happy relationship will be restored. This hope, the logical consequence of the Isaianic view of God, is reminiscent of 19.16–25; it recurs in a few places in Third Isaiah (60.5–7; 61.5–7), and it brings the rather dour section on foreign nations to a positive conclusion.

In the Isaiah tradition the rise and fall of cities and the sovereignty of Yahweh were directly linked. There were no great problems about this because great calamities could easily be seen as well-deserved. But here, as elsewhere, the editor is not satisfied with judgement. Beyond judgement is peace and true worship. We, too, live in an age of turmoil. The tragedies force themselves on our attention; rightly so, because we are all too ready to forget our corporate arrogance, unbelief and disobedience, and we need reminding of the consequences of such attitudes. But human arrogance and its judgement are not the last word. The end, as in v. 18, is the glory of the LORD. How to express this in concrete and corporate terms is probably the greatest challenge facing contemporary theologians and therefore contemporary preachers.

The Lord's judgement
24.1–27.13

The next four chapters look to the future and, as they stand, they provide a theological comment on the oracles of the previous section. In the end God's righteous judgements are secure and all things on earth and in heaven will bow to them. Isaianic themes continue to occur, but the section is different from what has gone before in several striking ways. It concerns, not immediate enemies and particular cities, but all nations and peoples, indeed, the whole creation. Ultimate history rather than immediate history now constitutes the agenda. The section has little to say about human action – nothing akin to Isaiah's exhortations to Ahaz is to be found in it – but much to say about divine action. The resolution of the world's injustices comes by direct action from above. Consistent with this is the affirmation, never hinted at previously in the prophecy, that death itself will be conquered.

The section is often called 'the Isaiah Apocalypse', because there is an easy-going tendency to describe all texts dealing with the distant future as apocalyptic, but that leads to confusion. Apocalyptic writing deals with revelation on the grandest scale; it has a much wider range than the end of the world. On the basis of visionary experiences, often of extraordinary complexity, and using highly imaginative and symbolic style, it offers resolutions of the divine mysteries of heaven and earth. Texts of this kind appear frequently in the last two centuries before the Common Era and the first century thereafter. There are, of course, links between prophecy and apocalyptic. Both claim to reveal the divine will and both have much to say about the future. For this reason texts, such as Joel, Zechariah 9–14 and these present chapters, which no longer speak of the future in precise, prophetic terms, and yet which are not apocalyptic in the fullest sense, are exceptionally interesting. Some scholars use the term 'proto-apocalyptic', but it is best to avoid labels if we cannot be precise about them. Certainly, if we regard apocalyptic as a fairly narrow technical term, we cannot apply it to Isa. 24–27.

The oracles of chs. 13–23 passed particular judgements in particular cases, but the basic problem of why the nations were able to cause such offence to Yahweh and his people was never resolved. Now, with the change of emphasis, it is possible to put all those outrages into true perspective. Yahweh reigns over the whole creation. All times are in his hands, all nations, even the power of life and death. In the end he will act to judge the earth, to punish the wicked, to vindicate his people, and to call them home to his holy mountain. Some commentators (Oswalt, Hayes and Irvine) attribute these chapters to Isaiah himself, but there is widespread agreement that the date must be some time after the exile; suggestions vary from the fifth century to the second.

So far we have been speaking of the section as if it were a unity in form and content, which is how we read it now, but the chapters are anything but homogeneous. Different kinds of literature, prophecies, psalms, prayers have been brought together and one editor of pronounced theological convictions has moulded them into a coherent piece; another (or perhaps the same person) inserted the compilation into its present position, so providing the fitting and all-embracing conclusion to what has gone before. This happened in the late stages of redaction, perhaps as late as the Greek period, when it had become clear to Israel that, so great was the power of the world empires (Persia first, then Greece, and Rome would follow), that never again could the tiny people of God hope to gain a position of ascendency simply by force of arms. If Israel was to stand high above the nations, then it could only be by Yahweh's intervention.

A great catastrophe
24.1–13

This passage sets the scene for the whole section. It describes a cosmic catastrophe brought about by natural disasters, and immediately the contrast is struck with the preceding section where disasters afflicted particular nations. The reason for the catastrophe is Yahweh's wrath over human sin. There may be room in the section for psalms of praise, even a message of hope for certain people, but the bottom line is exhaustive and inescapable judgement on a wicked world. No time scale is provided. The passage contains references to other prophetic texts, which suggests that it was composed when the writings of the great prophets had come to be highly regarded.

24.1 The image is of an earthquake, recalling the convulsions in Ps. 46 over which Yahweh alone has control. The word for *Beware* followed by a participle usually denotes the imminent future, which is encouraging for the readers but still imprecise. *the earth* – either the whole earth or the land of a particular nation; v. 4 really settles the matter in favour of the former.

24.2 Social distinctions will be meaningless. Some catastrophes leave certain groups untouched, even in profit, but this time none will escape. *priest and people* – there was no king in the post-exilic community; the priesthood constituted the aristocracy of Israel, so this phrase means 'high and low' as well as 'sacred and secular'.

24.3 The authenticating formula comes, unusually, in the middle of the passage. *this is the word* could mean, 'This, too, is a prophetic oracle', but it could also mean, 'This is the true interpretation of the oracles of Isaiah.'

24.4 The image changes to the equally terrible image of drought. Again the doom is universal.

24.5 The use of the word *desecrated* is interesting. Sin in the OT, especially that involving bloodshed, acts as a pollutant (Num. 35.33; Ps. 106.38; Jer. 3.2, 9). If the last two lines related only to Israel, they would present no problem, but how do they apply to all nations? The author takes the view that the divine law, revealed to Israel as a gift and privilege, is the law for everyone. An *everlasting covenant* was made with Noah and with all living beings in Gen. 9.16. Other nations, in their ignorance, break it consistently, but that reveals their confusion and ignorance, not the irrelevance of the law. Paul faced a similar problem in Rom. 1–2 and solved it by speaking of conscience and the law inscribed on the heart.

24.6 The *curse*, with its devastating effects, falls on all those who break the divine law (cf. Deut. 27.15–26). Nothing is said to indicate who the fortunate *few* are.

24.7 The picture now changes; it focusses upon small groups, showing how they will meet the catastrophe. The *wine* harvest is lost and those who should be revelling at the vintage festival *groan in sorrow*. Cf. 16.8–10.

24.8   No feast in the year was more exhilarating than the Feast of Ingathering or Tabernacles, of which the wine festival was a part (Deut. 16.14; cf. Judg. 9.27 and 21.19–25). The festival would not be abandoned unless there was a complete breakdown in social life. The purpose of the close-up is, therefore, to show that, in the time of disaster, all the stable factors of common life disappear.

24.9   What joy is there in *wine* if there is no festival? An interesting comment on the significance of cultic observance in Israel.

24.10   There are other references to cities in this section (cf. 25.2f.; 26.1–5), all symbolic. *The city* represents the acme of human culture; the ruin of the unnamed city is the symbol of human helplessness before Yahweh. Survivors barricade themselves in their shattered houses to protect themselves from thieves.

24.11   REB's rendering suggests that shortage of *wine* was the survivors' chief problem, which does not indicate serious catastrophe. People were *crying out* because the traditional way of enjoying the wine harvest had been lost. *all joy has faded* – the verb is linked with the word for 'evening' (cf. NRSV), and REB is very neat.

24.12   *gates* – see note on 3.26. If, after the calamity, the *gates are smashed*, the community loses it identity.

24.13   Cf. 17.6. The harvest is gone; the tree stands gaunt and empty. Will there be another harvest next year? That is precisely the note that the passage wants to strike.

The passage has a fearful topicality. The earth has been desecrated by those who live on it and the sufferings depicted are already with us. The difference is that the author sees the calamity as universal, whereas in our day, it afflicts some and leaves others untouched. The grim logic of the passage is correct – large-scale human sin does lead to large-scale calamity – but its outworking in history is more complicated than this author anticipates. If some ecologists are correct, however, the passage of time will yet justify him.

Joy for the vindicated
24.14–16b

The harsh prophecy in 1–13 is followed by two short passages showing opposite sides of the eschatological coin. For some, joy; for others, indescribable terror. Both passages look to the future. The first, 24.14–16b, picks out a group whose existence is not even hinted at in vv. 1–13. No attempt is made to explain how such a group could survive the catastrophe. These chapters look for resolutions in final, absolute and thoroughly divine terms. Practical problems do not impinge much upon the author's consciousness.

24.14 Who are the *people* who *raise their voices*? The Heb. simply has an emphatic third person pronoun. Some argue that 'they' are the community of Israel, spread around the world in the Diaspora. However, both the geographical references in 14–16 and the universal interests of the whole chapter require us to understand this as a world-wide worshipping community. It was not sufficient, in post-exilic eschatology, to proclaim the vindication of Israel. Other nations must also come in the end, willingly or unwillingly, to recognize the unique glory of Yahweh (Zech. 8.23).

24.15 The geographical terms are not specific, simply as comprehensive as possible.

24.16ab The author, in a vision, finds himself united with the survivors and even with the heavenly onlookers, observing the universal worship of Yahweh. There is no word for *nation* in the Heb., so there is a question as to what they ascribe *beauty* to. Some direct it to Yahweh, 'the Righteous One', in which case 'honour' rather than *beauty* is the best rendering. Others take it as a reference to the land of Israel, to which the word *beauty* (though not the word *righteous*), is often applied (Dan. 8.9; 11.16, 41). What is quite clear is that the worshippers are praising Yahweh for establishing righteousness in the earth.

The position of these verses is most illuminating and they show what theological force can be exerted by editors The universal worship praises Yahweh for establishing righteousness by enacting calamity (vv. 1–13, 16c–20). This is theological rigour to make us tremble, and as far from sentimentality as theology can go.

No joy for the traitors
24.16c–20

The pendulum swings to the other extreme and the bald statement of disaster carries on from v. 13. It is to be a calamity with no escape The images are piled up, adding to the horror but not to the precision.

24.16cd   The first line is uncertain, and each translator does what is right in his own eyes. *Woe betide me* is a cry of grief; it does not indicate that the speaker himself is in trouble, but that the news he relates is unwelcome. The rest of the verse is a string of five words in Heb., all beginning with 'b' and making a very impressive effect.

24.17   A threefold image of inescapable disaster. The first word means 'terror', but the REB conjures a consistent image drawn from hunting (see v. 18). More cautious translators stick to the Heb.

24.18   The first three lines repeat the image (recalling Amos 5.19). In the last two lines the image changes and we have a vision of cosmic disaster going beyond even what is described in 1–13. In Hebrew cosmology a chaos of water surrounds the inhabitable earth. There is water above the heavens and water beyond the mountains, kept in place by Yahweh's word (Job 38.8–11; Ps. 104.6–9; Prov. 8.29; Jer. 5.22). *The windows of heaven* are opened to allow for rain, but Yahweh in his wrath may throw them wide open and flood the earth (cf. Gen. 7.11; 8.2).[1] The shaking of the *foundations* recalls the language of 24.1. Again it is difficult to see how the faithful were to escape.

24.19   In the last two verses the earth is personified amid a jumble of images. *The earth* is completely broken, like a tool, *convulsed*, like a gravely sick person, and *reels wildly*, like someone who has lost all control.

24.20   The *watchman's shelter* is a makeshift affair, put up mainly as a defence against the sun and easily damaged by bad weather. Noah's flood was due to the corruption of the earth and this passage makes a similar point. The *inhabitants* have brought the doom upon themselves. There is no mention of the remnant of vv. 14–16b who escape.

Yahweh as judge and king
24.21–23

In the chapter so far we have heard of a catastrophe for the whole earth and a terrible judgement on the wicked. The up side is represented only by 14–16b, telling of the worship offered by survivors. We now have the climax: cosmic punishment, the kings of the earth disappear from view, and Yahweh reigns alone in Zion. No messianic figure has a place in this scenario.

24.21   Justice is meted out first in heaven. Nothing shows the distance of this section from classical prophecy more clearly than this detail. Increasingly in post-exilic writing, the important theatre of Yahweh's activity is heaven. The trials that take place on earth are secondary to and derivative from the strife that takes place in heaven. Yahweh's final triumph appears only when *the host of heaven* is subdued. The highest potentates in *heaven* are joined with more

---

[1] For a fuller discussion of Hebrew cosmology, see my *Groundwork of Biblical Studies*, pp. 105–14.

lowly potentates *on earth*. The term, *the host of heaven* may mean the heavenly bodies, created things which have wrongly received the worship of wicked men (Deut. 4.19; II Kings 17.16; 21.3; Jer. 8.2). Verse 23ab lends a little support to this view. Or it may mean angelic beings, members of the celestial civil service, who have attempted to gain power to which they have no right. According to one contemporary notion, preserved in the Greek text of Deut. 32.8 (but not in the Heb.), when Yahweh divided up the nations of the earth, he allotted an angel or 'son of God' to each of them. The apostasy of the nation could, therefore, be attributed to the failure of the guardian. On balance the second explanation is more probable.

24.22   Nothing is better news for suffering people than the vision of their persecutors being made to suffer the fate that they meted out to others. The *dungeon* probably has no connection with Sheol; it is a real place of punishment. REB opts for *over many years* but most translations have 'after many days/years', less dramatic but more accurate.

24.23   The reference to *shame* may imply that *moon* and *sun* are under judgement. But more probably they fade in embarrassment and fear, lest they appear to be competing with the light of Yahweh (cf. Rev. 21.23). There is an extensive background to the phrase, *the LORD of Hosts has become king*. In the cults of Israel's neighbours, the variation of the seasons determined the liturgy, and annually the king, representing the god, went through a dramatic ritual of death and resurrection, symbolizing the death and rebirth of the earth. The climax came when the king was triumphantly restored to his throne. How far these ideas penetrated into Israel's cult has been much discussed and certain psalms (e.g. 47; 93; 97; 99) feature largely in the argument. Two Heb. words provide the shout of triumph at the climactic moment (97.1; 99.1), but what do they mean? Most translations give, 'The LORD reigns' or 'The LORD is king', implying that Yahweh's rule is uninterrupted. But REB gives 'The LORD has become king', which allows the supposition that he is being restored to his throne. The Heb. of 23c closely parallels this exclamation and may be an allusion to such a ceremony. On the other hand, it can be argued that, at least in regard to this verse , the phrase marks the moment when Yahweh ascends the throne indisputably and for ever. Yahweh *is revealed in his glory to the elders* because it was to Moses and the elders that he revealed himself in Ex. 24.9–11.

No matter what has happened in the previous verses, at the great climax, Jerusalem and the people of Israel share in the glory. If there is a contradiction, it is because Yahweh can never be wrong, either in his demand for justice or in his choice of Zion and Israel.

A psalm of thanksgiving
25.1–5

These five verses provide an appropriate comment on the enthronement scene in 24.23, illustrating the art of the editor of chs. 24–27. The passage is written in the traditional language and style of psalms of thanksgiving; its theme is thanks for the overthrow of a city. It may look back to the sack of a particular city, but REB uses the plural, *cities*, giving the passage a general reference. The fall of cities is an indication that the highest human achievements collapse, but Yahweh's reign is for ever. The psalm may well have been composed or adapted especially for this section.

25.1 The language is reminiscent of worship in the psalms. *long-planned* – lit. 'counsels from a distance', implies a plan, formed in heaven, but filling all time and space. The meaning of history is revealed only in its totality, which includes its end; human understanding is confused because we see only a small section of the full course of history.

25.2 The city is seen as a centre of power, of governments, of palaces, of temples; but it is also the nature of *cities* to fall and be sacked, as the *tells* of the ANE reveal all too clearly.[2] The author is thus able to illustrate his central affirmation, 'Yahweh reigns in righteousness over human displays of power; ultimately they all collapse in violence.' Yahweh will have the last word. The *cities* are *never to be rebuilt*.

25.3 It is taken for granted that all aggressive nations suffer judgement in the end and these triumphs of Yahweh elicit grudging recognition that his will cannot be gainsaid. *cruel* – the normal sense

---

[2] A *tell* or (*tel*) is an artificial mound containing the ruins of an ancient city.

of the Heb. word is 'strong' (NRSV); the nations are powerful as well as *ruthless*.

25.4 A dramatic change. The recital of judgement on the strongest of the strong turns into a thanksgiving for Yahweh's faithfulness to *the poor*. Yahweh is their true defence. In the post-exilic period, when those least willing to compromise suffered most, righteousness and poverty often went together. Lacking power and prosperity the pinned their hopes on vindication by Yahweh.

25.5 The text is not good, but the psalm concludes with a reiteration of the basic affirmation of Yahweh's sovereignty.

These verses present two aspects of the biblical doctrine of God: universal sovereignty to the cost of powerful and ruthless nations and concern for the powerless. These two aspects must be held in balance; there is no Christian gospel if the balance is lost.

The final celebration
25.6–8

Ch. 24 concluded with Yahweh enthroned on Zion. This passage speaks of Yahweh giving a banquet there. It seems then that the psalm of praise has been inserted, quite appropriately, between 24.23 and its continuation in 25.6. This passage contains the first clear statement in the OT that Yahweh overcomes death. For that reason it appears, often with vv. 1–5, 9 and 10a, in lectionaries for All Saints, All Souls, the Easter season and for funerals.

25.6 The *mountain* must be Zion, as in 24.23. Nevertheless the echoes of Ex. 24.9–11, where the elders ate and drank with God on Sinai, continue. Mount Zion came to be regarded as a localization of Sinai within the land of Israel. There the stones from Sinai were preserved, there the law was read; the fire and smoke of the altar replicated the fire and smoke of Sinai (I Kings 8.1–11). The eschatology of Israel was never concerned with a happy land, far, far away; it was always tied up with Jerusalem and with Zion. The *banquet* is a common feature of future hopes. The peace offering involved a feast in the temple precincts, the pilgrimage festivals involved feasting, royal events involved feasting. It is impossible for the final enthronement of Yahweh not to involve a banquet. In 24.23, only the elders of Israel would be present on the great occasion; here the banquet is *for all the peoples*. There is much in the OT that treats other nations with contempt. The oracles in the previous section were scarcely flattering; Second Isaiah mocks Babylon unmercifully; Moab suffers later in this chapter. Nevertheless there are hints here and there that, if Yahweh made all the nations, they must have a place in his plan. In some cases only an inferior role is given to foreigners (Isa. 45.14; 66.19f.), but there are places where distinctions seem to vanish (cf. Isa. 2.2–4). Bearing in mind what Israel had suffered at the hands of other nations, the liberality of these verses is remarkable. The verse includes several technical terms for food and drink. RV and RSV try to render them accurately and produce a translation that must make readers wonder what sort of feast this is. REB interprets the general sense and provides a menu representing the longings of a people devoted to feasting but much practised in going hungry.

25.7   Another gracious act of Yahweh on behalf of *all the peoples*. In the past they have been metaphorically veiled, an image drawn from mourning rites. The nations, lacking the protection of Yahweh, lived perpetually in a state of loss. *the pall* of 7c implies a covering for a corpse. The verse cannot refer to the *veil* that covered the face of Moses in Ex. 34.33, because that veil shone with more divine glory than the people could stand, which does not fit this context.

25.8   The first line comes as a bolt from the blue. It is not certain when a positive belief in survival first appeared in Israel. There are hints in the psalms (49.14f.; 73.24), but this appears to be the first time in OT prophecy that the hope was held out so positively. Many commentators regard the line as a later addition. They may be right, for the passage would run smoothly without it. *He will destroy death* (lit. 'swallow up') means that people will no longer end in Sheol. That is a glorious hope, though it leaves unsolved the problem of those who have died already. It seems likely that a faithful community, which had struggled with the problem of death and reached at least a partial solution, added this line to bring to a climax a prophecy already glowing with hope. *for ever* is not simply a flourish. The seasonal conquest of death in nature was fundamental to the religion of Israel's neighbours, but the annual victory, celebrated in those cults, did not answer the personal problem. The present line witnesses to a victory that is irreversible. 8b continues the image of a release from mourning, as in 7bc (see Rev. 7.17 and 21.4). *throughout the world* indicates, not simply that the dispersion was an established fact, but that it had become a theological problem. The Hebrews had suffered *indignities* at home, not least that of being ruled by foreigners, but abroad members of the elect had to live in unclean lands and be beholden to non-elect neighbours day by day. This stigma had to be removed. So a passage that begins with a universalist hope concludes with a special hope for *his people*. The concluding formula provides the assurance that this will all happen. Yahweh does not speak in vain.

Here the grandeur of OT belief about Yahweh really emerges. The traditional belief of the Hebrews was that, at death, a person passed into Sheol (see note on 14.9). Plainly, if Yahweh was really to save his people, something must be done about Sheol. One resolution was an invasion of Sheol to release the dead; this notion was worked out in the last centuries before the Common Era and became the doctrine of resurrection. 8a, however, implies a different solution. If death is to disappear, Sheol itself must disappear. Sheol had a place within the cosmic structure, so Yahweh's action implies complete control of the universe. The destruction of death is as significant an action as the creation.

A thanksgiving and a repudiation of Moab
25.9–12

9–10a are a short thanksgiving appropriately added to the preceding vision; but someone with a strong antipathy to Moab has turned the thanksgiving into a diatribe against Israel's ancient neighbour (10b–11). V. 12 adds a more practical note.

25.9 To add assurance to the prophecy the editor pictures the happy community giving thanks on the great day.

25.10 The *hand* of Yahweh can often mean punishment (see Isa.

1.25, 5.25), but here it *will rest* on Zion in blessing. The dislocation after 10a is violent. Moab was an ancient enemy; the Moabite was traditionally banned from a share in Israel's worship (Deut. 23.3f.) and the ban continued until the time of Nehemiah (Neh. 13.1). Even so, the language is strong. It was common to speak of trampling down enemies and sometimes it was no metaphor (see Josh. 10.22–4); the addition of the *midden* adds force to the immage; *Moab* will not be trodden into nice, clean ground but into a dunghill.

25.11   *Moab* is now swimming, and drowning, in excrement.

25.12   In case the metaphor is not enough, the verse , in language borrowed from 26.5, describes the fate of Moab's cities in practical terms.

A song of victory
26.1–6

Another liturgical interlude, like 25.1–5; a song to be sung when Yahweh's righteous people enter the holy city in triumph. The background is the great procession that climbed the hill of Zion at the festivals. This procession, however, celebrates, not an annual feast, but Yahweh's final victory. The passage would fit neatly after 25.9 or 10a; perhaps the vindictive piece on Moab (25.10b–12) was a later insertion.

26.1   The third time that the formula *On that day* has been used in this section and there are more examples to come. No matter where the Jewish people are dispersed, the triumph must take place *in Judah*. The *strong city* is Jerusalem. The word that REB renders *safety* is the common word for 'salvation'. This term, which has assumed great importance in theology, has, as its basic meaning, physical security.

26.2   For the significance of *gates*, see the note on 24.12. Those who wanted to enter had to state their claim. Processions halted at the gates of Jerusalem and Ps. 24 provides the entrance liturgy. Only the righteous can enter (Ps. 118.19f.). Here the qualifications are similar. The *righteous nation* is Israel, so for the moment the song follows the Israel-centred focus of 25.8 rather than the universal vision of 25.7.

26.3   A well-known verse , much used as a text for sermons. AV provided a rendering so poetic and so satisfying that it took on a life of its own; now it seems churlish to demand a more accurate translation. Nevertheless REB makes an important point. The notion of stability has two aspects. There is the stability of the *city*, the *ramparts*, Yahweh himself, and there is the stability of attitude expressed in *faith, firm purpose, trust*. The two elements are inseparable, each contributing to the other. This is a truly Isaianic note; it provides the point of the pun in Isa. 7.9 (cf. 30.15). *untroubled* is a low key rendering of the Heb. *šālôm šālôm* ('perfect peace' in AV), a doubled version of the well-known Hebrew greeting. *Šālôm* means more than the absence of trouble; it indicates the condition of confidence and security, so much sought after, so rarely attained.

26.4   This short verse consists almost entirely of words suggesting security. The *rock* is one of the commonest images for Yahweh in the OT (see, for example, Pss. 18.2,31, 42.9, 61.2, 95.1). It was the only secure foundation for building, the only natural feature unaffected by wind or sun or seasons; it provided shade and shelter and a natural citadel from which defenders could look down on their enemies.

26.5   If the city of v. 1 is Yahweh's city, this *city* is the symbol of human achievement. It has the highest defences imaginable, but Yahweh *levels it to the ground* (cf. 25.12).

26.6   Vv. 5f. repeat the sense of 25.2–4, but the reference here to *the oppressed and the poor* is hardly a realistic detail. Poor scavengers might plunder ruined cities, but the Hebrew *poor* would not be in a position to rummage around a foreign city. The picture is, therefore, an ideal one. The mighty will be brought low and the humble will trample over the ruins of their proud achievements. From the exile onwards the powerlessness of Yahweh's elect was always a problem. It was made worse by the fact that the few Jews who did prosper were the compromisers and the apostate. Total reversal was needed, so, when the *righteous nation* at last emerged on top, it would be represented, in its triumph, not by its leaders, but by its *poor*.

Lamentation and resurrection
26.7–21

A passage, bristling with questions, but of the utmost interest, well-known because, even more than 25.8, it affirms the survival of death. Fundamentally the passage is a psalm of lamentation. The hoped for victory has not happened and Israel, having waited so long for the final resolution, finds herself still waiting. As in so many psalms, protestations of loyalty, pleas for intervention, sad recounting of present distress and confidence that all will be well follow one after another. There is, too, a note of certainty that seems to put everything right (as in certain psalms, e.g. 7, 31, 54, 71).

The crucial issue is the interpretation of v. 19. Some, including the great German commentator, Wildberger, have contended that this verse has been overinterpreted, that it is simply a powerful metaphor, a promise that suffering Israel will be restored and come to enjoy a new birth (cf. the vision of the dry bones in Ezek. 37). If this is the case, the whole passage can be taken as a unity and 20f. consists of sober advice to be patient a little longer. But if 19 is a specific affirmation of the resurrection of the dead, then it is another bolt from the blue, it turns the lamentation on its head, and 20f. has to be understood in quite a different way.

These questions will have to be discussed as we go along, but a word is necessary about the emergence of belief in resurrection in Israel (see note on 25.6–8). Traditionally the Hebrews believed that, though the service of Yahweh brought blessing and joy throughout earthly life, death brought this privilege to an end. Sheol had no such pleasures (see note on 14.9). If all faithful Hebrews had lived to a ripe old age and the apostate had died young, this belief would have been easy to accept; but it was patently not so. So puzzlement and protest appear in some of the psalms and, to some extent, in Job. Not until the persecutions of the second century BCE, when the most faithful suffered agonies because of their faithfulness and the apostate

157

flourished because of their apostasy, were some devout Hebrews at last convinced that the resolution of this problem must be attained after death (cf. Dan. 12.2). It was not easy to say how. The idea of an immortal soul which could manage perfectly well without a body was foreign to their understanding. So they had to envisage an invasion of Sheol and a restoration of the bodies of the dead. There are obvious difficulties with this and in pre-Christian Jewish literature the problems were never really sorted out.

If, as seems probable, v. 19 is a statement about the resurrection of the dead, then it must have been added to the psalm very late in the day. But once added, the verse changed the meaning of the whole, and 20f. and probably 14 appear in a new light. Nothing could illustrate better the depth of meaning of the OT and the significance of editors. When the passage is read in the Easter season or at All Saints, the impact it makes owes more to the editor than to any original author.

26.7   The lament begins with an expression of confidence. The statements are not consistent with the circumstances of the writer, but this is their strength. The writer is confident in Yahweh though the immediate evidence is discouraging.

26.8   Some psalms of lament have an air of self-righteousness (see Ps. 44). It is almost necessary for the logic. If the psalmist and those he represents have not been faithful, they have no right to complain. *laws*, Heb. *mišpāṭ*, (see Introduction, pp.00f. and note on 1.17). *your name and your renown* – names were important in the biblical world as symbols of the person; the name of Yahweh was so precious that it was never pronounced. *renown* – the record of Yahweh's mighty deeds in history, regularly rehearsed in worship.

26.9   Deep longing is most insistent in the wakeful *night*. *dawn* is a universal symbol of hope (Ps. 30.5). *justice* – Heb. *ṣedeq*, often associated with *laws* (see note on 1.21).

26.10   For most of the psalm the theme is the suffering of Israel in face of other nations, but a concurrent theme calls up the distinction between just and unjust within *the land of honest ways*, presumably Israel, though rarely do OT writers describe the nation in such terms. The *wicked* do not see the true state of affairs. Yahweh's *majesty* is not a theory of the faithful; it is an inescapable fact of life.

26.11   The *hand*, when it is *lifted high*, is a symbol of power for good or ill . By inserting *your* before *people* REB restores the theme of Israel against her enemies. Yahweh was often associated with *fire* (Ex. 19.18 etc.), sometimes in a destructive sense.

26.12   An expression of assurance in line with those laments that express certainty regarding the answer.

26.13   Another affirmation of fidelity. Submission to an overlord often meant servile acceptance of his gods, but not in this instance!

26.14   In an ordinary lament, the sense here would be straightforward, 'Human glory does not last.' The oppressors have their day now, but death will bring them low (cf. 14.9–11). The *memory* of them, so important to those who had no belief in survival, will be *wiped out*. But that argument is not so effective if the same fate awaits the righteous. If, however, we read the psalm with v. 19 in place, the message is transformed, 'Resurrection for us, but the grave for you!'

26.15   This verse looks backwards from the standpoint of the ultimate future to a national expansion that, from the author's standpoint, is yet to come. While other monarchs go their way to Sheol, *the nation*, Israel, enters into new prosperity, which means *honour* for Yahweh.

26.16   We now return to the *distress* which lies at the root of the lament. Adverse circumstances are interpreted as Yahweh's *rebuke*.

26.17   The *pains* of *labour* are often used as a metaphor of distress, surprisingly because the pain was so positive. Here there is pain, but no happy outcome.

26.18   Giving *birth to wind* is a mixed and clumsy metaphor, but we know what it means. The suffering led to nothing, though so much was expected.

26.19   The language is not easy, it is not certain who is the speaker, nor who is being addressed. Our view is that the verse does not refer metaphorically to the revival of Israel as a nation, that it is a second-century insertion, and that, unlike 25.8, it speaks, not of the conquest of death, but of resurrection from the grave. The verse answers the preceding complaints completely; indeed, if the author of the lament had been aware that this is how the psalm would end, he would not have written it in the way he did. Nowhere in the OT is this hope fully expounded; we never hear how the process of corruption is reversed nor what happens to the restored bodies, but the affirmation is sufficent. Yahweh rules Sheol; death is not the end; beyond it is joy and the praise of Yahweh. *dew* is a positive image; it represents precious moisture in the long hot summer.

26.20   Vv. 20f. are an addendum to bring the passage to a fitting conclusion. The original sense must have been, 'Terrible things are still to happen. Take care, don't look for trouble. Go home, settle down, and wait for better times!' Similar advice was given on the night before the escape from Egypt in Ex. 12.22f. If we accept that 19 refers to a restoration of Israel, there is no difficulty with this meaning. If 19 is treated as a later insertion and a prophecy of resurrection, the sense is different, 'There will still be a period of waiting in this world, even though the final hope lies beyond Sheol, so be patient.' It is also possible, in the light of 19, to understand the *rooms* as graves and to read 20 as meaning, 'Surrender yourselves peacefully to death for a little while, till the day of resurrection comes.' There is some evidence that this interpretation was current in early Judaism, though it seems forced and artificial.[3]

26.21   The final verse returns to the bad news; the danger comes, not from foreign enemies, but from Yahweh. It is always a comfort to the oppressed to believe that no crime will go unpunished in the end. The Hebrews had an almost mystical belief in the power of *blood*. Here it seems to endure as a permanent witness against the one who shed it (cf. Gen. 4.10).

The doctrine of resurrection appears clumsy beside the Greek idea of immortality, and for many Christians immortality is a more satisfying belief. We have to consider, however, the whole inter-locked pattern of biblical ideas. In the first place, the human race is made from the earth and to the earth it returns. A divine act of re-creation after death is consistent with this, but immortality as an

---

[3] See II Esdras 7 which deals at length with matters concerning the end. II Esdras is an apocalyptic book roughly contemporary with the NT. It is found in the Apocrypha.

inherent human quality is not. Secondly, immortality requires a division of the person into a mortal body and an immortal soul. This is inconsistent with the biblical view that the human person is an integrated whole; the whole person lives, praises God, sins, dies, and is raised. Thirdly, the narratives of the resurrection of Jesus can in no way be told in terms of belief in immortality.

We are, of course, commenting on the way the Bible handles the issue, not defining a belief for our own times. There is undoubtedly a culture gap to be bridged. This was already clear to Paul when he took his Hebrew ideas into the Gentile world, and I Corinthians represents a brilliant interpetation of the resurrection theme. Flesh and blood does not rise, but the person, the true body, does. The body of flesh is transformed into a spiritual body, appropriate to a new non-fleshly world.

It is well to remember in this discussion that we are here dealing with the imponderables of faith. No one has a map and a programme for the new age. We are seeking an authentic way of expounding Christian hope that fits consistently into the biblical story of God's saving acts, and the doctrine of resurrection supplies it. That does not mean that belief in immortality has to be firmly denied. Millions, who are not concerned with biblical concepts or theological consistency, find it expresses their Christian hope perfectly. And some theologians who are anxious to escape from the thought forms of an ancient Semitic people find immortality a more useful and comprehensible concept. This, however, is a commentary on Isaiah and it is our task to remain within the thought world of that book.

Leviathan

27.1

The last chapter in this section consists of four short pieces, all concerned with the events of the end. The first, a single verse, deals with Yahweh's slaughter of a monster, or monsters, of the deep. Attempts have been made to treat the references as if they related to actual creatures, whales or crocodiles, used as metaphors. On that reckoning there are two serpents here, representing the Tigris and the Euphrates. The argument is not persuasive, however. We have to recognize that this is the language of mythology, a strange language to many, but one that must be understood by anyone who wishes to enter the OT world.

27.1   In 26.21 Yahweh punishes the inhabitants of the earth for their particular sins; in 27.1 he destroys *Leviathan*, the mythical sea monster who is the symbol of all rebellion. Myth was a means whereby the ancients expressed their beliefs about ultimate things, creation, the gods, human destiny, etc. Records of some of these myths survive; perhaps the best known is the Babylonian creation myth, which tells of a battle between the young god Marduk and a sea monster representing chaos, called Tiamat.[4] Marduk triumphs and from the body of the monster the heavens are made, the human race from the blood of Kingu, her commander in chief. Different versions of this myth are found in the ANE and the question is how much influence it had on Israel. If we read Gen. 1, it is easy to answer, 'None'. There is no monster, no battle, no family of gods. There is a great deep, and the Heb. word for 'deep' has some similarity to the name Tiamat, but that hardly puts Gen. 1 into the category of creation myths. It is a mistake, however, to assume that the lofty concepts of Gen. 1 were universal in Israel. There are many references to sea monsters and to other-worldly battles. Ps. 74.12–17 relates that, as part of an act of creation, Yahweh slew a sea monster called *Leviathan* and various other dragons. In a similar context, Ps. 89 shows how Yahweh dealt with the pride of the sea and with Rahab, another name for the monster. Job 26.10–14 follows the same line of thought, and Isa. 51.9f. points out that it was Yahweh who dealt with the sea and with Rahab. Dan. 7.2 tells of four great beasts, coming up out of the sea, who were enemies of Yahweh and of his people. It seems then that Israelite culture did make use of the common mythology, ascribing to Yahweh victory over the chaos monster and consequent control over the seas. The double reference to Yahweh's *sword* in 27.1 is in line with these references and at odds with Gen. 1.

The myth does not belong to the world of time and space, least of all to the chronological world in which past, present and future are sharply distinguished. Yahweh's victory over the sea in creation is renewed in the exodus in Ps. 74.13, and Isa. 51.9–11 calls on Yahweh to repeat both his original triumph and his exodus triumph by leading the exiles home to Zion. Ezek. 29.3 sees Pharaoh as the great

---

[4] The Babylonian creation myth can be read in *ANET*, pp. 60–72.

dragon lurking in the waters of the Nile, and Isa. 30.7 gives Egypt the name Rahab. It is hardly surprising, then, that the monster *Leviathan* should appear in the present verse as the ultimate enemy of Yahweh. *On that day*, in the time of the end, Yahweh will repeat his primal victory and so deal finally with all rebellion against him.

The writers of the OT had their problems of theological language, much as we do. How is it possible to speak of realities that belong to a world outside our world of time and space? Myth provides a very acceptable answer. The truth is expressed in a story that makes use of earthly things like swords and serpents but that is actually located beyond the physical world that we see and know. It is a thousand pities that myth is so often regarded as a negative word; in fact myths represent the struggle of ancient peoples, including the Hebrews, to affirm their beliefs.

A second song of the vineyard
27.2–6

This passage deals with the relationship between Yahweh and his vineyard, Israel, when the great day comes, and there can be little doubt that the author intended his readers to recall the first song of the vineyard in 5.1–7. Both passages refer to Yahweh's ownership of and diligent care for the vineyard and to the briars and thorns which were a constant threat to husbandry. The present author, however, does not simply reproduce the thrust of the earlier song. The ending of 5.1–7 is harsh; here, at least in v. 6, it is hopeful. It seems as if the author, or, if 6 is a later addition, the editor wanted to re-use the imagery but to reverse the climax.

27.2   To whom does the invitation go to *sing of the pleasant vineyard*? In this context, not simply to Israel, but to all those who will be rejoicing when the great day draws near.

27.3   In both 5.1–7 and here Yahweh's care of the vineyard is the crucial factor. Israel is not in charge; Yahweh is. Israel's task is to respond, to bring forth fruit. Here Yahweh claims to *water* the vineyard *regularly*; in 5.1–7 he threatens to withhold water from it as a punishment. In 3c REB speaks of *leaves* wilting rather than enemies harming (as RV, NIV, NRSV), which means that Israel's failings are internal, not due to external pressure.

27.4 The normal meaning of the word rendered *wine* is 'wrath', so 'I have no wrath', (NRSV, cf. NIV, RV), which is a deliberate reversal of the promise of punishment in 5.5f. But in REB there is no reversal, rather a repetition of the charge made in the last line of 5.2. It is not clear what place the *briars and thorns* have in the argument as a glance at other translations will show. REB smooths out the difficulty.

27.5 The prosperity of the vineyard is in suspense until verse 6. In REB everything depends upon whether the vineyard *makes peace with me*. How far Israel's position is one of pure grace and how far it depends upon her moral performance is a subtle theological question. REB states the case slightly differently from NRSV where Yahweh rejects wrath in 4a. No single verse, no single book can strike the perfect balance, but Isaiah makes us constantly aware of the creative tension between the two factors.

27.6 Now there is no doubt that the vineyard is *Israel* and that her future is glorious. Many take the view that this verse is an addition to ensure that the passage, set in a context that is heavy with judgement, should contain an unambiguous promise for the elect. This is probably the view of the REB translators, for 6 is separated from 2–5. *the whole earth* will profit from Israel's prosperity. Either Israel's influence will spread over the whole earth from Zion or Israelites, already scattered, will be a blessing to the lands in which they live. The former is more likely because most Jewish eschatological hopes centre on the gathering of the people on Mount Zion (cf. 27.13).

A tale of destruction
27.7–11

No passage in the book of Isaiah is more difficult to unravel. The text is corrupt, the allusions imponderable, the links with the surrounding material obscure. Despite the use of scholarly imagination and various attempts to improve the Heb., the translators fail to provide fully comprehensible English. It is possible to read the whole passage as referring to Samaria and the Samaritans after the breach with the returned exiles had taken place. It then criticizes the original northern kingdom and reiterates the judgement on its people. This hypothesis works better for 10f. than for 7–9, and REB, preferring obscurity to insecure hypothesis, does not concur with it. On the other hand, the passage could be a backward glance at the southern kingdom from a date after 586. REB certainly reads 7–9 in this way, leaving us to speculate about 10f.

27.7   With no clear light to guide us, we assume that *them* is post-exilic Israel. The *enemies* and the *attackers* (see marg.) – Assyria and Babylon were both humiliated in time. For all her travails, had Judah suffered as much?

27.8   The Heb. does not mention *Jerusalem*, but only a feminine pronoun. REB resolves the difficulties of translation so that the verse can then be read as a reference to the Babylonian captivity. *the east wind* blows from the Arabian desert, scorching the earth and shrivelling vegetation; a good image for either Assyria or Babylon.

27.9   Some would like to remove this verse as an insertion: 10 would certainly follow 8 more smoothly than does 9. *Jacob* is another name for Israel as the elect community. The verse is concerned, not with how the expiation of *Jacob's iniquity* takes place, but with its practical results. One consequence is the destruction of the objects with which syncretistic shrines were furnished. The *sacred poles* or Asherim were symbols of the female deity, Asherah (see note on 17.8); *incense-altars* is probably the right translation, though some think it refers to the pillars that represented the male deity. The verse is reminiscent of Deut. 12.3, where such reforms were demanded, and II Kings 23.14f., where they were carried out.

27.10   At this point the argument for relating the passage to Samaria becomes stronger. The details of *The fortified city* would apply more easily to Samaria than to Jerusalem. Samaria was sacked by the Assyrians in 721 and the two verses could be a heartless reminiscence of that event.

27.11   Again the language would fit Samaria better than Jerusalem. A post-exilic author would readily have described the Samaritans as *a people without sense* and he would readily have prophesied that Yahweh would *show them no mercy*. It is less likely that he would have used such language of Judah. Nevertheless no hypothesis regarding these verses inspires much confidence. Sometimes it is necessary to remain baffled.

Even in our bafflement we can be sure that this passage, like so many others, affirms that Yahweh punishes wrongdoing inexorably and in just measure. But punishment is not the last word; there is a hint that Jerusalem will be purged and live again.

Final promises
27.12f.

The section ends with two great promises of hope. The final editor, who may himself have found some of his material uneven, wished to conclude with a stirring and unambiguous affirmation. These two verses paint separate pictures, and they may have been added at different times, but they are complementary and they bring the section to a triumphant conclusion.

27.12   The threshing image is ideal to express judgement, as John the Baptist realized (Matt. 3.12). Threshing is a violent action; it separates the good from the worthless; the good is preserved with care, the worthless scattered by the wind. This verse is concerned with the ideal land of Israel; it stretched from the sources of *the Euphrates* in the north to *the wadi of Egypt*, the modern Wadi el-'Arish, which flows, when it flows at all, northwards from Sinai into the Mediterranean. This is the land promised to Abraham (Gen. 15.18) and achieved by David (I Kings 4.21) but never again united in a single autonomous Jewish kingdom. The threshing deals with the occupants of that territory and the verse states that *Israelites will be gathered one by one*. Throughout the pre-exilic period Israel was considered as a community. The whole nation was punished or the whole nation was saved. In post-exilic times that communal way of thinking had to be modified. Apostate Jews could not be considered as part of the final, glorious, redeemed people of God. So individual selection finds a place in the judgement.

27.13   A picture of the faithful returning for a great festival on Mount Zion. A *trumpet* made from a ram's horn was used at festivals to attract attention, create excitement and inaugurate the event (Ps. 81.3; Joel 2.15), but the functional use of the trumpet is hardly the point. A trumpet was the sign of a theophany in Ex. 19.16 (cf. Ps. 47.5; Joel 2.1; Zech. 9.14) and that is more relevant here, for this is no ordinary festival. The area referred to is larger than that of the previous verse and we have to think of Jews of the dispersion. It is taken for granted that those Jews who dwell away from their homeland *are lost* and longing to return, though this was not the case with all who were deported to Babylon. The reference to *Assyria* indicates that, in the eyes of the author, faithful survivors of the northern kingdom still had to be reckoned with.

So the section on the great judgement reaches its climax. *On that day*, the great day of the end, Yahweh will be present on the *holy mountain* to receive the worship of his own, gathered at last where they belong.

Judah, Egypt, and Assyria
28.1–33.24

The core of this section is a number of reproachful oracles addressed to Judah at the end of the eighth century BCE. It is a period of foolish optimism (perhaps brought on by the death of Sargon in 705), of rebellious plotting against Assyria, and of ill-judged reliance on Egyptian promises. The overall tone of the section is gloomy; the word 'woe' occurs frequently. The oracles criticize Judah not simply for diplomatic and political errors but for the social evils of which we heard much in chs. 1–12. Positively the oracles urge patience, trust in Yahweh, the abandonment of confidence in Egypt, and hope for a Davidic king who will renew Judah's prosperity. These factors suggest that much of the basic material comes from Isaiah himself in the period just before Sennacherib came to Jerusalem and retreated in haste. The section has been carefully edited and other material has been added, as we shall see.

Drunkards of Ephraim
28.1–4

It may seem strange that the editor introduces a section on the shortcomings of Judah with an oracle against *Ephraim*, that is, the northern kingdom, but there are good reasons for his decision. The oracle, as most agree, was addressed to Ephraim in the crazy days before the fall of Samaria. Anarchy and misrule characterized the time. King followed king; there were six in the last two decades, at least four of whom were murdered. The ill-judged confederacy with Syria against Assyria indicates the kind of folly that the prophet describes as drunkenness. Up to the last the rulers in Samaria thought that Assyria could be defied. The first of the oracles against Judah (vv. 7–13) uses the image of drunkenness. What better way, then, to introduce the section than to reissue an oracle on a similar theme which had already been proved devastatingly true? Here was

Judah, twenty years on, suffering from the same arrogant illusions. No doubt Isaiah pointed out the parallel again and again in his lifetime, so it is reasonable that the edited version of his prophecies should do the same. Not all scholars accept this hypothesis. Kaiser calls the passage proto-apocalyptic and dates it a couple of centuries later, but few follow him.

28.1   We have a sorry picture of garlanded *drunkards* at the end of a feast; the *flowers* and those who wear them are both drooping. The *Alas* is not so much for the *garlands* as for the revellers. Some translators take 1c as a reference to 'the head of a valley', not to *the heads* of the drinkers, which means that the image relates to the city of Samaria, the crown of the northern kingdom (RV, RSV, NIV). In either case the wealthy leaders of the kingdom are in the dock for their appalling behaviour.

28.2   The *one* is Assyria, a dreadful threat apparent to all except these drunken leaders. The images of *hail*, *tempest*, *torrent* and *flood* fit the picture of an assault on a capital city rather better than an attack on drunkards.

28.3   We return to the revellers. In the final blunderings, the *garlands* fall off and are *trampled underfoot*. Or perhaps *garlands* should be rendered 'crown'; the streets of Samaria will be *trampled* by invaders.

28.4   The second half of the verse is not too difficult. The *early figs* came before the main crop so they were eagerly seized as a welcome delicacy. The enemy will do the same to Ephraim's precious fruit. But what do the *figs* represent? REB (NRSV too) has the invader eagerly grabbing the incompetent leaders. Sober RV, RSV, NIV continue to think of Samaria. No matter how much the city and its inhabitants were *fading*, they represented a rich prize to an invader.

The passage is not as taut and as economical as we should expect from Isaiah; the image at times seems out of control. Nevertheless the evidence is good that the oracle does come from him and that it represents an attack on the idle and inept rulers in Samaria in the last years before the city fell. Pride, self-indulgence and folly are the sins that call forth Yahweh's judgement.

A hopeful promise
28.5f.

These two positive verses appear between an oracle against Ephraim and an oracle against Judah. They are probably an editorial insertion. Yahweh will provide the complete reversal of the situation in vv. 1–4 and 7–13.

28.5   The word *garland* appears again; this time it represents a blessing that Yahweh will provide for *the remnant of his people*. This is not a prophecy that a remnant would survive but a promise made to a remnant that had survived. In view of the position of these verses between 1–4 and 7–13, it is reasonable to suppose that *the remnant* refers to a post-exilic Jewish community made up of those with origins in both the northern and southern kingdoms.

28.6   It is interesting and thoroughly in line with the Isaianic tradition that the first blessing is *a spirit of justice*. Those who suffered the kind of injustice that the prophets denounced made poor defenders; what had they to defend? The best security against external enemies is internal justice. The *one who sits as a judge* is probably a future Davidic monarch for the community. Together with the *spirit of justice* for the ruler goes *valour* for the defenders *at the gate*.

The corrupt and divided community described in 1–4 was ripe for destruction; they had brought it upon themselves. This community will be secure; the LORD of Hosts will bless it and it will be united against any enemy.

The drunkards of Judah
28.7–13

This passage picks up the theme of vv. 1–4 and applies it to Judah. There is no reason to doubt that the core derives from Isaiah himself, though there are some editorial touches. The imminence of an invasion, implied in v. 11, helps us to date the basic prophecy to around 703. An Assyrian thrust came uncomfortably near to Jerusalem in 711 (see Isa. 20), but the later date is more likely. Hezekiah was generally regarded as a good king because of his religious policy (II Kings 18.1–8), but his willingness to rely on Egypt for support in an anti-Assyrian policy did not meet with Isaiah's approval.

28.7 The passage begins with an obvious editorial link. *These also* ties up the priests and prophets of 7–13 with the drunken leaders of 1–4. In view of the fact that the leaders of the northern kingdom had led their people to disaster, the link is telling. In the Levitical law (Lev. 10.8f.) *wine* was forbidden to priests when on duty, and though the final codification of that law was much later than Isaiah's time, there can be little doubt that provisions like this were operative much earlier. The accusation refers not simply to actual drunkenness but to the stupid and unworthy actions that accompanied it. The conjunction of *priest and prophet* is interesting. Years ago it was common, especially in Protestant circles, to assume, on the basis of passages such as Isa. 1, that prophets had little time for priestly religion. More recently it has been recognized, on one hand that ritual is an essential element in all religion (the problem is *hypocritical* ritual), and on the other that some prophets had a place in the cultic system. Here *priest and prophet* appear to be colleagues, both incurring the same condemnation.

28.8 This disgusting picture suggests a celebration that had got out of hand. Feasting was an essential element in temple worship, and rooms and tables were provided. After the blood had been offered to Yahweh and the priests had taken their share, the carcase of the animal in the most common type of sacrifice was consumed by the worshippers.[1] So there was ample opportunity for over-indulgence once the sense of devotion was lost.

28.9 The next two verses are a puzzle. The first question is: who is speaking? Most commentators take the view that this is the response of the priests and prophets who are being upbraided, 'Who does he think he is talking to? Little children?' REB's rendering seems to

[1] This sacrifice (Heb. *zebaḥ šᵉlāmîm*) is traditionally called a 'peace offering' (AV, RV, RSV), but the term is variously rendered in modern versions: 'shared offering' (REB), 'sacrifice of well-being' (NRSV), 'fellowship offering' (GNB, NIV), etc.

represent the exasparated cry of the one prophesying, 'Who will take any notice? They are just like children.'

28.10   This verse is untranslateable; it consists of three pairs of short words, each pair repeated. The older translations jibbed at printing gibberish and struggled to produce a rendering that was not entirely meaningless. JB, however, accepts the fact and leaves the words untranslated. REB describes the words as *meaningless noises*, which is a comment, not a translation. The question is how the gibberish attaches to the previous verse. The most obvious explanation is that it is a continuation of the mockery, either rudeness on the part of the drunkards, 'This is how he sounds, blah, blah, blah', or the prophet's representation of the speech of the drunkards.

28.11   However difficult 9f. may be, the point of 11 is clear. *meaningless* the *noises* of v. 10 may be, but the *barbarous speech* of v. 11 will be tragically meaningful. An enemy will appear in Judah and his strange language will bring home to the Judahites Yahweh's word of judgement on his people significantly described as *this people*. It would be humiliating to learn this lesson from foreigners, and terrifying when the foreigners were the Assyrians.

28.12   This is Judah's tragedy. Yahweh's word had once offered true solace, but *they would not listen*. Rest from enemies was the perennial hope of Israel (Deut. 12.9f.; I Kings 8.56), but Judah had let the chance slip away. Whether this was Isaiah's summary of royal policy, foolish anti-Assyrian conspiracies, or whether this is the editor's comment on Isaiah's whole ministry cannot be determined, but the point is the same in both cases.

28.13   For the third time in the passage there is a reference to unintelligible speech; first from the drunkards (or from the prophet), then from the Assyrians, now from Yahweh. The verse not only borrows from 10f. but also from 8.15, and it is probably a later comment from someone anxious to drive home the moral, 'Ignore the word of Yahweh and in time it will become unintelligible to you.' The building up of verbs at the end of the verse ensures that we do not miss the point.

A treaty with Death
28.14-22

This passage is a similar assault on the Jerusalem establishment, but here *rulers* rather than priests and prophets are the target. The historical context is the same, a deal with some ally, probably Egypt, to set up resistance against Assyria. The thrust is that forgetting Yahweh and trusting Egypt is suicide, a view which suggests that Isaiah is the author. There are a number of editorial additions and comments.

28.14 *Therefore* is simply an editorial link: 14-22 does not depend on 7-13. The offence of the *rulers* is arrogance, the belief that they were wise enough to direct Judah's affairs without any help from Yahweh. As in 28.11, *this people* rather than 'my people' is significant.

28.15 The prophet quotes the boast of the rulers who are obviously pleased with their political acumen. But what does the *treaty with Death* mean? Some older commentators (Whitehouse, Skinner) thought that the *rulers* had betrayed Yahweh by seeking the help of other gods; one of the gods of Ugaritic mythology was called Mot, a form of the Heb. word for death. This may explain why REB renders *Death* with a capital. We must remember, however, that this speech is not genuine quotation; Isaiah is putting words in the mouths of the rulers and he is being bitterly sarcastic. They may boast of signing *a pact* with a powerful ally; Isaiah calls it *a treaty with Death . . . a pact with Sheol*. For *Sheol* see note on 14.9. *the raging flood* – the Assyrian army. The image suggests the wadis that suddenly become torrents after the winter rains; perhaps also the mythological flood that Yahweh's creative power holds in check. The last two lines make it clear that Isaiah, not the rulers, is composing the speech. Alliances with forces other than Yahweh, whether human or divine, were regarded by the prophets not simply as folly but as *falsehood*.

28.16 This verse and the first sentence of 17 represent Yahweh's counter to the boasting of the rulers. It could hardly be more positive or more apt; yet it is probably an insertion. 17c reads better as a continuation of 15. V. 16 expresses a promise, and an awesome one. The image is of a new temple, perhaps even a new city. The word that qualifies the *stone* may refer to some kind of testing; so we get 'a tested stone' or 'a stone by which things are tested'. This confuses the metaphor and it is better to follow NEB/REB in their *block of granite*. The last line of 16 seems to be an intrusion, but it is not. The edifice is not an actual building but a new Judahite society; the firmness of the edifice represents the firmness of the people. The Heb. translated *he who has faith* means 'he who is reliable' (cf. Isa. 7.9). This verse is used in Rom. 9.33 and I Peter 2.6.

28.17 The first sentence describes the builder at work; *justice* and *righteousness* will provide the standards of the new society. Amos 7.7–9 also uses the image of the *plumb-line* with similar meaning. In 17c we return to the direct assault upon the leaders. They hope to escape the *flood* of v. 15. Not so; Yahweh's *hail* (cf. 28.2; 30.30; 32.19 RV) will destroy their flimsy hiding-place.

28.18 The claim enunciated in v. 15 is now completely reversed. The *treaty* that was to have been a source of pride *will be annulled*; the *waters* they hoped to escape will overwhelm them.

28.19 A *flood* suggests a specific catastrophe and one subsequent reader was afraid that Yahweh's judgement might be regarded as a once-for-all calamity. So the punishment is generalized. The floods will keep on coming and the *terror* will become a regular experience. One can see why an editor would introduce such a comment, but it does dull the edge of the previous verse.

28.20 *The bed is too short . . . and the blanket too narrow* sounds like a proverbial saying for an uncomfortable situation, but it is out of proportion with the horror described above. The editor who added this failed to grasp the power of the text he was working on.

28.21 The judgement begins again in a new form. Yahweh will intervene as he has intervened before. The two examples given are David's slaughter of the Philistines at Baal-perazim (II Sam. 5.17–21) and Joshua's slaughter of the Gibeonites at Beth-horon (Josh. 10.1–11). In both cases Yahweh specifically ordered the onslaught. So he will do again, but this time his own people will be the victims. That is why it was so *strange a deed*, and *an alien task*.

28.22 The passage concludes with another addition which returns to the theme of *arrogance*. Some would argue that this verse threatens the whole earth with destruction (so AV, RV) and that it is very late. REB does not share this view. The word rendered *land* can mean 'earth', but that is insufficient evidence to sustain the case that the passage has been hijacked by an apocalyptist. The hand of the editor is revealed in *I have heard*. A prophet who could declaim 14f., 17cd and 18 would hardly conclude with a line like 22c.

An agricultural parable
28.23–29

This passage belongs to a different literary genre from what has gone before. It describes some agricultural processes and makes the simple point that the farmer learns his skills from Yahweh, which is a testimony to Yahweh's great *wisdom*. Such an observation is sound, but not what we expect from a prophet; it belongs to the category of 'Wisdom Literature'. But two points have to be made. First, it is an error to suppose that literary categories were so rigid that an exponent of one could never stray into another. Secondly, the inclusion of the passage at this point might give it a different meaning from that which it would bear if it stood alone. This second point is crucial. We cannot read the passage now – nor were we meant to – without seeing the agricultural processes as a paradigm of how Yahweh deals with the nations. If the passage is the work of Isaiah, it indicates a profound change from his normal style; more probably it is a wisdom saying which a shrewd editor included with the deliberate intention of making it into a parable. So in its present context it teaches that God both judges and saves, that he does everything according to plan, that he can be both violent and gentle, that his infinite wisdom always achieves the end he desires.

28.23 The introductory formula belongs on the lips of a sage; the prophet has a different way of introducing his oracles.

28.24 The answer to both questions is 'no'. There is a rhythm in the agricultural task. So too, we must understand, Yahweh does not punish for ever and without purpose.

28.25 Again we have stress on the order involved in farming. Finding modern equivalents for ancient botanical terms is hazardous. Michael Zohary[2] contends that *dill* should be 'black cummin' and *vetches* should be 'emmer', a kind of wheat, but this is not a matter of great concern to most of us. The important point is that different crops are given different treatment.

28.26 This is the end of the first stanza. Yahweh has provided an ordered creation and the farmer's skill lies in understanding that order.

28.27 In threshing the farmer does not act in a crude and undiscriminating way. The *threshing-sledge* is for hard grain well protected with husks. Finer seeds must be treated with a light *rod* or *a flail*.

28.28 Even the *Grain* is not *crushed* to destruction but threshed to exactly the right degree. There is a subtlety in this kind of work which reflects the subtlety of Yahweh.

28.29 The concluding formula states coolly and confidently the sage's message that Yahweh's *counsel is wonderful*. The application is left to the reader and the context. The message we infer is that Yahweh's counsel is wonderful, not simply in instructing farmers, but in judging and saving the nations of the world, and the nations of the world must find their peace in appreciating and accepting that counsel.

Jerusalem, punished and redeemed
29.1–8

The passage is in two stanzas, 1–4 prophesying that Jerusalem will suffer a siege and 5–8 that the enemy will be repulsed by Yahweh. Both these leading ideas are readily attributable to Isaiah, and the circumstances just before Sennacherib's siege seem to be indicated,

[2] Michael Zohary, *Plants of the Bible*, Cambridge 1992.

but could even Isaiah have made both prophecies at the same time? To predict a calamity against common expectation, as the prophets often do, requires insight, which Isaiah often displays; to predict, beyond that, that the siege will fail requires more than insight. Some, who see prophetic inspiration in absolute terms, will have no difficulty with this, but foreknowledge of this kind is not, in general, a feature of biblical prophecy. Given that there is at least an Isaianic nucleus here, there are two possible solutions. One is that Isaiah is the author of both halves, but that the prediction of the siege was made well before 701 and the prediction of deliverance much later; the two were brought together by an editor. The other is that Isaiah is responsible for the first prophecy and a later hand for the second. Jerusalem's escape in 701 prompted the conviction that Yahweh would always defend his own city; so an editor, writing a hundred years later, might have added the second prophecy to give the oracle balance and to stress this belief. Such editorial activity was taking place in the days before Jerusalem fell to Babylon (see Isa. 37–39, especially 37.35) and that particular conviction was shown to be unfounded.

29.1   One has only to read the passage to see that *Ariel* is Jerusalem. Why this strange name is chosen is not clear, though v. 2 gives a hint. The word means literally 'lion of God', which is not helpful. In Ezek. 43.15f. it is translated 'altar-hearth', not so much because the etymology is understood, but because it cannot mean anything else. If *Ariel* means 'altar', it is a fitting name for Jerusalem. David captured Jerusalem from the Jebusites (II Sam. 5.6f.), hence the reference in 1b. *When another year has passed* is rather too precise; the Heb. (lit. 'add year to year') probably means 'let a year or two go by'. The siege appears not to be imminent. The *pilgrim-feasts* were the festivals at the barley, wheat and grape harvests, which were given various names in Israel's history: earlier, 'Unleavened Bread, Harvest and Ingathering' (Ex. 23.14–17; 34.24), later, Passover, Weeks and Tabernacles. At these festivals all male Israelites were to show themselves at the temple in Jerusalem.[3]

29.2   The first two lines contain the direct threat. 2c contains a pun

---

[3] This was the case after the Deuteronomic law of 'the single sanctuary' had been promulgated (Deut. 12.13f.). No doubt before this time the males appeared at local shrines.

and is even more threatening. *Ariel* (Jerusalem) is going to become *Ariel, my fire-altar.* In other words the city will become a burnt offering.

29.3   The verse displays familiarity with the way sieges were conducted, but is more notable for its theology. The army, whether Sennacherib's or anybody else's, will have no will of its own. Yahweh alone will be the agent.

29.4   Jerusalem will be humiliated. The image is of a man beaten down or perhaps prostrate in penitence. With no power of his own he can only plead for deliverance. That is an appropriate end to the first stanza and a fitting prelude to the second. 4cd overloads the verse and brings in a new and scarcely necessary idea, that of necromancy (cf. I Sam. 28). The lines seem to be an addendum and not one that improves the meaning.

29.5   The tone changes. The *enemies* will disappear. Yahweh's power turns the most *ruthless foes* into *dust* and *chaff* (cf. 17.13). And it will happen *Suddenly.* Human armies fight long campaigns to achieve their goals; Yahweh achieves his *in an instant*.

29.6   Some want to connect this verse with the threat to Jerusalem in 1–4, no doubt because the the word rendered *punishment* contains the idea of divine visitation, but Yahweh visits other nations and the REB reading is perfectly sound. *thunder, earthquake, storm, tempest, fire* are regular means by which Yahweh reveals his presence and accomplishes his will (e.g. Ex. 19.18; Josh. 10.11; I Kings 19.11f.).

29.7   The author is now generalizing, perhaps an indication that this is not a prophecy in the way that vv. 1–4 are. In 701 Jerusalem was threatened by a single nation; here Yahweh's displeasure falls on *The horde of all the nations warring against Ariel.* All Jerusalem's enemies *will fade as a dream.* The theological point is powerful. To human beings, enemies were brutally real; to Yahweh they had no substance at all.

29.8   The image is reversed to hammer the point home. The

enemies are enjoying happy dreams of power, but when they awake, they will find themselves *empty* and *faint*. Again the reference to *the horde of nations* suggests a theological principle rather than a specific prophecy.

These eight verses display much of the bedrock theology of the book of Isaiah. Jerusalem, David's city, will not escape judgement; foreign armies will be the means, but Yahweh will be in charge; then, paradoxically, Yahweh will deal with all nations that war against Jerusalem; without effort he can call up the forces of nature to do his bidding.

Cautionary fragments
29.9–16

As the REB format shows, this passage has to be considered as four fragments, though it is easy to observe links between them. They all deplore a contemporary condition of national folly and obduracy; three of the fragments can reasonably be dated in the period just before Sennacherib's arrival, when Hezekiah was seeking help from Egypt; these three, for all their brevity, can fairly be attributed to Isaiah.

29.9 All the verbs are imperatives and more direct than REB suggests. They are presumably addressed to Judah's rulers. Deliberate avoidance of the truth destroys the capacity to recognize truth when it appears; wilful blindness leads to absolute blindness. They appear *drunk*, but it is moral confusion that causes their unsteadiness.

29.10 So *deep* is their *stupor* that it must be attributed to divine judgement (cf. 6.10). Paul uses the same argument in Rom. 1; when people resolutely choose evil, God's wrath is expressed in giving them up to the evil they have chosen. A later editor decided to be more specific regarding those addressed. The *eyes* of the nation were *the prophets*; the *heads* were *the seers*; Yahweh had silenced them both.

29.11 This prose fragment is a comment on vv. 9f. It describes the ultimate condition of an obtuse nation. REB speaks of *The prophetic* *vision*, but the Heb. means 'vision of every kind'. The word of Yahweh is like *a sealed book*, which implies that prophecy was thought of as a written record rather than as a spoken word, which in turn indicates a period after the exile.

29.12   When the literate fail, the illiterate can do nothing to help; when the leaders are found wanting, the common people cannot replace them.

29.13   This brief oracle recalls Isa. 1. As we have noted before *this people* is a negative term, unlike 'my people'. While the worship continues on Mount Zion, the people are devising plans which run counter to Yahweh's will. This suggests the occasion when Hezekiah sought help from Egypt to resist Sennacherib. The last line reads literally 'their fear of me . . .', but REB is justified in using the term *their religion*, because it makes more sense in English.

29.14   The term rendered *shock* appears as both noun and verb. The noun means 'marvel' or 'wonder' and is often used for great acts of deliverance wrought by Yahweh on behalf of his people, particularly the exodus (Ex. 15.11; Ps. 78.10–3; etc.). The terrible truth now is that Yahweh's saving power will be turned against Israel. The *wisdom* tradition was important to Israel; if it ceased the nation would be greatly impoverished. But 14cd suggests, not simply that the sages would disappear, but that *discernment* of every kind would go. It is hard to imagine a worse fate for a nation.

29.15   This verse implies that secret *plans* were afoot, kept from both prophet and people. Again the flirtation with Egypt suggests itself (cf. 30.1f. and 31.1), for diplomacy of that kind had to be secret. Isaiah so much disapproves of the scheme that he sees the secrecy as a futile attempt to deceive, not the people only, but Yahweh.

29.16   A further accusation that the leadership has lost its bearings. The image of *the potter* is found in Isa. 45.9, 64.8, Jer. 18.6 and Rom. 9.20f. In every case it draws attention to the absolute autonomy of the potter and the total impotence of *the clay*. The greatest folly is to suppose that the clay can challenge the potter, yet that is what is happening in Judah.

A blessed future for Israel
29.17–24

The tone changes, as it did after v. 4, and the remaining verses are full of promise. The situation is quite different from that of vv. 9–16. The happy future will come soon according to 17a, whereas 14 promises a series of unpleasant shocks. The nation is guilty in 9f., 13 and 15f., but there is no suggestion of a need for penitence in 17–24. The problem of 9f. and 13–16 is national folly and obduracy, whereas 17–24 operate on a grander scale; 17 deals with the renewal of nature. Nevertheless there are indications that this passage was included at this point for the deliberate purpose of responding to the previous verses. The post-exilic editor prized the oracles of Isaiah, moreover he was painfully aware of how they had been fulfilled. He had no intention of omitting or contradicting them, but, whenever possible, he was anxious to put the other side. His contemporaries needed the good news as well as the woe, so he followed the accusations with words of encouragement. This is another example of the sure touch of the editor; Isaiah would surely have approved.

29.17   The *very short time* suggests that the people are in dire straits and the author is anxious to bring good news. *Lebanon* is the high, wooded area to the north of Palestine, famous for its timber. The thrust of the verse is not easy to grasp; some commentators even suggest that it is a prophecy of devastation to precede the good news. REB, however, rightly interprets it as a prophecy of a renewal of nature which acts as a symbol of salvation for Israel. We have already encountered this idea in 11.6–9; it recurs in 32.15f. and becomes even more extravagant in later writings, such as II Baruch 29.5–8, I Enoch 10.18f. and 51.4. *Lebanon*, steep, rocky and sometimes snow-clad, will become like a *garden* and such fruitful *land* will be *as common as scrub* is now.

29.18   There is some discussion whether *the deaf* and *the blind* refer to the physically handicapped, in the way that v. 19 refers to the actual *poor*, or whether the reference is to those who are morally deaf and blind. The concreteness of vv. 19–21 suggest the former but the apparent link with 9–12 suggests the latter. In either case, the essence of the promised salvation is the reversal of the present situation.

29.19 The stress on *The lowly* and *the poor* is a true Isaianic note but it also derives from the precise conditions of the post-exilic world. Israel's overlords were the Persians, later the Greeks; they represented world empires with huge trading networks and something approaching a common culture. Fortunes were waiting for those, even Jews, who ventured into this new world and accepted its standards, but increasing poverty was the reward for those who rejected the alien culture and its compromises. Fidelity to *the Holy One of Israel* was a costly business. Salvation would mean a redistribution of prosperity; the faithful would find joy, not deprivation, in their fidelity.

29.20–21 The two verses are brought together because, in the Heb., *will be cut down* appears at the end of 20, leaving 21 without a main verb. The problem is not external enemies but *The ruthless* and *the arrogant* and other cheats and malefactors within the Jewish community. Once again the divine promise is concerned with social justice.

29.22 The new introductory formula implies that vv. 22–24 were added still later. *the deliverer of Abraham* is an unusual designation for Yahweh. In OT tradition (cf. Isa. 51.2) Yahweh called Abraham and he obeyed. Josh. 24.2f., however, states that when Abraham's family lived 'beyond the Euphrates', they 'served other gods'. Abraham's call was, therefore, a kind of deliverance. Later Jewish literature makes more of this.[4] Shame and pallor may represent Israel's present condition, but this belies the true facts.

29.23 Yahweh's deeds are not yet obvious to everyone, but soon they will be and Jacob's *descendants* will bow before Yahweh *with awe*. If social justice is promised in 19–21, here the promise is that sound theological understanding will abound. The verse looks back to 15f. and promises that that folly will be rectified.

29.24 This verse looks back to 9f. *the confused* and *the obstinate* are not the same as the villains of 20f. When the whole chapter is read as a unit, three categories emerge: the righteous poor of 19, the wicked of 20f., and *the confused* of 9f. and 24. The first will be vindicated, the

---

[4] See Jubilees 11.14–12.24 and Apocalypse of Abraham 8, in H.F.D. Sparks (ed.), *The Apocryphal Old Testament*, Oxford 1984, pp. 1–139 and 363–91.

second disposed of, and the third straightened out. The references to *understanding* and *instruction* suggest the wisdom tradition. Indeed it is interesting to compare the climax of the prophetic oracle in 17–21 with what we have here. Though different, both traditions contribute massively to Hebrew religion and theology.

Israel's rebellious tendency
30.1–18

This chapter follows the pattern of 29 in that there is a series of condemnations followed by a glowing promise. There is little doubt that vv. 1–17 originally represented five short oracles (1–5, 6f., 8–11, 12–14, and 15–17): careful study reveals differences between them and the second, fourth and fifth each have their own introductory formula. Nevertheless their general thrust is similar and the editor who brought them together treated them as complementary rather than as separate units. The modern reader is thus able both to consider the precise point of each oracle in its earliest form and to read them as they now appear, together, each interpreting the others. The main theme of vv. 1–5 is the familar one of the folly of trusting Egypt: practical folly because Egypt will fail them and blasphemous folly because Yahweh's will has been ignored. There were several Palestinian plots against Assyrian overlordship in the last decades of the eighth century. 711 is one possible date (cf. Isa. 20), but around 703 is more likely. There is no reason to doubt that Isaiah is the author.

30.1 It is the nature of children to obey, so, if the *children* are *rebellious*, they are perverse. Rebellion is not so much a specific act as an ingrained characteristic. *rebellious children* have no place in the community; hence the draconian provisions of the Deuteronomic law (Deut. 21.18–21). Evidently a plot was being hatched at court of which Isaiah disapproved and from which he was excluded (cf. 29.15f.). The plot, a consequence perhaps of Sargon's death in 705, involved making overtures to Egypt. Isaiah's attitude throughout is that Judah should trust Yahweh to deal with Assyria and not be lured into rebellion by untrustworthy allies. *piling sin on sin* implies that this was not the first plot, and indeed we know of others in Isaiah's lifetime in which Judah might well have been involved.

30.2 Kings often consulted Yahweh, even bad kings (cf. I Kings 22). To some extent that is what prophets were for. Isaiah is shocked that this plan was made in haste without any attempt to seek Yahweh's guidance. The Pharaoh at the time was Shabako, an Ethiopian, who ruled Upper Egypt and who had but a few years previously extended his sovereignty northwards to the delta.

30.3 This verse spoils the rhetoric by anticipating the climax; v. 5 would be more effective without it. It may well have been added as a gloss.

30.4 To whom do the *officers* belong? Some suppose that they are Hezekiah's officers who have been received at Pharaoh's court. Others argue that they belong to Shabako. It matters little; the point is that, however well negotiations are going, Egypt will let Judah down in the end. *Zoan*, Tanis to the Greeks, was on Egypt's Mediterranean coast; *Hanes*, probably to be identified with Heracleopolis, was further inland.

30.5 Isaiah's sad prophecy was correct. In 711 Egypt, *that unprofitable nation*, failed Philistia in her time of need, and when the leader of that rebellion fled to Egypt from Ashdod, he was handed over to the Assyrians. Judah was saved by good fortune, not by Egypt. The deliverance of 701 owed nothing to Egypt. Moreover that deliverance was not quite as complete as some interpreters suggest. II Kings 18.13–16 acknowledges that Hezekiah had to pay an enormous tribute to Sennacherib, and Assyrian inscriptions claim that forty-six cities of Judah were laid waste, which might reasonably be described as *humiliation*. This oracle proved, therefore, to be remarkably prescient despite the fact that Jerusalem was not taken and Sennacherib had to beat a hasty retreat.

30.6 Leaving aside the heading, 6f. could well be taken as a continuation of the previous oracle. The subject, the situation, and the thrust are the same. The heading, however, means either that 6f. originally existed separately from 1–5, or that someone inserted a heading into the middle of 1–7. The heading recalls the formula used to introduce many of the oracles in chs. 13–23. Perhaps the editor wanted to link this passage with those solemn warnings. *the South* is the Heb. Negeb, the name of the arid area south of Judah and northeast of Sinai. It is uncertain who *The Beasts* are; presumably contemporary readers were able to pick up a reference that is lost on us. The rest of the verse expands on the fortunes of the diplomatic mission mentioned in v. 2. There was a coastal route to Egypt, but it would hardly have been described in these terms, so we assume the caravan travelled by an unfrequented and dangerous route, perhaps for secrecy, perhaps for fear of the Assyrian army. The *flying serpent* is a species unknown to herpetologists, but its appearance here is understandable. OT writers had no comprehensive taxonomy of desert fauna. They knew only that the desert was vast and full of unpleasant creatures. It is not surprising that fearful imagination added to the actual dangers (cf. Num. 21.6–9; Deut. 8.15). The diplomatic mission is represented as a caravan hoping to trade with Egypt. They would find, however, that the customers were *unprofitable*.

30.7 *Rahab* is one name for the mythical serpent who represents chaos in the Babylonian creation story (cf. the note on 27.1). How far this mythology was current in Israel we do not know, but *Rahab Subdued* was evidently the ultimate name for the 'spent force'.

30.8 The speaker in vv. 8–11 is either Yahweh addressing Isaiah (cf. 8.1 and Hab. 2.2), or, more probably, Isaiah addressing his disciples (cf. 8.16 and Jer. 36). The charge is slightly different from that in 1–7. The purpose of the writing is to make the charge more durable and more concrete, but what is to be written? Some commentators suggest the whole series of oracles against alliance with Egypt in chs. 28–31, but the word *tablet* does not suggest a long inscription and the word for *engrave* implies an incision on hard material. On the other hand, *write* could imply a long message and the word rendered *inscription* could mean 'a book'. On the whole it is best to assume that a short inscription is indicated, probably a brief summary of the charge set out in this oracle.

30.9 The rebellion is unspecified, but, interpreting the term from the present context, we conclude that the people are accused of rejecting Yahweh's word regarding alliances with Egypt (cf. v. 1). The Heb. word for *listen* expresses every nuance from 'hear' through 'listen' and 'understand' to 'obey'. *the Lord's instruction* means the word given through the prophet. The Heb. word is *ṭôrâ*, which came in later times to mean the Law (see note on 1.10).

30.10 We come now to a precise charge, that the people have rounded on the faithful prophets and tried to silence them. Neither *seers* nor *those who have visions* are to be distinguished from prophets (see I Sam. 9.9). 10cd confirms what we already know from I Kings 22, Jer. 28, Micah 3.5f. and many other references, that time-serving prophets were ever-present in Israel; *smooth words* were available for kings who wanted them. Equally, faithful prophets often suffered obloquy (Amos 2.12; 7.10–12; Jer. 11.21; 18.18; 20.1f.). This is an age-old story. Conscientious prophets are ever a problem for self-assured and self-opinionated leaders. Every effort has to be made to silence or manipulate them.

30.11 This is Isaiah at his most caustic. We cannot suppose that anybody actually said these words, but this is what they meant. They have gone beyond disobeying the divine command to wishing to be rid of Yahweh altogether: a much more serious charge than that of rejecting the prophet's word about Egypt.

30.12 Vv. 1–11 have been mainly concerned with accusations; we now come to the consequences. The emphatic *Therefore* comes again at the beginning of 13 and again in 16. This verse is a summary of the accusations. As it stands now, the *warning* relates to the charge in vv. 9–11. Translating *devious* rather than 'oppressive' involves a slight change in the Heb., but it has the effect of tying in this prophecy more closely with the accusation of secretiveness in vv. 1f.

30.13 The doom is represented in terms of two images. The first is that of an unstable *wall*. When the *crack* first appears it is hardly perceptible, but it will not go away, *and suddenly* the whole edifice *comes crashing down*. The *iniquity* may be long lasting, the degeneration imperceptible, but the doom will be instantaneous.

30.14 The second image represents completeness. A pot may be broken but the pieces may still have a use; this *jar* will be so broken that not even the smallest *fragments* will survive to fulfil a useful function.

30.15 No pair of lines in the whole prophecy encapsulate Isaiah's message better than 15bc. They are reminiscent of his advice to Ahaz in 7.4. REB's *calm detachment* is but one attempt to render an elusive phrase. The Heb. has two words, rendered in AV, RV and NRSV, 'returning and rest'. Many think that the first means 'returning to Yahweh', a sense ruled out by REB. Other possibilities are that it means 'drawing back' from a particular policy, that is the alliance with Egypt, or 'returning' to the former policy of subservience to Assyria. 'Rest' might mean inactivity as a positive policy, or 'standing firm' by the treaty with Assyria. The ambiguity is positive, perhaps even deliberate; all translations contain an element of truth. *quiet trust* is a little more precise. Quietness sums up the appropriate attitude to Assyria: without fear or foolish bravado. The *trust* is in Yahweh, who, if Judah could believe it, controlled the destiny of all nations. The depth of meaning here cannot be plumbed. The AV of 15c, 'In quietness and in confidence shall be your strength', adorned the walls of many Victorian drawing rooms. The way our forefathers interpreted it was probably as good as any other, with the one condition that it does not and could not mean 'self-confidence'. A sad comment on the prophet's message is that the words appear here as a summary, not of Judah's faith, but of the belief that the people had rejected.

30.16 The people state their wilful plans; Isaiah points out the consequences. Translators struggle to express the subtlety of this conversation without complete success. The same verb appears in the boast (*flee*) and in the consequence (*put to flight*); it works in Heb., but not in English, for fleeing is not a proud action. In the second part the people boast that they will *ride apace*; the riposte is that greater *pace* will mark the pursuit, presumably by the Assyrians.

30.17 Though this is hyperbole, it is not so far removed from battlefield experience. Once morale cracks and defeat looms, it needs little to turn the host backwards. The double image in 17cd seems odd, but Jerusalem is *on a mountaintop*, and the lines are a not inaccurate description of what happened in 701. The fact that Jerusalem was saved tends to make us forget that the rest of Judah was savaged.

30.18 There is every reason to see this verse as a later addition, but a very constructive one. In vv. 1–17 Isaiah or his editor used 'therefore' as a keyword to introduce a promise of punishment. Here the same word introduces a promise of grace which hardly follows from the preceding oracles. REB tries to avoid the difficulty by translating it as *Yet*. Perhaps the verse is an editorial attempt to link the harsh words of 1–17 with the more hopeful material in 19–26. If so, the editor shows deep theological perception. Isaiah is predominantly a prophet of judgement, but the same cannot be said of the Isaiah tradition. Disciples who lived in more hopeful times had no difficulty in reading the prophet's austere words as a theology of grace. This verse is an example. In the end Yahweh's *favour* outweighs Israel's foolish pride. So both Yahweh and the faithful are *waiting*. Yahweh's patience and fidelity provide an example that the wise and the blessed follow. Note that *justice* is used positively; the Heb. word *mišpāṭ* suggests an all-round rightness. Yahweh and the faithful are waiting for the day when *justice*, that is to say the vindication of the faithful, will come to pass.

A promise of plenty
30.19–26

This passage simply glows with hope. As it stands it provides a balance to the severities of 1–17, though closer inspection shows that it is not addressed to the same people, nor is it of the same style, nor of the same date: another good example of the way in which a modern reading of the text in its present form and position yields a different, and perhaps fuller, meaning than study of the individual units in their historical contexts.

30.19 The citizens of *Jerusalem* are addressed, partly because Jerusalem is a symbol of the land and the people and partly because, as capital city and site of the temple, Jerusalem had suffered most. The second sentence does not mean that Yahweh is at present deaf. *hears* means, not simply an act of hearing, but Yahweh's complete response (cf. note on v. 9 above).

30.20 *adversity* and *affliction* are indications of the present condition of Israel which give point to the assurances of 23f. There is much discussion about who the teacher is. It may be Yahweh himself, despite the tradition that Yahweh must never be seen (Ex. 33.20–3). Alternatively it may refer to the faithful teacher of Jewish Law and Jewish faith who, in days of persecution, had to work underground. This would imply a much later date. In the second century BCE, when the faithful were suffering under Antiochus Epiphanes, prophecy had ceased and the rallying point was the collection of Jewish Law, custom and theology that we know as the Torah. The teacher of the Law was a crucial figure. The Heb. of the verse is difficult which makes certainty on this point impossible.

30.21   This verse suggests a society in which right conduct had been exhaustively prescribed and there was never doubt about the right thing to do. Such a notion could apply to the Jewish people only after the Torah came to be accepted as Yahweh's final word, that is to say, after the fourth century BCE.

30.22   The cult of *images* appears in different forms. These seem to be personal possessions, domestic ornaments rather than temple furniture. The latter part of the verse alludes to notions of clean and *unclean* that dominate post-exilic Judaism. Idols, of course, were a source of uncleanness. *foul discharge* – bodily discharges were the most immediate source of pollution (Lev. 15).

30.23   *rain* could not always be relied upon and crops often failed. Pasturage for *cattle* was hard to find and never enough. When the great *day comes*, those difficulties will be over. There is a joyful acceptance of material prosperity in OT pictures of the glorious future. While gross materialism is no ally of religious faith, disdain for the joys of the natural order and preoccupation with the 'spiritual' life have no foundation in Scripture.

30.24   Agricultural processes will continue but in blissful circumstances. So bountiful will be the crops that farm animals will be fed, not with chaff, but with food of the highest quality.

30.25   Irrigation was always a problem, especially in hilly country. Water had to be carried laboriously up to the higher terraces. Springs appearing on the tops of all the mountains would solve that problem. The rest of the passage refers to three features of the end-time. The first is the great battle that must precede the end. The reference to a *massacre* seems to fit badly into a sequence of resplendent promises, but every hope for the future had to begin with a prodigious battle in which the dominant world power was destroyed to make room for Israel (cf. Rev. 16.14–6). *fortresses* symbolize the arrogant power of the nations that presumed to oppose Yahweh by dominating Israel.

30.26   The second feature of the end-time is the transformation of the heavenly bodies. Their positive features would be enhanced; negative features are not even mentioned. The writer is painting a glorious picture; he does not want to spoil it by prosaic references to sunstroke. The third feature leaves hyperbole behind and the passage reaches its climax, not with cosmic turbulence, but with Yahweh tenderly binding up *the broken limbs of his people*. The passage demonstrates the full range of Jewish imagination, but it begins and ends with the most basic longings, an end to weeping and the healing of *wounds*.

Judgement on Assyria
30.27–33

This passage prophesies a violent judgement on Assyria while Judah celebrates. It is difficult to fix a historical setting because the passage has been adapted and re-used more than once. Some would deny that there is anything of Isaiah here, but a more likely hypothesis is that a first draft, relating to 701, belongs to him; more detail was added in the period just before Assyria was destroyed (Nineveh fell in 612) and perhaps again in the days when prophecy was giving way to apocalyptic and the Greeks had taken on the role of the ultimate enemy, 'the Assyrians'. This hypothesis would explain the mood of bitterness throughout. It would also explain the 'unrealistic' elements in the picture. Eighth-century prophecy was vigorous, but not wildly imaginative; the same could not be said of post-exilic writing. The immeasurable power of the world empires under which Israel then suffered led to hopes of divine intervention on the grandest, supernatural scale.

30.27   The verse deals with the advent of Yahweh under the image of an approaching storm. *from afar* relates both to the storm-clouds that appear first in the distance and to the fact that Yahweh's historic abode lay away to the south on Sinai (cf. Deut. 33.2; Judg. 5.4). The difficulty of the Heb. is shown by REB giving *his doom heavy* where RV and NRSV render 'in thick rising smoke'. *fire* is associated with Yahweh in the burning bush story (Ex. 3), in the Sinai theophany (Ex. 19.18), and in many other places (Ex. 24.17; Deut. 4.11; Isa. 6.4; Ps. 144.5).

30.28 *breath* – the Heb. is *rûaḥ*, which can mean a rushing wind, very suitable for the *breath* of Yahweh. REB's translation of the verse contains four images of Yahweh's power. First, the *torrent in spate*, which was used in 8.8, where it represented Assyria overwhelming Judah; now the situation is reversed and Assyria is overwhelmed. Secondly, the *yoke*, always imposed by the master and usually resented by the beast. Thirdly, sieving suggests arbitrary power. The operator decides what to save and what to throw away. Fourthly, the driver inserts the *bit* to give him power over the animal. All the images suggest a power that is both irresistible and irksome.

30.29 Subjection for Assyria but *songs* for Israel. Some argue that this verse and 32a are out of place because the text appears heartless. Unhappily this is no argument at all. There is venom in almost every line of the passage and we cannot be surprised that an element of smugness also appears. Scripture sometimes has the function of revealing ourselves to ourselves. Festivals were joyful occasions. The fact that the festival indicated takes place at *night* suggests the Passover, the supreme celebration of deliverance, but the allusion to a procession in the latter part of the verse argues in favour of Tabernacles (II Sam. 6; I Kings 8.1–5; Pss. 24.3–10; 68; 118; 132). There is no reason why the author should not amalgamate festivals to strengthen his image. The *Rock of Israel* is a common name for Yahweh, derived no doubt from the stability of rocks and the fact that a rock, enclosed today within the Dome of the Rock, crowns Mount Zion (Deut. 32.4; Ps. 18.2, 31; Isa. 17.10; 26.4).

30.30 This verse describes a theophany, an appearance of God on earth; it does not describe, in realistic terms, how the Assyrians will be dealt with. Theophanies are usually accompanied by dramatic natural phenomena; see, for example, the fire, smoke and earthquake of Ex. 19.18, and the wind and earthquake of I Kings 19.11f. (cf. also Pss. 18.7–15; 29.3–9; 77.16–20).

30.31   This is the only mention of *Assyria* in the passage. No doubt it originally related to Assyria, but in the course of time it was elaborated to apply to the enemy of the day, the current Assyria.

30.32   The Heb. is difficult, which leads to this improbable picture of the rhythm of the celebrations keeping time with the blows that fall on the enemy. The sistrum is a percussion instrument in which metal rods are agitated. For musical instruments in the Bible, see footnote on p. 35.

30.33   The fire is ready to consume Israel's enemy, another example of imaginative rather than realistic prophecy. *Topheth* was the rubbish dump in the valley of Hinnom to the south of Jerusalem where the refuse was burnt. It was also linked with human sacrifice to the god *Molech* (II Kings 23.10; cf. Jer. 7.31f.), for whom Solomon built 'a high place' (I Kings 11.7).[5] Human sacrifice is, of course, banned in both the Deuteronomic (Deut. 12.31; 18.10) and the Levitical (Lev. 18.21; 20.2–5) codes. *Molech* was linked with Ammon rather than Assyria.

The unreliability of Egypt
31.1–3

This oracle is close in meaning to 30.1–7. Circumstances and date appear to be the same. Hezekiah is seeking help against the Assyrians from Egypt just before 701 and Isaiah is outraged. The comprehensive dismissal of Egypt as an ally may indicate that the Assyrian defeat of Egypt at Eltekeh had already taken place (see Introduction, p. xxii). Hezekiah's policy may seem wise: the Assyrian forces were large and ruthless, and it was only common sense to seek the help of a country with plenty of horses and chariots

[5] One cannot speak with absolute certainty about the god *Molech* because other interpretations of the word have been put forward, but the best supported hypothesis is that the term is a contemptuous name constructed by the Hebrews from consonants that frequently occur in the name of a foreign deity and the vowels of the word for 'shame'.

to put in the field. But, as Isaiah pointed out, Egypt could not be relied upon to commit her forces, and even if she did, there was no certainty that she would prevail. This, however, does not get to the root of Isaiah's objection. He affirmed that history was not made, nor battles won, by horses and chariots. The affairs of the nations were in the hands of Yahweh and, unlike Egypt, Yahweh was infinitely reliable and waiting to give succour to his people. Nevertheless Hezekiah preferred to put his trust in forces he could see. In the event Egypt, when brought to battle by the Assyrians, was defeated; whereas Yahweh delivered Jerusalem. Whatever the truth about Sennacherib's retreat in 701, Isaiah and his disciples saw the series of events in precisely these terms.

31.1 Judgement is due for Hezekiah and his advisers because of their misplaced faith. Judah had few *horses* and *chariots* of her own and conventional wisdom dictated that *vast numbers* and good armour won battles. So it was prudent to seek a well-equipped ally. But according to Isaiah, conventional wisdom is no wisdom at all. To seek help from Egypt and not to *look to* Yahweh is grievous folly.

31.2 This verse is a comment by the prophet between the two verses constituting the oracle. The reference to Yahweh's *wisdom* is a jibe at the expense of Hezekiah's advisers. Assyria may be the current threat, but, if Yahweh is offended, he will prove a much more troublesome adversary.

31.3 The argument relies upon one of the most basic elements of biblical thought, the contrast between *flesh* and *spirit* (not to be equated with the contrast of body and soul that we have inherited from the Greeks). *flesh* is the medium of mortal life, it is vulnerable and limited, it exists for a span and then suffers corruption; *spirit* is unseen, unlimited, and unpredictable power, evidenced in the wind, ever active, deriving from Yahweh himself. *spirit* blows into inert bodies and they live (Ezek. 37), the more spirit, the more energy (Judg. 14.6, 19; 15.14), and when *spirit* departs, death and corruption ensue. *Egyptians* and their *horses* belong to the world of *flesh*; Yahweh is the source of all *spirit*. So Judah has chosen the wrong ally and will suffer. In fact, Judah and Egypt did not *perish together*. History moved on and 701 was remembered as a year of deliverance.

At no point is the difference between Isaiah's view and our own more clear than in this matter of national strategy. We arm ourselves and make alliances and trust that God will support us if our cause is just. Isaiah argues that Yahweh's help is on a different plane from human alliances. To pay the moral price of allegiance to Yahweh is true wisdom besides which the cleverest human diplomacy is folly. Isaiah's argument is put down as soft-headed idealism by modern political realists, but this raises three questions for us to ponder. What authority does Isaiah's affirmation have for Christians? Has his argument ever been tested? And has so-called political realism been successful in bringing peace and prosperity to the world?

Yahweh will defend Jerusalem
31.4–9

If this passage is approached from the direction of historical criticism, it proves to be full of deep complexities, but if it is taken as a single integrated text, it can be made to yield a coherent message: Jerusalem will be saved, the power of Assyria will be broken, and Judah will give up her idols. Neither the Heb. nor any translation reads smoothly.

31.4   The formula is meant to claim prophetic, perhaps Isaianic, authority for what follows, but it is hard to attribute more than the odd line to Isaiah or his immediate followers. The image of the *lion* is puzzling. If it is to be read positively, Yahweh is the *lion*, Jerusalem *its prey*, and *the shepherds* Assyria. Yahweh protects Jerusalem and is not *daunted* by clamouring forces attempting to frighten him off. It is odd, however, to represent Yahweh as a threatening beast and the Assyrians as *shepherds*. A negative reading sees the image as a threat: Yahweh will not let Judah escape judgement, no matter what Hezekiah and the Egyptians do. Fighting 'against Mount Zion' is as good a rendering of the Heb. as *on the heights of Mount Zion*. If the image is taken negatively the coherence of 4–9 is lost and 4 continues the threatening sense of 1–3. On balance the positive reading is preferable.

31.5   Here is a straightforward and impressive image of protection. There is a veiled reference to the exodus, for *sparing* translates a Heb.

term that occurs in verbal form only here and in Ex. 12.27. The noun means 'Passover'.

31.6f. The privileged protection of v. 5 is inappropriate unless *Israel* is pure and faithful, so these verses attempt to indicate the necessary conditions. Judah was presently in a state of disobedience, if not rebellion.

31.7 This verse recalls 30.22 and shows that *idols* were domestic ornaments as well as fixtures in temples.

31.8 Yahweh will deal with *Assyria*, a view that is consistent with Isaiah's rejection of alliances with Egypt. *but not by man's sword* – in the eighth century prophets were inclined to see Yahweh working through normal human forces; the present notion of supernatural invasion becomes common only in post-exilic times when no other hope was viable. 8cd is more matter-of-fact. Israel had suffered this experience from the Assyrians and there is obvious pleasure in the thought of a reversal, though, if the text is late, *Assyria* must be a code word for some other enemy.

31.9 The rendering *officers* is justified by the context though the Heb. word means 'rock'. The line completes the picture of abject defeat. The concluding formula links Yahweh with *fire* and *furnace*, images which gather together various awesome overtones. Fire burnt on the altar; fire consumed the city's waste; fire could break out and destroy crops and whole cities; fire destroyed human bodies (Isa. 30.33); Yahweh appeared as fire to Abraham (Gen. 15.17) and to Moses on Sinai (Ex. 19.18).

It can scarcely be doubted that, in these six verses we have a number of short prophecies of different dates, some of which may go back to the late eighth century. The context of these prophecies is lost and there is a good chance that one of them (v. 4) has been 'turned', so that in the final text it carries a different meaning from that which it had originally. By an editorial process, probably by more than one, the verses have been joined into a single prophecy which both looks back on the deliverance of Jerusalem in 701 and out to Jerusalem's contemporary condition. The *Assyria* of v. 8 indicates both the historic and the present enemy. The thrust of the edited version is that Yahweh delivers his people when they repent. The modern reader can choose between historical analysis of the text, which, in this case, leads to a number of fairly empty fragments, or the integrated version, which expresses the theology of the editor's day.

A kingdom of righteousness
32.1–8

This chapter is concerned with the ideal kingdom where government is just, counsels are wise, the faithful are honoured, and villains are revealed in their villainy. This standard of values is, not surprisingly, common to all strands of Hebrew thought, prophecy (Isa. 11.1–5), psalms (Ps. 72), wisdom writing (Prov. 21.1–3). For this reason it is difficult to supply the original context of vv. 1–8, but the sense is clear without it. After the criticism of king and court in the last few chapters, the editor has introduced a passage to show what wise government is like; an ideal lesson for Sundays concerned with social and political issues. Vv. 1–5 describe the righteous kingdom; 6–8 turn to moralising about the nature of villainy, which suggests a later insertion by a writer in the wisdom style.

32.1   The reference to a future *king* recalls 11.1–5 and 9.6f., but this passage is not so lyrical about the king and is more concerned about a just society. For *righteousness* see Introduction, p. xxviii. The reference to *ministers* shows that this is a more practical picture than the hopes normally termed 'messianic'. The establishment of real *justice* depends, not simply on the *king* , but upon the activities of those around him.

32.2   The excellence of the members of the government is described in four images related to the climate. The first two represent the rulers as a protection from *wind* and *storm*, words denoting attacks on the people's security. The irony is that all too often the rulers were the cause of the oppression, not the *refuge* from it. *runnels* stresses that the channels are artifical; agriculture in the Middle East is entirely dependent on irrigation. The rulers will provide blessings as vital to the people as *water* is to the fields. The sun could quickly shrivel anything without deep roots, so *shade* was important (cf. Isa. 4.6; 25.4.).

32.3 Once true justice is established, there will be an end to the confusions which always benefited the manipulators. This verse should be linked with passages like 6.9f. and 29.9–12 which point out that deafness to the truth afflicts recalcitrant people. Here we have the opposite.

32.4 There is profound understanding here, not simply exuberant optimism. Impetuousness is often caused by insecurity, stammering is the result of the speaker being overawed. When true peace and justice arrive, these conditions will disappear.

32.5 There is no better indicator of the health of a society than the kind of person who prospers and is honoured within it. REB is right to preserve NEB's *scoundrel*. A more common rendering of the Heb. word is 'fool' (NRSV), but folly in Heb. was not an unfortunate shortcoming, rather a corruption of thought, word and action.

32.6f. The editor now turns to the basic contrast of the wisdom literature, that between the wise man and the fool (cf. Prov. 13–5). The verses strip away the disguise of the rogue and reveal his true nature. In word, thought and conduct he is false, even false before Yahweh. The most notable index of his villainy is his attitude to *the needy*. Here the editor or the wisdom writer lines himself up with the prophetic tradition (Amos 2.6f.; 4.1; 5.11; 8.4–6 etc.).

32.8 The one *of noble mind* is the exact opposite. The word means 'generous' 'open', 'willing'. In AV and RV it is rendered 'liberal', that is, the opposite of 'mean'. The noble man is not simply open, as opposed to devious, generous as opposed to mean, but *he stands firm*, unlike the villain who can never be relied on.

A harsh warning

32.9–15a

The chapter, which in 1–5 and 15b–20 is so hopeful, is interrupted by this very threatening section. The passage follows the prophetic tradition in the minimal sense, that is to say, it foretells a period of distress; but it does not interpret the disaster in terms of moral judgement, nor attribute it to Yahweh.

32.9 The attack upon *women* is reminiscent of Amos 4.1 and Isa. 3.16–26, but it is hard to see why they are singled out when men and women will suffer together. There is no suggestion that the women were guilty of any particular sin, so it may simply be that women were more given to public celebration than men. *listen attentively* (cf. 28.23) represents the style of wisdom writing rather than prophecy, as in vv. 6–8. The force of 9f. is the sudden change of fortune between the present condition of living *at ease* (alluded to five times in three verses) and the desperate trouble to come.

32.10 It was at the autumn festival, when the long hot summer was over and the year 'turned', that the most *carefree* celebrating took place (cf. Judg. 21.19–22; Deut. 16.13f.; Isa. 16.10). *quaking* in fear is the perfect antithesis to dancing for joy. No reason is given for the *failure* of *the vintage*.

32.11 The contrast continues. Mourning rites included tearing clothes and wearing sackcloth (Gen. 37.34; I Sam. 4.12; II Sam. 1.2; 3.31).

32.12 Beating the breast appears as a sign of distress in Luke 18.13 and 23.48. It was a graphic way of expressing to the world that one was enduring pain. Similar actions are widespread in the modern world. The British 'stiff upper lip' tradition is not a very healthy way of handling grief.

32.13 *my people* shows that the writer is a member of the doomed community. Not only will the harvest be lost but the whole *land* will produce only *thorns and briars* (cf. 5.6). The women will mourn for homes, at present *happy*, but soon to be wrecked. *the bustling city* is presumably Jerusalem.

32.14 Only animals roaming *wild* will be found in the *streets* and this situation will last *for ever*, which seems like hyperbole.

32.15a By making a break at the end of 14, GNB and JB emphasize that 9–14 is a foreign body in the chapter. Other translations have no break and so link the warning and the promise. REB, by including 15a in the warning, puts a time limit on the desolation. The *spirit from on high* is a source of power *lavished upon* the people by Yahweh, but we must be careful not to identify this term with the Holy Spirit of Christian theology. Attributing personality to spirits from God in the OT often means overinterpreting the text. Translators frequently have difficulty deciding whether the word needs a capital letter. Compare RSV and NRSV.

A peaceful future
32.15b–20

The chapter closes with an idyllic picture of a land of righteousness and peace. It brings to an end one section of the book of Isaiah, for nothing in chs. 34–66 can reasonably be attributed to Isaiah, the son of Amoz, and the same is probably true of ch. 33. There are few clues to indicate the authorship of this passage. There is no suggestion that exile and return must intervene before the peaceful future arrives, so the author must have functioned well before 597. Isaiah himself is not ruled out. REB's decision to make a break after 15a has the effect of separating the gift of the spirit in 15a from the new age of 15b–20. This pleases few commentators. They draw attention to the fact that elsewhere the advent of the golden age is linked with the spirit (Isa. 44.3–5; Joel 2.28f.; Zech. 12.10), and that REB is working against the Hebrew author, who intended to make the advent of the spirit the connecting link between the disaster that precedes and the peace that follows. The vision pictures a world from which all the un-pleasant realities of the present, land shortage, drought, war and other disruptions, are removed. The tranquility depends absolutely on the prior establishment of justice and righteousness.

32.15bc   These lines closely resemble 29.17. There were vast deserts and huge areas of scrubland in the ANE; the problem was that so little of it could support agriculture. If *garden land* was *as common as scrub*, then prosperity would have arrived.

32.16   The fecundity of the land was the gift of Yahweh, but he would never grant it simply to satisfy his people's greed. *Justice* and *righteousness* were the key. They, too, were gifts of Yahweh, but gifts that had been consistently rejected. Once they were accepted and established, all the rest would follow.

32.17   If not Isaiah, the author certainly understood Isaianic theology. The ideal condition for a people and the consequence of *righteousness* was not fretting or intriguing or plotting but *quiet trust* in Yahweh. 32.17 echoes 7.4 and 30.15 and uses some of the same words. *peace* is a sublime word in Heb., meaning the best of everything.

32.18   The word translated *security* is used for *at ease* in 32.9, 11, but there is a world of difference in the overtone. This is a cardinal point in Isaiah's theology. You can be *at ease* now, on your own terms, or you can live in *security* under Yahweh's will. The difference is that the former state can be suddenly shattered; the latter is as stable as Yahweh himself.

32.19   The literal meaning of the Heb. is very difficult, though most commentators believe that it implies disaster for the *forest* and the *cities* (RV, RSV, JB, NIV, and NRSV). One explanation is that the verse is displaced and belongs between 14 and 15. Another is to relate the verse to Israel's enemies; they are the *forest* (of soldiers) and theirs are the *cities* that suffer. NEB and REB solve the problem speculatively by changing the verse into a happy continuation of 18.

32.20   There will be no irrigation problems and, so extensive will be the pastures that there will be no need to keep *ox and donkey* confined.

A prophetic psalm
33.1–24

This chapter is often referred to as a prophetic liturgy, though there are no real signs of cultic usage. It is better to regard it as a discourse within the prophetic tradition which repeatedly crosses the boundaries between oracle and psalmody (cf. Micah 7.7–20; Hab. 3;

conversely, some psalms have a prophetical element, e.g. 60). As far as sense is concerned, there are changes of direction every few verses; woe, prayer, lamentation, affirmation, promise tumble out one after another. In these circumstances it is not easy, and perhaps not necessary, to define the constituent parts. Broadly speaking, the subject matter is lamentation at the presence of an enemy and assurance that he will be destroyed and that Jerusalem will at last enjoy peace and prosperity. The enemy is never named and guesses range from Babylon to the Greeks. Though there are allusions to Isaianic language, few think that the passage belongs to the period of the Assyrian threat. We shall read the passage as a whole but note the changes of style and address as we go along.

33.1 *Woe* formulae are found in 3.9 and 11 as well as elsewhere in the OT. They amount to a mild form of curse without any magical element. The object is an unnamed *destroyer* who is, for the moment, still standing strong. It is vain to seek for a particular occasion. Enmity always leads to the attribution of every kind of villainy to the other party, so there could hardly be a crisis where this language did not fit. The last two lines are very confident. No grounds are given for this confidence, but the context shows that Yahweh alone provides the author's never-failing security.

33.2 The author turns to prayer in language similar to that of psalms of lamentation. From bitter experience arises devout petition. *troubles* – a vague term; the context suggests that they are caused by the *destroyer*. The sufferer needs courage *every morning* to face the new day.

33.3 Elemental forces are often used to describe Yahweh's power. They demonstrate the difference in scale between Yahweh and the human race. A man's shout will scatter pigeons; Yahweh's *roar* scatters *nations*.

33.4 The author's mind wanders to a less exalted aspect of victory. When the *destroyer* and his forces have been defeated, the victors – surely the Israelites – will descend on the battlefield like *locusts* to strip the dead of their valuables.

33.5 The writing now assumes the form of a hymn. It is a statement about Yahweh's nature, not about the people's virtue. *justice and righteousness* belong to *Zion* by divine decree. That does not mean that they can always be found there. See v. 14.

33.6   The Heb. is difficult and REB achieves three parallel lines only by emending it. Even so the result is imperfect, for in REB, 6a is addressed to Yahweh, whereas 5 and 6c refer to Yahweh in the third person. 6b makes an unusual point. *deliverance*, often translated 'salvation', lies in *wisdom and knowledge*. Traditionally salvation lay in victory over circumstances. Here it lies in the virtues of the people, which suggests a background when *wisdom* was prized more than victories in battle; perhaps a time, after 586, when the work of the sages had come to the fore and Israel was not operating as a military power. In both senses the salvation is a gift from Yahweh.

33.7   The next two verses return to the lament theme. The lack of evidence regarding date means that we cannot be certain who the *envoys*, lit. 'messengers of peàce', were. Presumably they were Israelites who had been sent to negotiate *peace* and failed.

33.8   A picture of a land in turmoil. The fact that the *highways* were *deserted* meant that the caravans had ceased to operate, which in turn meant that life was reduced to subsistence level (cf. Judg. 5.6). Normal trading had broken down; people did not stand by promises. The MT has 'cities', not *treaties* but long ago scholars suggested that 'cities' was a scribal error for a similar word meaning 'witnesses'. Then, when the Isaiah scroll was discovered at Qumran, there was the word 'witnesses' in the text – a reassuring piece of evidence that scholarly guesses must be taken seriously. REB carries the process one stage further with the rendering *treaties*.

33.9   It was too dangerous to work the *land*, and its neglected condition gave rise to this metaphor drawn from the experience of drought. The four places named were well-known for the luxuriance of their fields or forests. *Lebanon* was in the far north. See note on 14.8. *Sharon* was a fertile coastal plain west of Samaria. *Bashan*, famous for its cattle, lay north-east of the Sea of Galilee. *Carmel*, well forested in biblical times, was the ridge that runs north-west to south-east across the land to the north of Samaria.

33.10   As often in the psalter, Yahweh speaks in response to the lament with an oracle of salvation. This is one reason why many scholars are persuaded that prophets had a function in the cult: to provide Yahweh's response to a petition.

33.11 Yahweh addresses his enemies. The metaphor in 11a is clear, if unusual. *a wind* – (Heb. *rûaḥ*); the fact that *rûaḥ* can mean 'wind', 'breath' and 'spirit' gives rise to some of the most interesting questions of interpretation in the OT (cf. 32.15).

33.12 The *nations* are Israel's enemies. REB's *white ash* follows the previous line neatly.

33.13 The break between 12 and 13 in REB is hard to defend. V. 13 represents a final appeal to all nations to recognize how things are. A new section begins with 14. *afar off* and *near at hand* is a way of including everybody.

33.14 The author turns on the present occupants of *Zion*. The form of vv. 14–16 is liturgical and has parallels in Pss. 15 and 24. Only the righteous have a place in *Zion*, hence the need to question those who arrive at the gates (Ps. 24.3–5). But here the wrong people are in possession of the city. So the questions are asked by the *Sinners* within, not the pilgrims without.

33.15 The issue is not whether Yahweh will deliver his chosen city, but who is fit to live in it when he does. The same theme occurs in Mal. 3.1–3, another of those OT passages made famous by Handel. The qualifications of those who will survive the 'refiner's fire' are similar to those set out in Ps. 15 and more briefly in Ps. 24.4. They are ethical and practical. The righteous do not pretend that *murder* and *evil* do not exist, but they refuse to have any part in them.

33.16 Zion represents *the heights* in both a physical and a moral sense. Zion is *a fastness* in both senses too. The last line is a reminder that the author, visionary though he may be, has his feet on the ground. One problem of lofty fortresses was that *food* had to be laboriously carried up, but an even greater problem was *water*, as Hezekiah's tunnel bears witness (II Kings 20.20).

33.17 Another change of emphasis and the passage becomes a prophetic promise of a glorious future similar to 32.1–5. Some understand the *king* as Yahweh, but a human king is more probable.

ANE kings were often tyrants, but the Israelite ideal was a king of Davidic qualities, who was Yahweh's son, Yahweh's chosen, and a guarantor of Yahweh's protection (cf. Ps. 2). This verse, therefore, falls within the Isaiah tradition of messianic expectation. The *land stretching into the distance* is the full Davidic kingdom, not a land hedged in, as it so often was in history, by enemies. The *king* and his people would be able to *look on* it, that is to say, oversee and enjoy possession of it.

33.18   The two questions refer to the predatory habits of conquerors who invariably demanded tribute (see II Kings 18.13–6). The inhabitants of the liberated land would be able to look back on such horrors with relief. *treasures* requires a slight emendment, but makes better sense than the MT 'towers'.

33.19   No humiliation is worse than seeing the government of one's homeland conducted by those who do not speak the language and who are therefore deaf to the pleas of the local people (cf. Isa. 28.11). All that will be a thing of the past.

33.20   How different the new *Zion* will be! The term *sacred feasts* indicates how impossible it is to separate social and religious life in Israel. Festivity was inextricably entwined with worship. *Jerusalem* is described as a *tent*, reminiscent of the tabernacle of the wilderness story, but it is a *tent* that is not *moved*. Tent-dwellers kept moving, not because they enjoyed touring, but because local resources were quickly exhausted. A permanent place represented an ideal. The last two lines seem an unnecessary addition.

33.21   Yahweh *in all his majesty* will reign in Jerusalem. But after 21a the image begins to break down and it requires all the ingenuity of commentators to provide a coherent reading of the last four verses, to say nothing of a climactic end to the section. The prophecy tends to lose touch with the realism that marks pre-exilic prophecy. Jerusalem becomes *a place of rivers and broad streams*, though, in the normal course of things, broad streams do not spring from rocky outcrops like Zion. Ezek. 47 shares a similarly supernatural vision. It is denied that foreign or hostile *ships* will be able to enter the waters, lest we think that rivers will make Jerusalem worse off.

33.22   This verse has the form of a liturgical exclamation akin to 'The

Lord reigns' in the psalms (93.1 etc.). It seems strangely placed after
v. 21, but it would follow well after 20c or 21a. *judge, lawgiver* and *king*
are all positive words with a firm place in Hebrew hopes. Just as the
king, properly understood, heralds a peaceful and godly society, so
the *judge* signifies a just one. If Yahweh fills all these roles, peace and
prosperity are assured.

33.23 Commentators have long puzzled how to explain the first
three lines. They seem to be a rude comment on a ship; but which
ship? Can 21ab possibly be an image of Yahweh as a boat? If so, the
lines are an enemy's taunt against Yahweh. But, as they come near
the end of the passage and are never answered, we can hardly be
satisfied with that explanation. We have to say that, for a reason we
cannot now divine, foreign material has crept into the text creating
nonsense. That, no doubt, is why REB puts the lines in brackets. The
last two lines are a little easier, though the text needs emendation. In
the great day the victory will be so complete that even the least
capable of military prowess (cf. II Sam. 5.6) will be able to take their
share of the spoil.

33.24 Relying on the Hebrew belief that sickness follows sin, the
author promises that, by Yahweh's grace, the sinners *will be pardoned*
and sickness will be no more.

Edom and Israel
34.1–35.10

Chs. 34–35 are sometimes called 'the Little Apocalypse', notably by those who refer to chs. 24–27 as 'the Isaiah Apocalypse', but once again caution is necessary. These chapters are about great future events, but that does not make them 'apocalyptic' in the true sense (see pp. 143, 160). The chapters describe the downfall of Edom and the glorious return of the Lord's people to Zion, with unrestrained enthusiasm.

The position of chs. 34–35 allows for different theories about their origin. If they are taken separately, 34 must be related to 1–33 and 35 to 40–55 (chs. 36–39 are an obvious insertion). But, if, as is more reasonable, they are taken together, they may be regarded as a final, summarizing comment on the ways of Yahweh as set out in chs. 28–33 (or even 1–33), or as an introduction to 40–55, perhaps by the same author, whom we call Second Isaiah. The most interesting hypothesis, however, is that the chapters were composed by an editor who was dependent on both First and Second Isaiah and who was anxious to tie the two books together with a piece that looked both backwards and forwards. Whatever the truth may be, it is as a link passage that we read the chapters today.

While few complain of the exuberant prophecy in ch. 35, the language of 34 is, quite simply, malevolent and crude. The author appears over-confident, not to say self-righteous, on Israel's behalf. The only defence is that, if they are taken together, chs. 34 and 35 point to a God who acts in history in righteousness and love. Unworthy motives surface because not all editors were saints and visionaries and the meaning of history is not so easy to read.

Doom for Edom
34.1–17

Ch. 34 describes the terrible consequences for Edom of the final intervention of Yahweh. It is not prophecy in the straightforward sense; the framework is cosmic (v. 4) and no earthly forces are involved. This indicates a post-exilic background, when Israel was more inclined to look for salvation from overt divine intervention than from a divine ordering of the common affairs of the nations. The antipathy between Israel and Edom was deep rooted. In the tradition it went back to the dissension between Jacob and Esau (Gen. 25.24–34). Hebrew annals record the refusal of Edom to allow the wandering Israelites to pass through its territory (Num. 20.14–21). Throughout history Edom coveted Israel's land (and vice versa), and it appears that, when Judah was depopulated and vulnerable in 586, Edom tried to profit from it (Obad. 11). Not surprisingly Jeremiah (49.7–22) and Ezekiel (25.1–14) have little good to say of Edom (cf. Ps. 137.7). It is wrong, however, to link the whole of the chapter with Edom. The first four verses are about all the nations and Edom emerges in vv. 5f. as a specially selected representative rather than as the only guilty one.

34.1 The *nations* are invited to observe a divine act of justice. The formula suggests a court, but there is no trial. The question of guilt is settled; all that remains is the sentence. Second Isaiah makes use of the same grandiloquent style (41.1; 43.9; 45.20; 48.16). In harsh reality only Jews would hear or read these words, but they were able to draw comfort from the belief that Yahweh would one day call the *nations* to order.

34.2 No reason is given for Yahweh's *anger*. In the post-exilic period the guilt of the nations of the world, all seen in one way or another as oppressors of Israel, was taken for granted. The sentence is that *the nations* be given up to holy *slaughter*. The complete destruction of an enemy, including women, children and cattle, was a chilling feature of life in the ANE. Joshua 'devoted' Jericho (Josh. 6.21) and Saul, instructed to 'devote' Amalek (I Sam. 15.3), was punished for sparing some cattle! Such wanton destruction offends our humanitarian instincts and, as a divine action, presents us with the gravest theological problems, even though, in modern times, we have been able to reconcile ourselves to saturation bombing as consistent with the divine will. The ancient argument depended on the belief that a community could so offend the divine majesty that it had to be removed from sight altogether so that it could never reappear. Such a notion of divine majesty (and, indeed, of the real being of communities) is impressive, though the rest of the logic is intolerable.

34.3 There is not much exaggeration in this verse. Unburied bodies in Palestine quickly stink and add to the horror.

34.4 The author now departs from realism and, in apocalyptic style, foretells the end of *the host of heaven* and *the heavens* themselves. Astral deities were worshipped by Israel's neighbours though the practice was banned in Israel (Deut. 4.19; 17.3). Here they are dealt with radically; even *the heavens* themselves, sometimes referred to as a kind of curtain (Job 9.8; Ps. 104.2; Isa. 40.22), will be disposed of. The final simile is powerful; if *the foliage* of *the vine* can wither when the season is over, so can the heavenly lights when their time is called.

34.5 There is no hint of a human agent and the vision is totally unrealistic. Yahweh's metaphorical *sword* descends on *Edom*, now picked out for representative destruction. The last line in Heb. is difficult, but it includes another reference to the total destruction of an enemy as a religious duty (Heb. *ḥerem*).

34.6 The image is puzzling because it associates the blood-letting in Edom with *sacrifice*. The killing of animals was linked with sacrifice, but the most common sacrifices (peace offerings, 'shared-offerings' in REB) were joyful celebrations in which a spotless animal, first offered in the sanctuary, was eaten by the worshippers. In this verse the destructive elements in sacrifice are abstracted from the rest of the rite. There is a neat rhyme between *sacrifice* and *slaughter* in Heb. (6de), which may explain why the metaphor is used in this way. *Bozrah*, 25 miles south of the Dead Sea, was the chief city of *Edom*.

34.7 Evocation of the *ḥerem* and of the rite of sacrifice is not enough. Even wild animals will pour out their blood on this unhappy land.

34.8 The word *vengeance* has bad overtones in English suggesting bitter passions, festering hatred, loss of control. Few would describe the proceedings of our courts as exacting vengeance. The Heb. word was not so negative; it implied a just requital, a putting right of wrongs, the restoration of dues to the ill-used. In a generally harsh and unjust world, such requital was properly longed for. This is the first hint of a reason for the great doom. Yahweh acts as *the champion of Zion*, which suggests that the guilt of the nations lay in their oppression of Israel.

34.9 The Heb. reads 'her' *torrents*. REB includes the name for clarity's sake, but it is notable that Edom is not mentioned again. Vv. 9f. describe volcanic phenomena. The slopes of a volcano remain barren for years after eruption. This language, however, may be derived from the description of the end of Sodom in Gen. 19.24–8.

34.10 The author piles up words, *never, for ever, age after age, ever again* to stress the utter desolation and unfruitfulness of the doomed land. The passion of the author is inescapable.

34.11 Passion is not always a reliable guide. The author is now led into a series of wild predictions scarcely consistent with those just expressed. Birds, who could never exist in the land of v. 9, will find a *home* there. Several species cannot be identified with certainty. This hardly matters. The intention is to describe an area, formerly prosperous, now completely broken down, so that only wild and dreadful creatures can survive there (cf. 32.14). The words *chaos* and *jumble* translate *tōhû* and *bōhû*, words that appear in Gen. 1.2 with the meaning 'without form and void' (REB 'a vast waste'). Yahweh, who had ordered the world in creation, was now returning the land to its pre-creation formlessness.

34.12 This verse reads like an anti-climax. NRSV provides a more dramatic rendering by translating *mᵉlûkâ* (an abstract noun meaning 'kingship') as 'kingdom' rather than *king*.

34.13 The next three verses extend the sense of 11ab, but fail to increase the horror of 9f. The point, however, that human civilization has of itself no permanence in Yahweh's world, is well and truly made.

34.14 There are some grounds for saying that the *he-goats* and *the nightjar* were really demons. The former is rendered 'demons' in Lev. 17.7 and the latter, which occurs nowhere else in the Heb. Bible, came to be used in a demonic sense in later Judaism. The line between feared, but rarely seen, creatures and imaginary, demonic creatures could not be clearly drawn in ancient Israel. Unpleasant birds or beasts might, therefore, be supposed to have even more unpleasant relations. The terms used are meant to inspire fear.

34.15   The author extends his argument by showing that the intruders will not simply arrive for a brief call but will stay and breed.

34.16   Every detail of this future is recorded and it will be possible to check that it is all true. Nothing will escape Yahweh's attention (cf. 40.26). It is not so clear what *book* is meant. Presumably some prophetic text is indicated, but whether the present one, or some other prophetic writing, or all the books of all the prophets is not certain. *his own mouth* and *his spirit* are again allusions to the creation story of Gen. 1. What Yahweh did then he can undo and reorder his creation as he wishes.

34.17   The verse affirms the absolute authority of Yahweh over his world. The essence of the creation was imposing order on chaos. Now Yahweh imposes a new order to the disadvantage of Edom and the sinful nations she represents. The intruders will have their place *for all time*.

If this chapter seems venomous and terrible, we must remind ourselves of two cardinal principles of OT interpretation. First, the text must be seen in its cultural setting. We cannot assess OT writing from the standpoint of our more sophisticated (but often equally venomous) culture. Secondly, the book must be read as a whole. Ch. 35 contains a very different message.

The glorious return to Zion
35.1–10

The denunciation of evil nations is over and the author turns to the glorious prospect for the faithful. Language, imagery, style are suggestive of Second Isaiah, but close attention to the text shows that it goes some way beyond Second Isaiah in expectation. Second Isaiah spoke of a return of the exiles from Babylon; ch. 35 envisages a return of all Yahweh's people together with a transformation of the natural order. This casts doubt on the theory that chs. 34–35 were composed simply as a link. They are a link, but they are more than a link. They carry the prophecies of both chs. 1–33 and 40–55 on to a new point where they bear on a situation, the author's situation, which was in some ways worse than the Babylonian exile and yet which was inspired by an even greater hope. In origin, therefore, the chapters probably come from the days of Israel's sufferings under Persia, the first of the great world empires. But, in their present context, they serve not so much to illuminate the dark days after the exile as to intepret all the prophecies of the book of Isaiah in terms of ultimate judgment and hope. The basic theme is a divine self-manifestation which involves a transformation of nature and which culminates in the triumphant return of Yahweh's people to Zion. Due, no doubt, to its ringing optimism, the passage is one of the best known and most favoured in the OT.

35.1   Vv. 1–7 deal with a series of reversals, most of them in the order of nature. A similar hope regarding *the wilderness* is found in 43.19f., but Second Isaiah keeps his feet on the ground more than the present author. In this passage the *desert* will simply disappear; better still, it will *burst into flower*. The glorious line from the AV, 'The desert shall rejoice, and blossom as the rose' has to be abandoned because the last word of v. 1, giving us 'as the rose', truly belongs to 2a.

35.2   *asphodel* is probably right, though 'lily' and 'crocus' have their defenders; the word occurs only here and in S. of Sol. 2.1. Lyrical Heb. readily personifies natural features (cf. 55.12); here the desert will *rejoice and shout for joy*. It will produce, not simply grass, but all the luxurious growth of *Lebanon, Carmel and Sharon* (cf. 33.9). Nature transformed will both exhibit and *see the glory of the Lord*.

35.3   The hard facts of the present, however, are that the faithful are drooping. So they must be encouraged by the vision of future deliverance.

35.4   Salvation, in this case, means putting right the wrongs that Yahweh's people have suffered for decades. For *vengeance*, see note on 34.8.

35.5f.   Some commentators are inclined to treat these dramatic reversals as metaphors for a change in the spiritual condition of the people, but the OT is more down-to-earth than that. What better way to communicate the glorious hope than by reference to the people who need it most? Nature will be transformed, and so will afflicted humans. There were more *blind* and the *deaf* in ancient times than we see today; they constituted an ever-present reminder of the broken-ness of human life. Hope continually focusses on their plight (cf. 61.1–3; Matt. 11.5).

35.7 This verse continues to expatiate on the renewal of nature, though there are difficulties. The first noun means literally 'burning heat' and few commentators accept NEB/REB's *mirage* (but see RV marg.). The real question, however, is how to read the image. REB suggests that pastures will take the place of swamp, that is, *reeds and rushes*. RSV/NRSV reverse this and see swamps with *reeds and rushes* taking over from the grass or scrub, where jackals now live. The latter makes better sense.

35.8 The general picture of renewal becomes more specific. The return of the exiles, as forecast by Second Isaiah, provides the starting-point. When the Hebrews were in Babylon, 400 miles of scorching desert separated them from their homeland. The normal route passed round the northern edge of the desert; hence the name 'fertile crescent'. But Isa. 40.3 conceives of a direct route through the desert and our author follows this. Indeed, in his enthusiasm, he sees the *causeway* as the means to bring all Yahweh's scattered people home. The Heb. is again difficult. Both REB and NRSV make constructive guesses and provide reasonable, but not identical, translations. *the Way of Holiness* is the processional route that leads to the holy hill of Zion (cf. Ps. 24). The *unclean* are are not fit to enter the temple area. Folly, in Hebrew tradition, was a moral, rather than a mental, matter (cf. Pss. 14.1; 74.18), so the *fool* had no place on the highway.

35.9 Preying beasts provided one of the hazards of travel in the ANE, but not in the renewed world of this vision (cf. 11.6–9). The redemption in 9d is all-embracing. The Heb. word translated *redeemed* refers to the function, usually carried out by a senior member of the family, of obtaining the release of dependants who, for whatever reason, found themselves in trouble.

35.10 Chs. 36–39 are a historical narrative, so this verse concludes the prophetic oracles in Isa. 1–39 and it could scarcely be more fitting. It is taken verbatim from 51.11. The Hebrews not only shared with all peoples a love of their homeland, but they believed that it was given to them by Yahweh. *Zion* was a sanctuary appointed, not by them, but by him (Deut. 12.5; 16.2; 26.2). History, however, had dealt badly with the Hebrews and by the fifth century BCE they were scattered all over the Mediterranean world. Nevertheless *Zion* was still their only hallowed place and *everlasting joy* would come to them only when, at last, they were able to return.

The Jewish people, through all their troubled history, have never lost this sense of attachment to the land and to Zion. Some Jews, though not all, still read verses such as these in a concrete and practical sense and, as all the world knows, the question has now become highly complex and political. The Christian church claims to have inherited this promise, but has de-localized Zion, seeing it partly in the universal existence of the church and partly in the heavenly Jerusalem beyond time and space (Gal. 4.26; Heb. 12.22; Rev. 3.12; 21.2, 10).

Jerusalem delivered
36.1–39.8

The presence of this section, inserted after chs. 34–35, obscures the link which chs. 34–35 make between the first part of the book of Isaiah and the second. Chs. 36–9 are not prophetic oracle but historical narrative. They recount three narratives: the first (36–37) describes the deliverance of Jerusalem from Sennacherib in 701, the second (38) Hezekiah's illness and recovery, and the third (39) the arrival of envoys from Babylon at Hezekiah's court. The whole, apart from 38.9–20 (Hezekiah's poem), is a close parallel of II Kings 18.13–20.19. As we shall see, the evidence shows that Isaiah's editors borrowed from II Kings, so the section first appeared as part of the Deuteronomistic history (Joshua–II Kings), not as part of Isaiah.

The Deuteronomistic history, however, itself had sources, including narratives about prophets, Ahijah, Micaiah ben Imlah, Elijah, Elisha. II Kings 18.13–20.19 is somewhat similar; it refers several times to Isaiah the man and makes occasional allusions to his recorded teaching. But taken as a whole, it is more concerned with Hezekiah and the fate of Jerusalem than with Isaiah. Neither Isaiah nor Hezekiah appears here in the same guise as in the prophecy. In the first two narratives (II Kings 18.13–20.11; Isa. 36–38), Isaiah, who had warned consistently that judgement would follow disloyalty to Yahweh, becomes a confident prophet of hope, as if there had been no disloyalty, and Hezekiah, who, in his overtures to Egypt, had revealed his folly and deafness to the prophetic word, becomes the pious and obedient monarch who goes readily to Isaiah for advice.

There is no doubt then that Isa. 36–39 has a long and complicated literary history. A simplifed and still very controversial sketch of that history is as follows. (a) In the early seventh century BCE, soon after Isaiah's death, an account was made, perhaps more than one, of the events in which Isaiah and Hezekiah played a part; of these sources we know little. (b) Towards the end of the seventh century editors took over the sources and revised them according to their own theological convictions and precise needs. Their most prominent convictions were that Yahweh would defend Jerusalem, though other cities of Judah might fall, that the throne of David would be preserved, and that Hezekiah and Isaiah were, in their separate ways, symbols of Yahweh's presence in Israel. The survival of Jerusalem in 701 was regarded, not as a humiliating event with a fortunate conclusion, but as a divine deliverance revealing Yahweh's care for his chosen city. The first two narratives must have appeared at this time, before these convictions were challenged by the fall of Jerusalem in 586 BCE. The narrative of the envoys from Babylon (II Kings 20.12–19; Isa. 39) is later and informed by different convictions, as we shall see. (c) In time the compilers of II Kings incorporated these highly theological narratives into the Deuteronomistic history, from whence, very late in the day, they were taken into the book of Isaiah, no doubt so that all the material regarding the great prophet might be brought together into a single document. (d) Even this is not the end because a summary of the same events occurs in II Chron. 32 with yet a different slant, though we may fairly set it on one side as being only marginally relevant to our purpose.

A final point needs to be made regarding the nature and purpose of these narratives. There is a widely held view that narratives having the form of historical records are interesting and important only in so far as they reveal what actually happened. In the Bible, however, quasi-historical narratives are often used for making non-historical points. 'History' is written, on the basis of the scantiest evidence, to affirm faith, not to record facts. Appreciation of Isa. 36–9, therefore, must be determined by how the section reads as a paradigm of Yahweh's saving activity; it must not be surrendered if we discover elements that, in terms of what actually happened, are insecure.

The repulse of the Assyrians
36.1–37.38

The first fact to be noted is the way the passages begin. II Kings 18.13 equals Isa. 36.1, but the next three verses from II Kings are missing from Isaiah. The rest (II Kings 18.17–19.37 and Isaiah 36.2–37.38) is common to both. It tells of an Assyrian envoy calling for Jerusalem's surrender, Hezekiah's consultation with Isaiah, Isaiah's confident response, and the swift departure of Sennacherib and his troops after an angel of Yahweh smote them. The three verses missing from Isaiah (II Kings 18.14–16), however, tell a different story. Hezekiah sent a message of penitence to Sennacherib at Lachish confessing his disloyalty. Sennacherib demanded a huge tribute. Hezekiah paid up, even stripping the gold from the doors of the temple to meet the demand.

By good fortune the Assyrian account of Sennacherib's campaign has been preserved (*ANET*, pp. 287f.). It confirms the capture of many Judahite cities (Isa. 36.1; II Kings 18.13); it also confirms Hezekiah's humiliation and, though the figures differ slightly, his giving of tribute (II Kings 18.14–16); but it says nothing about the rest of the narrative. There is no mention of the envoy calling for surrender, Hezekiah's reaction, the confident utterances of Isaiah, the staggering loss of 185,000 troops, nor of Sennacherib's hasty departure.

These facts strongly suggest that the text of II Kings contains two accounts of the same event, a brief and tragic account in 18.13–16, confirmed by the Assyrian record, and a long and much more positive one in 18.17–19.37.[1] At some stage in the editing the two have been uncomfortably joined together. The Isaiah version includes only the latter, but, because that longer account lacks an introductory verse giving the date and the circumstances, the Isaiah version borrows the first verse from the brief account. This surely indicates that Isaiah is dependent on Kings rather than the other way round.

The first part of our passage, 36.1–37.7, consists of three scenes, the envoy's speech, Hezekiah's reaction, and Isaiah's comment. Then, in the second part, 37.8–35, those scenes are repeated in different words. It is possible that the actions took place twice – negotiations do tend to be repetitive – but it is more likely that we have another repetition, the same story in two different forms, perhaps from two different authors. II Chron. 32.1–22 assimiliates the two forms. In the present passage, therefore, we have a narrative in two cycles, each with three scenes, together with a finale in 37.36–38.[2]

---

[1] Some commentators have argued that the two accounts belong to different occasions and that both can be taken as fair reports of what happened, but there is little hard evidence that there was any second occasion when an Assyrian army threatened Jerusalem.

[2]
Introduction	36.1	
Link		37.8
1st scene	36.2–22	37.9–13
2nd scene	37.1–4	37.14–20
3rd scene	37.5–7	37.21–35
Conclusion		37.36–38

The first scene of the first cycle takes place before the walls of Jerusalem. It is largely concerned with the speech of the Assyrian envoy, and may well have a factual basis. That basis, however, is of little importance beside the brilliant composition of the author. To suit his purpose the speech had to contain the Assyrian case argued in the most persuasive way; the more arrogant and aggressive, the better. But, at the same time, the speech had to show how totally ineffective it all was. The readers had to be reminded that the Assyrian plan failed and Jerusalem was delivered by Yahweh. In this first scene Assyrian power is built up so that, later, it can come crashing down. The second scene, 37.1–4, shows Hezekiah behaving with all modesty and piety. The third reveals Isaiah's absolute confidence in Yahweh (37.5–7).

The second cycle begins with a connecting verse in v. 8. In 37.10–13 the messengers press an argument similar to that of 36.18–20 and, therefore, to the boast of 10.8–11. In 14–20 Hezekiah goes to the temple again and falls to prayer. The prayer is profoundly theological and calls to mind the great prayer attributed to Solomon at the consecration of the temple (I Kings 8.22–53; cf. David's prayer in II Sam. 7.18–29). There follows (21–35) Isaiah's response, much longer here than in the first cycle, probably because an original, short version (37. 33–5) has been expanded and made even more telling by insertions.

Finally in 37.36–8 there is the conclusion to the whole story. V. 36 recounts a staggering miracle. Vv. 37f. provide a tidy end.

In the whole of this narrative, Hezekiah and Isaiah never meet, though, in the embattled city, they could never have been more than a few hundred yards apart. This shows that the author is not recounting events as they happened but proclaiming a faith, in which king and prophet stand out separately as living symbols of the supremacy of Yahweh and his word, not as fearful human beings in need of mutual support.

36.1 Pre-exilic chronology is problematic, but this formula must refer to the year 701. The two accounts (II Kings 18.13 and Isa. 36.1) share this introductory verse acknowledging that *Sennacherib* took many Judahite *fortified towns*. Assyrian records give the number as forty-six and add, 'Himself (Hezekiah) I made a prisoner in Jerusalem, his royal residence, like a bird in a cage'.

36.2 Sennacherib, at *Lachish*, was twenty-five miles away. He sent *his chief officer* to demand Hezekiah's surrender. The confrontation took place at the spot where Isaiah accosted Ahaz in 7.3.

36.3 Two of the court officers, *Eliakim* and *Shebna*, have appeared before in 22.15, 20. REB has done its best to provide accurate designations for these functionaries, but the designation of government officials varies from nation to nation; *secretary of state* does not mean the same thing in the USA as in the UK and probably neither has much in common with the position of *Joah*. Reference to other translations reveals the difficulty.

36.4 We might assume that Sennacherib's representative would go straight to the point; he had not come to persuade but to dictate terms. But the speech begins by raising the question of whether the defenders' *confidence* was securely grounded. This is precisely the point that the author was anxious to press upon his readers.

36.5 The officer conveniently raises one of the critical questions of Isaiah's prophecy: on what or *On whom* do the people of Yahweh *rely*?

36.6 Isaiah had repeatedly complained of Hezekiah's willingness to pursue an anti-Assyrian policy on the basis of faith in, and alliance with, *Egypt* (19.1–15; 30.1–7; 31.1–3). Sennacherib's officer neatly sums up what Isaiah himself had often said. The staff that is supposed to support you actually harms you.

36.7 In II Kings 18.3–7 *Hezekiah* is credited with a religious reform along Deuteronomic lines; he *suppressed* the syncretistic sanctuaries and concentrated sacrifice in *Jerusalem* (Deut. 12.1–14) . The author knows that his readers would see this as a good reason why Yahweh should intervene to deliver Hezekiah. So with brilliant irony, he writes a script in which the Assyrian officer reveals understanding of Hezekiah's religious policy and makes use of it, apparently to set one faction in *Judah* against another, but in fact to draw attention to Hezekiah's virtue. This helps to offset the folly alluded to in the previous verse.

36.8 This seems like a generous offer but it is probably meant as a boast. Israel had no cavalry and *Assyria* had horses to spare.

36.10   Surely a direct reference to Isa. 10.5f. It is hard to imagine an Assyrian officer arguing like this, but not at all difficult to see it as the contention of a Deuteronomistic author.

36.11   *Hebrew* was the local demotic tongue; *Aramaic* was used more widely and was the language of diplomacy. By NT times it had taken the place of *Hebrew* for common (but not for religious) purposes. Evidently common people were within earshot and the officials were hoping for secret negotiations.

36.12   The *officer* replies that it is the common *people* who will have to suffer the siege with its attendant horrors.

36.13f.   More irony. Beside *the king of Assyria, Hezekiah* is *powerless*, but in the real situation, of which the officer was ignorant, both the king of Assyria and Hezekiah were powerless before Yahweh.

36.15   The speech is splendidly aggressive, but the author and his readers know perfectly well that the officer is wrong. The more he rants, the more they enjoy it.

36.16   The offer recalls the idyllic picture of prosperity in the time of Solomon (I Kings 4.25); an attractive contrast to what is implied in v. 12.

36.17   The horrors of transportation were well known to the author and his readers. The officer is used by the author to make some shrewd points, but the falsity of his promises is also made clear.

36.18   The next three verses make another theological point. To those who lack understanding Yahweh is just like all the other gods. History, however, and especially the events of 701, has shown that this is not the case. The boasting in vv. 18–20 seems to indicate that the author was familiar with 10.8–11.

36.19   *Hamath*, in the north on the Orontes, occurs frequently in the

OT. *Arpad*, further north still, is not mentioned previously in the historical books; it does occur, however, in Isa. 10.9. The site of *Sepharvaim* is uncertain; the name occurs only in this narrative. *Samaria*, by Deuteronomic understanding, was not saved because of her apostasy.

36.20   A neat argument on the lips of a heathen for the uniqueness of Yahweh, for Jerusalem *was* delivered.

36.22   The curtain comes down on scene one with the Jerusalemites in despair. *their clothes* were *torn* because, by Hebrew usage, deep feelings called for dramatic outward expression, and they were not only in deep trouble but they had just heard blasphemy against the name of Yahweh.

37.1   Scene two shows *Hezekiah* reacting to the crisis. There is little evidence from earlier chapters that Hezekiah was often as demure as this, but part of the author's purpose was to represent the Davidic monarchy in the best possible light. Both cycles point out that the temple was the pre-eminent place where Israel's king could meet with Israel's God.

37.2   Hezekiah had not been so ready to consult *Isaiah* when he was planning his Egyptian alliance. Here, however, he recognizes the prophet's authority at once. Even *the senior priests* went dutifully to him to hear the word of Yahweh. There was no High Priest before the exile; the king had control of the temple.

37.3   *contumely*; 'disgrace' is a more obvious word (cf. NRSV, JB, NIV, etc.). The simile of the woman in childbirth seems hardly fitting; we must assume that it was a common, perhaps proverbial, way of alluding to a dreadful tragedy.

37.4   *give heed to* in English usually suggests compliance, quite the opposite of what is intended. Yahweh will hear and be outraged. An important element in prophecy was intercessory prayer (I Sam. 12.19,23; Amos 7.2,5; Jer. 7.16; 14.11; etc.). *those who will survive* seems to indicate the inhabitants of Jerusalem, the only town not desolated by Sennacherib.

37.5   Scene three: the *officials* approach the prophet. Despite the authority attributed to *Isaiah*, this story is really about Hezekiah and the royal city. The prophet appears as an *éminence grise*, an adviser of recognized authority but without the status and responsibility of the monarch.

37.6   Apparently the officials had no need to say anything. Isaiah answers before the message can be delivered. The reply requires from Hezekiah an attitude totally at odds with that revealed in the shorter account in II Kings 18.13–16.

37.7   The Heb. rendered *I shall sap his morale* means 'I will put a spirit in him'. Yahweh was thought to be responsible for spirits of all kinds, malign as well as good (Judg. 9.23; I Sam. 16.14; I Kings 22.22). The reason given for Sennacherib's withdrawal is *a mere rumour*, presumably of unrest somewhere; not a sudden slaughter as in 37.36. Sennacherib did die a violent death according to 37.38, but not until much later.

37.8   This verse is a link between the first cycle and the second. *the chief officer* returns to the *camp* to find it *moved*. The second cycle, therefore, begins in *Libnah*, a town probably located a few miles north of *Lachish*.

37.9   On the face of it, Sennacherib hears news that leads him to put further pressure on Hezekiah, but there is no other evidence that the two cycles are sequential. The reference to *King Tirhakah* is simply the chronological starting-point of the second cycle. *Cush* is Ethiopia. The Ethiopians controlled Egypt at the time, but it is hard to see how they could have been much of a threat to Sennacherib when he had just defeated Egypt at Eltekeh. The word *again* is not in the Heb., though it does appear in II Kings 19.9.

37.10   As in the other cycle the message is by word of mouth and the argument is exactly the same (cf. 36.18–20).

37.11   The Heb. verb rendered *utterly destroyed* is the horrific word used for the slaughter of every living thing as a religious act (see note on Isa. 34.2). The question, of course, demands the answer no, but every reader knew that escape they did.

37.12   The list of towns in the fertile crescent is impressive, as it was meant to be, but Jerusalem was never to be included in the list.

37.13   Not only the nations were destroyed, but the royal houses too. Conversely, not only would Jerusalem survive, but the Davidic line too. These were the convictions of the author in the days of Josiah when Assyria's power was broken. Some of these place names also occur in 36.19.

37.14f.   The communucation from Sennacherib is now said to be a *letter*. This hardly constitutes a problem despite 37.9f. (and 36.22), because we may reasonably suppose that *Hezekiah* received the news in both a written and an oral form. Hezekiah took the scroll into *the temple*. To *spread it out before the Lord*, that is to say, to present the problem to Yahweh, was itself a *prayer*.

37.16   Israel's teachers never suggested that Yahweh could be *enthroned* at any spot on earth (I Kings 8.27). Neverthless they regarded the ark in the Holy of Holies as a symbolic throne. At each end of the ark stood *the cherubim*, large winged figures whose purpose was to affirm the glory of Yahweh (I Kings 8.6f.; cf. I Sam. 4.4; II Sam. 6.2; Ps. 80.1). The prayer affirms the universal sovereignty of Yahweh and the fact that he created *heaven and earth*, themes of astonishing boldness, even in Josiah's day.

37.17   Sennacherib's offence was not to harry Hezekiah, nor even to threaten Jerusalem, but to *taunt* Yahweh.

37.18   It was essential to the author's purpose that the harsh facts of the case should be fully stated.

37.19   The cults of the ANE were central to the existence of the various nations. Their *gods* were housed in fabulous temples, served by powerful priesthoods, celebrated in elaborate festivals, worshipped with costly sacrifices, and revered as the arbiters of the nations' fortunes by kings and peoples alike. For one nation to say that its gods were more powerful than those of a neighbour was a reasonable expression of local chauvinism; but for one nation to say that all other gods *were no gods* at all, and that all their elaborate cults were founded on nothing is, in the context, scarcely believable. We are so familiar with the monotheist position that we have lost our sense of amazement at the writer's boldness.

37.20 The prayer shows a theological sophistication that is all too often lacking in wartime prayers. Salvation is claimed, not for Israel's own comfort, but so that *the kingdoms of the earth may know* the truth. This kind of universalism reappears in Second Isaiah. It does not imply that all nations will share Israel's privileges, simply that they will know that Yahweh *alone* is *God*.

37.21 In the first cycle Isaiah was given a question to answer. Here he is simply aware of the content of Hezekiah's prayer. This is another sign that the author sees the narrative as theological drama.

37.22 Vv. 22–32 are probably an insertion, perhaps two insertions (22–29 and 30–2). Yahweh addresses Assyria in a brilliant song of mockery. *Zion* is represented as a marrigeable *daughter* who treats Sennacherib's advances with contempt. Only a writer of great skill and confidence could successfully portray an invading army as a suitor.

37.23 Again we meet the idea that Sennacherib is not threatening Hezekiah or Jerusalem or Israel, but Yahweh; it is doubtful whether those actually in Jerusalem at the time would have been able to see it this way. But, with the benefit of hindsight, the author is able to read the situation theologically and so come to what is for him the essential point.

37.24 After a victory no joy is greater than recalling with what proud confidence the enemy entered the battle. The author has a fine turn of phrase. The Assyrian envoy, who is now supposed to be speaking, would hardly have been so poetic.

37.25 Assyria did defeat Egypt at Eltekeh, but this is a ridiculous claim. The whole point, however, is that Assyrian pride was, and must be remembered as, grotesquely inflated.

37.26 Yahweh continues after the supposed boast of the Assyrian. The logic has already been set out in 10.5. Assyrian conquests took place within the pattern of Yahweh's will, though the Assyrians themselves were too arrogant and ignorant to recognize the fact. The *fortified cities* are those Assyria was permitted to conquer. The introduction of *your* does not help the sense.

37.27 The last two lines are similar to Isa. 40.6–8, but there can be no question of dependence. This author cannot have been writing after Jerusalem had fallen to the Babylonians.

37.28 Cf. Ps. 139.2. Yahweh knows all there is to know about human beings, not simply in terms of what they are doing, but in terms of penetrative understanding of thoughts and motives.

37.29 Sennacherib's retreat is seen as Yahweh's triumph, though the way it is put is rather different from what is said in v. 36. The *ring in your nose* is a perfect image, for it represents a way in which one, apparently weak, can control another who is impressively strong. *the way on which you came* (cf. 34a) emphasizes the totality of the reversal. The route taken by the army is the same, but the mood in which it travels will be dramatically changed.

37.30 Vv. 30–32 are probably a further addition. They are in prose and the style is different, though the message is the same. In 22–29 Yahweh addresses Assyria; in 30–32 his prophet addresses Hezekiah. It has often been noted that these verses would fit better after v. 35 than here. We have encountered signs already in 7.11–4. They are mysterious and powerful. A sign, which is easily apprehended, moves parallel to a greater reality, which is not so easily apprehended (see notes on 7.11 and 20.3). Here *the sign* is the way the people will be fed: in the first year from what is left, *in the second* from what has grown naturally in the unploughed fields, *in the third* from a full harvest. So the deliverance will come.

37.31 The idea of a remnant that survives the coming crisis is a well-known element in Isaianic theology; the identity of the remnant is, of course, different in different crises. *The survivors* here are those Judahites still in position after Sennacherib's depredations.

37.32 This *remnant* will consist only of dwellers in *Jerusalem* which is in accord with the facts, though not with some of the more optimistic hopes maintained in Israel. For the last sentence, see Isa. 9.7.

37.33 In the original form this verse probably followed v. 21, hence the word *Therefore*. Again the prophecy is in accord with the facts viewed in the best possible light. By all accounts Sennacherib got no nearer to Jerusalem than Lachish. Nothing is said, however, of the high price paid by Hezekiah to buy off Sennacherib according to II Kings 18.13–16, but equally nothing is said of the calamity that befell the Assyrians.

37.34   For the first line, see note on v. 29; this verse is probably the original, v. 29 the quotation. Later writers interpreted the event as an indication of divine intervention; naturally they assumed that it had been prophesied. *the word of the LORD* and the event to which it relates are closely tied together. Yahweh gives both.

37.35   This promise provided the driving force for much of Israel's hope in the years before 597. Jerusalem had survived Sennacherib's advance relatively unscathed, and by the author's day, the Assyrians had been brought low. What could be inferred from that? That Yahweh regarded Jerusalem as his chosen and its king, considered as the successor to *my servant David*, as his chosen representative (cf. I Kings 11.13, 34; 15.4f.; II Kings 8.19). This may explain why Hezekiah is represented in such glowing terms; if the city was saved, then the monarch must have been deserving.

37.36   This verse also appears in II Kings 19.35 and something similar is found in II Chron. 32.21, which, we may safely say, is dependent upon it. It is, however, incompatible with II Kings 18.13–6 and, of course, with the Assyrian record. It is also at odds with the prophetic statements made in the rest of the longer narrative of chs. 36–37. In the first cycle, 37.7 attributes Sennacherib's withdrawal to *a mere rumour*, and in the second, he is led away by some unnamed but irresistible force (vv. 29, 34). The number 185,000 is logistically incredible, but numbers in the OT are commonly exaggerated. It should also be added that, in pre-exilic prophecy, Yahweh is seen acting in the affairs of the nations by means of kings, prophets, armies; for all the many prophecies of destruction, reference to direct intervention by an *angel of the LORD* is almost unknown. It is reasonable, therefore, to conclude that this verse is an addition to the narrative made when the story had become legendary. Perhaps 31.8 provided the stimulus. There have been attempts to provide a rational basis for the verse, most notably by reference to an Egyptian tale, cited by Herodotus, the Greek historian, to the effect that, on another quite different occasion, mice gnawed through the bowstrings of Assyria's archers. But this provides no support for happenings at Jerusalem. On the contrary, it witnesses to the fact that stories of battle often gain legendary accretions. What is remarkable is that our narrative, written so long after the event, is elsewhere so free from such accretions. For all these reasons, the verse must be regarded as an over-enthusiastic insertion meant to enhance a story that needed no enhancing.

37.37 The original finale to the narrative. *Sennacherib*, no doubt feeling that he had got all that Judah could give him, and having duties and perhaps a crisis elsewhere, simply returned home.

38.37 The editor's final comment. 37.7 prophesied that Sennacherib would *fall by the sword*, so here is the fulfilment. The details are cloudy. Sennacherib was murdered twenty years later in 681. The Assyrian record (*ANET*, p. 288) suggests that he was battered to death by persons unnamed with 'statues of protective deities', which partly confirms the reference to *the temple of his god*. We should not miss the editor's irony. The temple was the place where the troubled Hezekiah found salvation and in a temple proud Sennacherib met his death. So much for Assyrian deities! The name *Nisroch* is a puzzle that commentators cannot solve. *Ararat* is an area in the mountains to the north of the fertile crescent. *Esarhaddon* reigned for twelve years; the Assyrian empire still had seventy years to run.

This passage is full of theological insights and it would be a pity if all attention was concentrated on the single fact that the city of Jerusalem was saved. The assertion of 37.35 needs to be pondered deeply before it can be accepted as an example of a general rule regarding God's activity in human conflict. Certainly human conflict is not governed simply by big battalions; nor is it outside the realm of divine action; certainly the faithful are called to put their trust in divine providence. But the ways of God in history are not always as clear as 37.35 implies, as the tragic events of 586 revealed to the OT writers themselves, and as the subsequent history of Jerusalem has revealed to all the world. This narrative requires us to think again about what divine protection means and whom God counts as 'his own'. The conception of a providence that sees us through, not simply the occasions of unexpected relief, but also the experiences of bewildering tragedy, alone meets our theological and our personal needs.

Hezekiah's sickness healed
38.1–6, 21f., 7f.

Another narrative exalting both Hezekiah and Isaiah. The king is healed from mortal sickness in recognition of his piety and Isaiah plays a leading part in the action. Vv. 7f. of the II Kings 20 version appear at the end of the chapter in the Heb. text of Isaiah (see NRSV). Presumably when the Kings passage was incorporated into Isaiah, these two verses were left out in error, and then later brought in at the wrong point. NEB and REB put them back in what is surely their right place.

38.1 *At this time* is vague; a more positive chronological link appears in v. 6. The *message* Isaiah has to deliver is most unusual; one suspects that its purpose is to heighten the effect of the miracle.

38.2 *Hezekiah*, anxious to commune with Yahweh and unable to go up to the temple, simply *turned his face to the wall*.

38.3 The king had no need of penitence; he simply draws attention to his record, set out in II Kings 18.1–8. In the earlier part of the book of Isaiah, however, the prophet complains bitterly about Judah's pursuit of Egyptian alliances and lack of faith in Yahweh (e.g. 29.9–16; 30.1–11; 31.1–3). It is interesting that nowhere in those oracles is Hezekiah mentioned by name.

38.5 Again, *Hezekiah* is regarded as the faithful and fitting descendant of *David* (cf. 37.35). The point of the narrative is that, because of the king's virtue, the *city* is saved.

38.6 This verse places the narrative firmly in the year 701. Hezekiah died in 687 so the arithmetic is correct. Many commentators take the view, however, that a legendary story of the healing of a king has been adapted and pressed into service by an author with a clear theological intention. His message would have been most relevant in the period just before 597.

38.21 It is right that the process of healing should follow the promise and precede the thanksgiving, so the transposition of these verses is sound. We do not know the nature of the illness, but there is nothing essentially miraculous in what is described here. *Isaiah* simply reveals more medical knowledge than anyone else at court. In such ways heroic figures of the past are magnified.

38.22   Unlike Ahaz in 7.12, Hezekiah asked for a sign or *proof* (see notes on 7.11, 14; 37.30). His question refers back to a detail found in II Kings 20.5 but omitted from Isaiah, that Hezekiah would *go up to the house of the LORD* on the third day. The order is still slightly odd because Hezekiah asks for a sign after he has recovered.

38.8   We infer that there was a *stairway*, visible to Hezekiah, on which a building cast a shadow indicating the passing of the hours. *the shadow* was to go up *ten steps*, and so add a few hours to the length of the day: a sign that Yahweh would add fifteen years to Hezekiah's life. This would mean that *the sun* had to go back across the sky, a striking miracle, even to a people without modern knowledge of physics. In this way Hezekiah is magnified. Signs are not necessarily miraculous, as we have seen before (7.11–14; 8.18; 20.3).

Hezekiah's psalm of thanksgiving
38.9–20

This passage has the form of a psalm of thanksgiving such as would be offered, together with a sacrifice, by a worshipper in the temple after recovery from illness (e.g. Ps. 30). It was common for such psalms to rehearse all the misery before coming at the end to an outburst of praise. The psalm is rich in theology, particularly in what it says about death. Like most of those who gave us the OT, the author has no hope of a glorious life hereafter; for him, the grave is the end of all proper existence. According to some sceptics, this means that there was no motive for his religious belief at all, but in fact, the awareness of the blessings he has enjoyed in this life leads to a deep sense of gratitude and so to joyous worship. The poem is not in the II Kings version, which means that it must have been added very late in the history of the book's development. It fits the context perfectly, though the attribution to Hezekiah is doubtless artificial. The Heb. text is bad and for the most part we shall follow REB without comment. All translations have the same problem.

38.10   The Hebrew was extremely 'down to earth' on the subject of death. Observation showed that the corpse retained its identity for a little while and the skeleton for much longer; so the person continued to have a vestigial existence, though it could not be called life. *the rest of my days* means the period when the corpse suffers corruption in the grave. *Sheol* is a figurative way of describing the existence of the tomb. *the gates* signify that those delivered to *Sheol* could never escape (see note on 14.9).

38.11   To *see the Lord* was to worship. The prime disability of the dead was that they could *no longer* worship. To our secular age, that is an astonishing sentiment. Does worship really head the list of this earth's pleasures, and why worship at all if there is no 'pie in the sky'? But that is how the OT sees it (cf. Pss. 6.5; 30.9; 88.5, 10f.; 115.17).

38.12   Death is represented in two powerful images, a *tent pulled up* and a length of cloth cut from its loom. *the thrum* is the ends of thread left on the loom when the cloth is cut off. Yahweh's absolute authority is taken for granted.

38.13   A bitter part of the human tragedy is that death, the last and worst enemy, has to be encountered in the midst of weakness and bodily pain.

38.14   *twitter* and *moan* hardly convey the true emotion. The poet is deeply affected and he appeals to Yahweh as his only hope.

38.15   Yet the absurdity of this plea comes home to him. According to Deuteronomic belief, Yahweh is responsible for his plight. So the poet faces an intolerable paradox.

38.16   This verse is the crux; the paradox must be broken. Either the last word is death or it is life, either anguish or joy. The poet affirms his faith that it is *life* and *rest*.

38.17   *love saved* him from his proper *lot*. Yahweh acted to deal with his *sins*. This is NT theology in embryo.

38.18f.   The poet is now in smooth water. In the tomb there is no confession of faith or *praise* or *hope*, but he claims a place among *the living*. The fact that he will eventually have to face death is no longer a problem. Mortal beings are dust and must come to an end, but, because of his present release from suffering, he can happily *confess* the *faithfulness* of Yahweh.

38.20   The shout of praise, with which the poem closes, is the more moving because it preserves within it the note of mortality. *the music of our praises* will *resound all our life long*.

Passages of this kind are a useful corrective to the belief that human problems can only be resolved in the hereafter. Too much other-worldliness represents theological weakness rather than strength.

Hezekiah and the envoys from Babylon
39.1–8

This narrative recounts an incident that took place before the threat to Jerusalem in 701. *Merodach-baladan* was a Babylonian prince who reigned over a small kingdom at the northern end of the Persian Gulf. He managed to keep his throne despite uneasy relations with Assyria, but after Sargon's death in 705 he began plotting against his overlord and we may assume that his contact with *Hezekiah* was not unconnected with the conspiracy. There may, therefore, be a factual basis to this narrative, but that is not where its true significance lies. The author is anxious to correct notions about the virtues of Hezekiah and the inviolability of Jerusalem. Some of the polish is knocked off Hezekiah. He behaves unwisely and a calamitous prophecy is put in the mouth of Isaiah. The treasures of Jerusalem would be carried off to Babylon and princes of the royal house would be made servants there. The promise that Yahweh would always protect Jerusalem (37.35; 38.6) is thus withdrawn.

Vv. 6f. refer to the events of 597 (II Kings 24.10–17) but not to the full horror of 586, when temple, palace and city were destroyed (II Kings 25). So one hypothesis is that the narrative was composed after the fate of Jerusalem was sealed but before the final disaster. At the same time, the narrative has a strange dispassionate quality which is hard to locate in the period between the two attacks, which suggests a period much later, when the pain had, to a large extent, been absorbed. We conclude that this narrative was written much later than the previous two, though it refers an event a few years before the date, 701, with which they are concerned.

39.1 The reference to Hezekiah's illness is a neat way of tying the three narratives together, though here it cannot be correct unless he was *ill* for a very long time. The *gift*, we may be sure, was not to cheer Hezekiah's convalescence but to persuade him to join the conspiracy.

39.2 The resources of the *treasury* suggest a date before the humiliations caused by Sennacherib (II Kings 18.14–16). Some scholars accuse *Hezekiah* of the heinous offence of *hubris*, which, in Greek tragedy, was enough to bring even the noblest down, but there is nothing here to suggest that he was behaving untowardly. Wealth could be a sign of divine favour (I Kings 10. 9, 24). Isaiah's wrath is not commensurate with the offence. There is irony in the fact that what Hezekiah proudly shows to the Babylonians, they eventually took.

39.3 *Isaiah*, apparently unaware of where the envoys came from, is suspicious, which is consistent with his disapproval of foreign alliances.

39.4 Hezekiah cheerfully owns up to what he had done. If he was supposed to feel remorse, the language fails to convey it.

39.6 The author was aware of some of the facts of the deportation. This verse is consistent with II Kings 24.13. It is hardly credible, however, that Isaiah was similarly aware. In the normal course of prophecy he would not have been able to name *Babylon* as the plunderer when the Assyrian empire still had almost a hundred years to run. The author has constructed a story in which Hezekiah is humbled and Isaiah makes an accurate prophecy about the fate of Jerusalem.

39.7 Cf. II Kings 24.15. There is no mention of the sack of the city or the end of the Davidic line. Either the worst had not yet happened or the author knew that his readers were familiar with the whole sad story.

39.8 Again, no guilty breakdown by *Hezekiah*. He simply accepts the situation as *good*. This comment makes Hezekiah out to be rather small-minded, but that may be misleading. The author knew what had happened to Hezekiah, and he simply records that the king acknowledged that he would live out his own time in *peace and security*, according to Yahweh's *word*.

II Kings 20.20f. rounds off the section with a concluding note about Hezekiah's famous conduit and his death. The book of Isaiah has no need of this ending, for it now continues with rich material from the Babylonian exile. We are transported from the gloomy prophecy (in vv. 6f.) to an unexpected but glorious reality.